Making Sense of
Academic Life

SRHE and Open University Press Imprint
General Editor: Heather Eggins

Current titles include:
Catherine Bargh, Peter Scott and David Smith: *Governing Universities*
Ronald Barnett: *Improving Higher Education: Total Quality Care*
Ronald Barnett: *The Idea of Higher Education*
Ronald Barnett: *The Limits of Competence*
Ronald Barnett: *Higher Education: A Critical Business*
John Biggs: *Teaching for Quality Learning at University*
David Boud *et al.* (eds): *Using Experience for Learning*
Etienne Bourgeois *et al.*: *The Adult University*
John Brennan *et al.* (eds): *What Kind of University?*
Angela Brew: *Directions in Staff Development*
Anne Brockbank and Ian McGill: *Facilitating Reflective Learning in Higher Education*
Ann Brooks: *Academic Women*
Sally Brown and Angela Glasner (eds): *Assessment Matters in Higher Education*
Frank Coffield and Bill Williamson (eds): *Repositioning Higher Education*
John Cowan: *On Becoming an Innovative University Teacher*
Heather Eggins (ed.): *Women as Leaders and Managers in Higher Education*
Gillian Evans: *Calling Academia to Account*
David Farnham (ed.): *Managing Academic Staff in Changing University Systems*
Sinclair Goodlad: *The Quest for Quality*
Harry Gray (ed.): *Universities and the Creation of Wealth*
Diana Green (ed.): *What is Quality in Higher Education?*
Elaine Martin: *Changing Academic Work*
Robin Middlehurst: *Leading Academics*
Sarah Neal: *The Making of Equal Opportunities Policies in Universities*
David Palfreyman and David Warner (eds): *Higher Education and the Law*
John Pratt: *The Polytechnic Experiment*
Michael Prosser and Keith Trigwell: *Understanding Learning and Teaching*
Yoni Ryan and Ortrun Zuber-Skerritt (eds): *Supervising Postgraduates from Non-English Speaking Backgrounds*
Tom Schuller (ed.): *The Changing University?*
Peter Scott (ed.): *The Globalization of Higher Education*
Peter Scott: *The Meanings of Mass Higher Education*
Harold Silver and Pamela Silver: *Students*
Anthony Smith and Frank Webster (eds): *The Postmodern University?*
Imogen Taylor: *Developing Learning in Professional Education*
Peter G. Taylor: *Making Sense of Academic Life*
Susan Toohey: *Designing Courses for Higher Education*
Paul R. Trowler: *Academics Responding to Change*
David Warner and Elaine Crosthwaite (eds): *Human Resource Management in Higher and Further Education*
David Warner and Charles Leonard: *The Income Generation Handbook* (Second Edition)
David Warner and David Palfreyman (eds): *Higher Education Management*
Graham Webb: *Understanding Staff Development*
Sue Wheeler and Jan Birtle: *A Handbook for Personal Tutors*

Making Sense of Academic Life

Academics, Universities and Change

Peter G. Taylor

The Society for Research into Higher Education
& Open University Press

Published by SRHE and
Open University Press
Celtic Court
22 Ballmoor
Buckingham
MK18 1XW

email: enquiries@openup.co.uk
world wide web: http://www.openup.co.uk

and
325 Chestnut Street
Philadelphia, PA 19106, USA

First published 1999

A catalogue record of this book is available from the British Library

ISBN   0 335 20184 9 (pb)   0 335 20185 7 (hb)

Library of Congress Cataloging-in-Publication Data
Taylor, Peter G., 1951–
   Making sense of academic life;   academics, universities, and
change   /   Peter G. Taylor.
       p.   cm.
   Includes bibliographical references (p.   ) and index.
   ISBN 0-335-20185-7 (hbk).   ISBN 0-335-20184-9 (pbk)
   1. College teachers.   2. College teaching.   3. Education. Higher—
Aims and objectives.   4. Universities and colleges—Administration.
5. Educational change.   I. Title.
LB1778.T39   1999
378.1'2—dc21   99–12582
                                                                        CIP

Typeset by Graphicraft Limited, Hong Kong
Printed in Great Britain by St Edmundsbury Press, Bury St Edmunds, Suffolk

Contents

Preface

If it is possible to distinguish the current 'crisis' in higher education from crises of earlier times then that distinction would focus on the current need to address discontinuous change, and the sheer speed of change. Change of this type has to be managed in systematic ways, unlike former times when change was more incremental – more an extension of 'what was'. Now 'what was' is seen as a problem rather than a solution. Like 'growing up', incremental change tended to happen without too much parental or other assistance.

Universities and academics are facing challenges that require more active and self-interested management as they develop radically new responses. While others have written about how universities might be better managed, this work looks to issues of self-management for academics. In these times, the strategy of 'working harder' simply will not work. Even if they have a reassuring familiarity, these challenges require responses based on new ways of thinking, thinking that engages with these challenges in self-interested ways. In this way academics become players rather than pawns in the process of change.

I recently received an email message from a colleague, which I have adapted for use here. The adapted form reads:

> Dakota tribal wisdom says that when you discover you are riding a dead horse, the best strategy is to dismount. However, in universities we often try other strategies with dead horses, including the following:
> 1. Buying a stronger whip.
> 2. Changing riders.
> 3. Saying things like 'this is the way we have always ridden this horse'.
> 4. Comparing the fate of horses in today's environment.
> 5. Hiring contractors to ride the dead horse.
> 6. Harnessing several dead horses together for increased speed.
> 7. Declaring the dead horse is 'better, faster and cheaper'.
> 8. Promoting the dead horse to a managerial position.

A cynic might suggest that this project involves 'writing a book about the future of dead horses'. But I am not cynical about the future of universities or academics. I see no reason to think that universities will have anything other than an increasingly important role in our societies, or that academics are an 'endangered species'. They are not. However, the roles of both universities and academics are changing.

In universities, the tradition *is* to change. And academic work is constantly engaged with change – in the form of learning. In fact it would be difficult to think of a profession which is better placed to respond to the challenges of change, and to develop work practices which are adaptive to and supportive of change. Therefore my approach is optimistic. My intention in this book is to raise broader issues that might inform thinking about – and therefore reactions to – academics' experiences of their changing roles in changing universities.

I use three strategies to pursue this intention.

First, I convey a sense of the 'big picture' of change in higher education, and in academics' work and work environments. This picture is not a neat one – it is blurry, the images overlie each other, it is disorderly. And my argument is that the future will be no more ordered – that it looks very much like things will become more complex, more fractured, less bounded, and academics are going to have to learn to live with this level of complexity and contradiction.

Second, I suggest that, while academics' work will change, that change will focus more on the intentions that underlie it, and the 'tools' that are used, than on the development of entirely new roles, or the loss of existing roles. To use an analogy, the change will be similar to that which doctors are experiencing as their work evolves from restorative to preventative medicine. That has not meant that doctors no longer 'set' broken bones, or involve themselves in providing intensive care for the very ill. But it has meant that their role is now more focused on keeping people healthy, rather than waiting for them to become unhealthy. For academics, the change will involve a new focus on structuring learning environments and helping students to make use of information, rather than being their *primary source* of information.

Third, I review the relationship between academics and their institutions. Here my focus is on the issue of academic careers. Learning to live with expanding expectations and roles, and increasing complexity and contradiction, is an urgent challenge facing all academics. This work offers some ways of thinking about the nature and future of 'academic' work, particularly in terms of the relationship between academic and institutional values, priorities and practices.

I offer a cautionary tale, arguing that change is never just about *progress*. It inevitably involves *regress* and *loss* as well. I also argue that the present and the future constantly intrude into each other, and that 'what is' and 'what can be' are the outcome of a complex set of interactions and limitations. These arguments draw on the experiences of those many academics with whom I have worked, and a broad literature.

My caution should not be mistaken for pessimism. This is also an optimistic tale. I trust that readers find this work useful and encouraging as they engage with the challenges that they face. These are challenging times, but, as the adage reminds us, 'it is what you learn after you know it all that counts'. May your learning be rewarding and rewarded!

Acknowledgements

I have had the pleasure of working with staff in a number of Australian universities, as they have engaged with change-related challenges over the last six years.

That work extended to researching the experiences of academics, general staff, and senior managers in two Australian universities, as they have grappled with moves to increase the use of communication and information technologies to support student learning (Taylor *et al.* 1996). This was an Evaluations and Investigations Project (EIP), funded by the Australian Government, through the Department of Employment, Education, Training and Youth Affairs (DEETYA). I wish to acknowledge my profound debt to those who assisted with and contributed to that project.

As I write I am involved in the pragmatics (and politics) of establishing a new campus for my university – the Logan Campus. Engagement in this work has extended and enriched the work of the EIP project. My thanks go to the many colleagues who have shared their experiences of this work with me during the last eighteen months.

There is another group of individuals who have more directly contributed to this work – sharing stories, challenging my thinking, commenting on drafts of ideas. In particular I want to acknowledge the contributions of Lee Andresen, Janine Collins, Barry Collier, Paul Draper, Wendy Dyer, Cheryl Gilbert, Linda Hort, Kees Hulsman, and Sue Johnston. And then there is Erica McWilliam – a colleague and friend whose scholarship continually challenges and inspires. Thank you!

1

Setting the Scene

That people live, ideologically, by stories that they have invented is no disgrace. In any case, it is inevitable. The danger to be feared is that we'll forget – either innocently or out of self-interest – that our stories are made up, and therefore subject to change as well as blame.

(Herron 1988: 103)

Academics' roles within the changing institutions of higher education – universities – cannot remain as they are, nor retreat to some former idealized times. Furthermore, the intentions of and directions for change continue to be both ambiguous and contested. This is readily seen in the multitude of conflicting stories about the need for change available in the media and the scholarly literature, and in conversations in places where academics meet, including the Internet.

The following is an extract from a colleague's reactions to involvement in the initial stages of development of the new (Logan) campus of my university. It exemplifies a sense of loss and uncertainty in the context of quite significant change:

Q. How, if at all, has your involvement with the Logan Campus initiative changed your view of your role as a lecturer?

A. Given that the duties of developing materials for Logan has come at pretty short notice, and on top of our normal workload, there has been very little time to develop this sort of perspective.

   I suppose the main change is that I have lost any illusions I might have had about being part of a community of scholars, and I now see myself – or I think the university sees me – simply as a production or office worker in a large hierarchical organization.

Q. What assumptions are you making about the locations, resources, roles of, and support for, your students?

A. As few as possible. Frankly, the goalposts seem to keep moving, so we are developing our subject in as 'disaster-proof' a way as possible.

Q. What questions and/or concerns remain unanswered, or continue to challenge your thinking?

A. It would be useful to know exactly what the university thinks flexible learning is. The descriptions of [some] people . . . make sense, but the university's presumptions seem quite different.

It would also be useful to know what the educational justification for this approach is, i.e. does flexible learning work? Nobody really seems to know.

Q. What major changes do you expect in your practices and/or role over the next two years?

A. No time to think this far ahead. We are just coping.

I hasten to add that this person is now seen as having developed some of the most successful flexible learning practices on this campus, has shared enthusiasm for the outcomes at numerous forums, and has asked to be permanently based on the Logan campus. The more important point is to acknowledge that those whose work is changed during any innovation are likely to experience a sense of loss and uncertainty during the initial phases of the change process. They cannot know the outcomes. But they can approach these challenges and be supported in ways that maximize the chance of success, even if the nature of that success cannot be fully anticipated.

In universities, the tradition *is* to change. Their very longevity as institutions is the most compelling evidence anyone could offer for this capacity to adapt to changing social, cultural, and political circumstances – their external environment. But much of what is written about the crisis of universities ignores this reality. Indeed, historically what is written tends to suggest a constant sense of crisis. That is, contemporary commentary on the state of higher education seems to portray a sense of crisis irrespective of the particular historical period in which it was written. Crisis and change can be two sides of the same experience, as the initial anecdote suggests.

This tendency to ignore their historical evolution, and thus to see current practices as merely an outcome of the relatively immediate past, leads me to suggest that universities are, paradoxically, amongst the oldest non-literate organizational cultures in existence. There are two claims I am making here – that academic communities often show little sense of their histories, and that academics' knowledge of how to undertake their educational work is largely accumulated and transmitted orally, rather than through texts or formal educational activities. The first claim is explored in Chapter 2, the second in Chapter 6.

While universities have changed since their origin, what marks the current experience of change is its scale – it is discontinuous rather than incremental (Nadler and Tushman 1995). Incremental change involves relatively minor changes, or changes which are limited in their scope. These types of change are manageable, involving relatively predictable outcomes – extensions of well-understood strategies. Discontinuous change is more systemic – it is broad-based, and difficult to manage. It involves simultaneous change in many aspects of a university, with outcomes that are difficult to predict or even foresee. The comments of my colleague, quoted earlier, illustrate this sense of discontinuity. Discontinuity is one of the defining features of the challenges facing academics.

Contemporary challenges

Two years ago my university organized a three-day international symposium on the topic 'Preparing University Teachers'. The symposium began with an invitation to participants to react to a scenario of academic work – a scenario with a decidedly entrepreneurial and virtual flavour – in universities in 2010. The scenario drew on ideas gleaned from the Brown and Duguid (1996) paper that I discuss in Chapter 2. Discussion started slowly, with most respondents reacting in disbelief, even horror, to some of the propositions that were floated. After some 50 minutes of increasingly animated and angry discussion, an international participant stood and observed, 'I don't know why you think of this as the future. In New Zealand we have been doing some of this for several years now.' Thus, there is little reason to believe that 'the future' will have any more uniformity than the past. The future will always involve an amalgam of practices, no individual component of which is likely to be absolutely novel. The discontinuity tends to lie in the particular orchestration of practices, which are themselves located in quite specific circumstances.

So what are some of the challenges that are facing higher education in the next twenty years? At the outset it is important to acknowledge that there is a profound sense that the challenges facing higher education are not local phenomena:

> As nations around the globe confront a similar educational options map, and one which is markedly different from earlier versions, new educational strategies must be explored . . . All nations, in terms of the educational options map, must confront and configure a set of interrelated policy issues involving the cost, scale, quality, relevance, portability, futurity, flexibility of and access to education.
>
> (Morrison 1995: 193)

This commonality reflects the globalization of economic activities and communication technologies, and the extension of the concept of mass education from the compulsory to the post-compulsory sectors. Thus, it is a truism to suggest that universities in most OECD countries are facing a number of challenges that are quantitatively if not qualitatively different from those they have faced in their more recent histories.

The report of the National Committee of Inquiry into Higher Education in the United Kingdom (the Dearing Committee), *Higher Education in the Learning Society* (NCIHE 1997), provides a thorough and current statement on the state of higher education in the UK. It suggests that 'external changes' will be a significant source of challenges: 'External factors have affected the development of higher education since the Robbins report on higher education in the early 1960s. We judge that external changes will be even more influential over the next 20 years' (Introduction, para. 16). The report also includes a list of 11 'potential changes' (para. 4.1) which are likely to impact on the future of higher education over the 20-year period nominated in their terms of reference. One challenge not acknowledged in this list is the impact of change itself. This is a telling omission, given the acknowledgement elsewhere in the report of the low morale of university staff, and of the potential deleterious effects of accelerating change. Specifically, the report acknowledges that: 'there are strains resulting from the pace of change, especially in the last few years, which must be addressed if higher education is to continue to be able to develop and serve the nation well' (para. 3.3). It is somewhat surprising then to note that in the chapter which deals with staff, Chapter 14, this issue is not discussed explicitly. Surely, if morale is declining (and the more recent work of Martin (1999) clearly indicates that this is the case), then the possibilities of creatively responding to the impact of the other trends would also be decreasing.

The report of the Committee of Review of Higher Education Financing and Policy, also known as the West Committee, acknowledges the likely impact of 'increasing globalization of education services and advances in communications technology' in its opening paragraph (CRHEFP 1998: 1). Later the report identifies six challenges facing the Australian higher education sector (pp. 55–6):

- community expectations of higher education will rise;
- the information and communications revolutions will provide many opportunities for higher education administration, teaching and research to be undertaken in better ways;
- competition will intensify, adding to the pressures on providers to deliver their services in the most cost-effective ways possible;
- taken together, the information and communications revolutions and growing competitive pressures will generate pressures for change in the overall structure of the higher education sector;
- international demand for higher education services will grow significantly in the long term; and
- demand for learning in Australia, particularly among the older age groups, is also likely to grow in the long term.

There are many other recently written versions of these challenges, but I want to draw on three versions – those of Terrence Morrison (1995), Stephen Ehrmann (1996), and Rachel Hudson, Sian Maslin-Prothero and Lyn Oates (1997) – to illustrate the discontinuity and scope of the challenges. But first a brief overview of what each sees as key challenges.

Morrison (1995), as the title of his paper ('Global transformation and the search for a new educational design') suggests, takes a very broad view – national rather than institutional. He suggests that the very success of higher education has led to some of the new challenges. In particular, he suggests that higher education has moved from the periphery of national political agendas to their centre as a result of a belief in the relationship between participation rates and national economic well-being. His 'new educational design' focuses on the challenge of providing lifelong learning. While he lists 14 factors that intrude upon higher education and training today, he argues that these raise issues which are discontinuous with those of previous times. In particular he notes a need to switch attention from a concern with *what* to teach and learn, to issues related to provision, e.g., *how* to access learning, *how* to manage institutions and systems, *how* to link with technology. It is as though the traditional, taken-for-granted practices of universities now provide inappropriate responses to the national imperatives that he identifies.

Extending this focus on provision, Ehrmann (1996) challenges campus-bound learning as an ideal and identifies three interacting challenges for universities:

- to increase accessibility so that higher education is available to 'the full range of adults who deserve a chance at education, despite their location, schedules, cultural differences or physical disabilities' (p. 9);
- to ensure the quality of 'learning for the 21st century' in order 'to improve the life chances of each of their adult learners, as individuals and as members of economic, cultural and political communities' (p. 9); and
- to do so in cost-effective ways, 'in the face of slow economic growth and other urgent social needs' (p. 9).

He sees these as 'the triple challenge' facing universities – to increase accessibility to high-quality higher education in cost-effective ways – and points to the potential value of communication and information technologies as a basis for responding to these challenges.

Hudson *et al.* (1997) provide a list of challenges for academics as part of an introduction to their case studies of flexible learning. They suggest that the key concepts underpinning the move to adopt flexible learning practices are access, control, responsibility and support. They list and discuss (pp. 4–6) six 'drivers for flexibility' in the teaching practices of universities, namely:

- pedagogy which aims to improve the quality of student learning experiences through promoting active, experiential and reflective learning;
- cuts in funding;
- increasing diversity in the student population;
- requirements to increase the equity of access to higher education – referring to potential students 'with disabilities, those from different ethnic cultures, residents of remote areas, shift workers, those who work in varying locations, and those who need to make one or more mid-life career changes, and so on' (p. 5);
- labour market requirements, especially the expectation that universities will develop lifelong learners, and provide lifelong education; and
- transferable skills – the demand for graduates who are employable as members of 'a multi-skilled, responsive and adaptable workforce' (p. 6).

The three versions each address relatively distinct dimensions of higher education: national systems (Morrison); individual institutions (Ehrmann);

and academics (Hudson *et al.*). Each takes the position that the contemporary context offers new challenges, challenges that in some senses are based on the very success of higher education in responding to the challenges of previous eras. The most significant success has involved the development of higher education as a system of mass rather than elite education, a development that began in America in the post-World War II era, and later in other countries. This has led to increased demand on public funding.

The general area of post-compulsory education and training is undergoing rapid expansion and refocusing. In developing policy to guide this evolution, governments have had to balance competing expenditure claims. In the context of higher education, the rationale for expanding participation has reflected both human-capital theory (the economic well-being of the nation depends on the development of a highly skilled workforce) and equity principles (the extension of mass education to the post-compulsory sectors). Thus the expansion of higher education can be argued for on economic *and* equity grounds. This means that, in an age of shrinking public sector expenditure, there is a politically attractive rationale for increased, but targeted, educational expenditure.

This sort of argument is well represented in the report of the Dearing Committee (NCIHE 1997) in Britain, and the West Committee (CRHEFP 1998) in Australia. Both reports recognize that while public funding for higher education has decreased on a per-student basis, the increasing rates of participation mean that the total impact on the public purse continues to increase. The trade-off for this increased total contribution has taken several forms. One involves increasing reliance on a user-pays approach to the funding of public higher education. The second involves the outcomes of 'targeted' expenditure. Here, paradoxically, as governments have reduced the per-student funding, they have used the extension of access as a basis for increasing national control over the governance of higher education. As a result, one of the new challenges facing universities is increasing levels of surveillance and accountability to national governments. My point is that institutional decision making in most OECD countries is being increasingly dominated by an agenda set by the state. Universities are becoming less autonomous, reacting at times to issues that are not initiated internally. It follows that staff have less time to focus on internal agendas, and they are often focusing on issues not of their own choosing or preference.

Let me now return to the issues of scope and discontinuity. It is evident that the scope of these challenges ranges across institutional and national boundaries, and involves anything from the funding of national systems of higher education to the provision of support for individual students participating in flexible learning programmes. If it is possible to distinguish the current 'crisis' in higher education from earlier times then that distinction would focus on the need to address the discontinuous nature and the sheer speed of current changes.

Change of this type has to be managed in systematic ways, unlike former times when change was more incremental. Like 'growing up', it tended to happen without a lot of assistance. Now universities and academics are faced by challenges that require more active and self-interested management. Adaptation in this more hostile environment requires active and systematic intervention, rather than the passive *laissez-faire* approaches of former times. This is not limited to the management of universities – it applies equally to the work of academics. New practices that respond to these challenges will represent both continuity with past practices, and very important discontinuities. However, not all of these challenges represent problems that are about to be 'solved'. Some are paradoxes and dilemmas with which we, like our predecessors, will have to learn to live.

Themes in this work

A number of leitmotifs are central to the discussion in this book, and tend to distinguish it from other more heroic tales. They suggest strategies for learning to live with challenges of the types listed above, and for engaging in self-interested self-management.

One theme of this book is its engagement with change at the level of the individual academic as well as at the level of universities as institutions, and higher education as a sector and system. At the level of the individual the discussion addresses personal issues such as identity, role, career, self-management. It invites a consideration of how issues such as these, particularly the sense of academic identity, are experienced and affected by change within the local meanings, values, and relations – the microcontexts and microhistories – of particular institutional settings.

A *second theme* involves *respect for ambivalence and a valuing of scepticism* – those who resist and/or express uncertainty, and those who question visions of certainty, should be listened to. Ian Craib provides a perspective on this theme in his book with the provocative title *The Importance of Disappointment* (1994). He speaks of disappointment as 'what happens, what we feel, when something we expect, intend, or hope for or desire does not materialize' (p. 3). The achievement of change necessarily involves the materialization of something new. Whether this materialization represents something intended, hoped for, or desired is open to question – failures can also be created, generating much disappointment.

In addition, whether what is lost as a result of the change was also intended, hoped for, or desired is also open to question – to scepticism. There is every reason to be sceptical of the long-term value of, and the sustainability of, desired changes. That is, it is entirely sensible, given the current rapid pace of change, to acknowledge that what is desired today may be out of favour tomorrow. As Craib argues: 'If the future is unpredictable, then it is a good reason to be afraid of it' (p. 120). But being sceptical is not the same as being fearful, and I regard the former as much more productive.

The *third theme* involves the characterization of my approach to the challenge of discussing academics' changing roles as *sensemaking*. Here I draw on the work of Karl Weick (1995), who describes sensemaking in terms of 'a developing set of ideas with explanatory possibilities rather than as a body of knowledge' (p. xi), ideas which involve 'identity, retrospect, enactment, social contact, ongoing events, cues, and plausibility' (p. 3). I regard his commentary on this process as a description of how one might constructively and effectively engage with the complexity of the changes in academics' roles within changing universities. My task here, therefore, is 'to construct, filter, frame, create facticity, and render the subjective into something more tangible' (p. 14) – to author as well as interpret, to create as well as to document change.

The implication is that sensemaking 'structures the future': 'sensemaking is about plausibility, coherence, and reasonableness. Sensemaking is about [creating] accounts that are socially acceptable and credible' (Weick 1995: 61). Individuals create their own reality within the frameworks of opportunities for both actions and sensemaking that are available to them at any time. That they see, and therefore experience, any situation differently from one time to another serves as a reminder that those 'creations' are under constant revision – 'even though people are immersed in flows [of information], they are seldom indifferent to what passes them by' (p. 45). However:

> A crucial property of sensemaking is that human situations are progressively clarified, but this clarification often works in reverse. It is less often the case that an outcome fulfils some prior definition of the situation, and more often the case that an outcome *develops* that prior definition.
>
> (Weick 1995: 11)

Thus, the 'structuring' is not *of* the future, but a process of *making* the immediate past meaningful, and of *updating* a relatively fuzzy sense of what the future might offer. Rationalizing is alive and well!

A *fourth theme* involves the need to acknowledge and deal with *issues of loss* associated with change, and with the importance of the *non-rational* in the sensemaking process, and in any other engagement with change. What is seldom acknowledged is that change is always *from* something, not just *to* something.

Loss is seldom mentioned by those who comment on the issue of change. Resistance is, and it is to be overcome. Anxiety is, but less frequently, and it invites reassurance. Uncertainty is also discussed, and here the usual response involves calls for vision and leadership – calls that may deny any experience of loss. Actions of resistance, expressions of uncertainty, questioning of visions of certainty – all these tend to be seen as obstructionist by those who write about change in higher education, and, in my experience, those who see themselves, or are employed as, agents for the achievement of that change. For example, staff who promote the use of the new technologies tend to be dismissive of those who exhibit such behaviour. The literature tends to provide mutually exclusive discourses – a binary formulation of pro- or anti- any focus for change.

It is also appropriate to 'fear the future', and to acknowledge that the present and future constantly intrude into each other. While Buddhism teaches the value of living in the moment, most people think in ways that continually involve projections into the future and remembering of the past, intuitively engaging in a version of sensemaking. It seems helpful to engage more *deliberately* in this task of sensemaking.

Sensemaking conceived in this way involves choice, and therefore values. Issues of significance, or attention, of expectation are based on individual values. This, in turn, hints at the importance of the *non-rational* in the sensemaking process. Issues of choice and sensemaking are too often presumed to lie in the terrain of the cognitive and the rational. Academics value the rational, the intellectual – it is how they make sense of and contribute to the formal knowledge which is their stock-in-trade. But, they often misrecognize change-focused learning as *necessarily* based on informed and rational processes. It may be, but it is more likely to be a form of rational sensemaking structured around a particular set of criteria – one's values. Thus, it may be more useful to regard initial engagements with change as involving values-based reasoning until outcomes-based sensemaking allows for a more informed updating of understandings. Of course this invites the question, 'Whose values? Academics' values or market values?'

Thus sensemaking is framed by expectations, intentions, desires whose achievement is 'anticipated' more at an emotional than cognitive level. It often involves the creation of meanings that allow individuals to feel good/ better/disappointed rather than to see more clearly. The latter requires additional effort – the sort of critical reflection that involves what Craib (1994) refers to as 'articulation' and 'internal arguments':

> The most important aspect is the toleration of the arguments, the recognition that when I am thinking or feeling one thing, I will be thinking and feeling something different fairly shortly.
>
> (Craib 1994: 171–2)

Thus, internal arguments allow for ambivalence. Craib speaks of the constant play around what individuals can and can't decide, about themselves and about the outside world. But choices are limited, individuals are condemned to choose:

> Such judgements are never purely rational, but they are surrounded by rationality: they need to be thought about, argued about internally and externally. The toleration of argument and the making of choices both require sacrifices and their attendant disappointment.
>
> (Craib 1994: 172)

All academics are condemned to making sense of changes in their roles, and to making choices with their 'attendant disappointment'.

Academics' roles are changing, and they will experience the emergent roles with varying degrees of satisfaction. My optimism centres on the possibility of engaging in the more deliberate forms of sensemaking and identity formation – articulation and internal argument – and the external debates that are likely to frame the choices which will be available in the future. Academics need to put their capacity for intellectual scepticism to work in the context of their experiential learning – their experience of change.

Some conceptual resources

I want to introduce two sets of conceptual resources that are important to this project. First, there are understandings of 'the postmodern condition', 'boundaries', and 'the end of enclosure', which are drawn from the wider literature. Two additional concepts, *tribalism* and *lone ranging*, are artefacts of my previous work.

The postmodern condition

Debates rage as to the nature, and uniformity, of the broad cultural conditions that we are experiencing. The terms 'modern' and 'postmodern' are used to signify a sense of discontinuity between a culture underpinned by Enlightenment thought, and cultural values and practices which resist this unified version of cultural advancement. Given their wide use in popular as well as academic conversations, the terms and their use defy tight definition. Indeed, there is a profound sense that the modern and postmodern constantly interact, that the latter is in constant engagement with the former, as reflected in the work of authors such as Bauman, Giddens, Habermas and Lyotard. 'Post' does not mean anti-modern. It insists on engagement with the modern, in part because 'modernism' provides the fixed reference point from which the postmodern perspective is distinguished.

Some are already 'writing postmodernism's obituary'. This reflects renewed interest in 'the re-emergence of the cosmopolitan and the universal, ideas stigmatized by the bias of the postmodern toward the particular and local . . . to recover the intellectual is to recover a cosmopolitan universalism' (Posnock 1997: 323–4). That interest is consistent with the academic worldview, a view which I discuss in greater detail in Chapter 3. However, my work attempts to raise issues that are global in their significance, while connecting them to more local consequences.

A concern with the postmodern can be understood as a recognition that 'things have changed, they aren't as we expected them to be' in quite challenging and discontinuous ways – that is, a concern with 'the postmodern condition'. This condition involves an array of challenges:

- A sense of moral purpose underpinned by 'constant and unrelenting dissatisfaction with what (an individual) has done' (Bauman 1998: 16).
- An experience, for intellectuals, of 'loss . . . loss of certainty, universality and their own privileged role as legislators of knowledge', leading to 'anxiety and loss of direction' (Kellner 1998: 75).

- Contingency – the idea that there are no acts or consequences that can be 'known'. There are no set categories, no final meaning, no all-powerful authorities to tell what 'the real world is'. There is instead dissonance, difference, diversity, dispersion, and a myriad of other possible uncertain states (Bloland 1995; Bauman 1998).
- Games of truth and error, and also play, rather than an historical search for truth (Foucault 1985).
- Challenges to the authority of higher education, with new forms of consumer culture, which include the consumption of symbols rather than commodities, and call into question the value of university credentials. These include challenges to the modernist metanarratives which frame much thinking about higher education – 'the ideas of merit, community, and autonomy' (Bloland 1995: 542).
- Changes in organizations 'typified by fragmentation, inconsistency, and a mix of organizational structures, policies and procedures', a capacity for detachment and a tendency to oral forms of communication (Bergquist 1995: 10–13).

Boundaries and 'the end of enclosure'

'Boundaries' (Bergquist 1995) and 'enclosed environments' (Deleuze 1992) are terms used to describe attempts by institutions to create contexts – enclosed territories – in which only the occupants define the particular rules and practices which govern internal operations. This intention is often expressed in terms of a need for operational cohesion, stability and autonomy. Bergquist, for example, suggests that 'in the modern world, boundaries (and identities defined by roles and rules) served as "containers" of anxiety' (p. 11). Deleuze speaks of the function of enclosed environments as 'to concentrate; to distribute space; to order time; to compose a productive force within the dimension of space–time whose effect will be greater than the sum of its component forces' (p. 3). He also refers to the replacement of disciplinary societies by '*societies of control*' (p. 4 – his italics), and of the substitution of socio-technological (i.e., computerized) mechanisms of control 'for the disciplinary sites of enclosure, whose crisis is everywhere proclaimed' (p. 7).

In the postmodern context, Bergquist, Deleuze and others characterize these 'sites of enclosure' as failing – an outcome captured by the expression 'the end of enclosure'. The link between this failure, and the 'spilling out of anxiety' is easy to anticipate. So too is the arrival of the 'boundary riders' – those charged with managing these sites, who 'never cease announcing supposedly necessary reforms' in the interest of 'operational cohesion, stability and autonomy' (Deleuze 1992: 4). Unlike Deleuze, who offers no reforming agenda (and indeed rejects the idea of 'tidying' responses), Bergquist nominates some 'reforms' which he considers to be appropriate responses to the postmodern condition:

To survive, most postmodern organizations have had to formulate clearer mission statements, in part because they can no longer retain clear boundaries. In the modern world, boundaries (and identities defined by roles and rules) served as 'containers' of anxiety. In the postmodern world, we must look to a clear sense of mission and purpose (both organizational and personal) to overcome this boundariless anxiety, the sense of living on the edge.

(Bergquist 1995: 11)

These new practices of enclosure are necessary because old forms of gatekeeping directed against unwanted intrusions (like changing roles), and against fragmentation, are failing. Of course, I question whether the 'former times' were really as some imagine them to have been.

Bender's (1997) analysis of the development of American universities over the last fifty years offers an interesting footnote to this discussion of 'the end of enclosure'. Specifically, he suggests that the degree of disciplinary enclosure in those universities has increased significantly since the 1960s, particularly in the fields of the humanities and social science. He disapproves of the outcomes:

in much current practice there is little or no effort to bridge the gap between academic theory and the local politics of everyday life . . . the dissolution of a public sphere and the limited role of academic intellect in whatever survives of that sphere is worrisome.

(Bender 1997: 28–31)

It seems that rebuilding boundaries and increasing enclosure can present a rather pyrrhic victory.

The work of John Seely Brown and Paul Duguid (1994) engages with 'boundaries' in quite different ways. They use the term 'border' to signify the phenomenon of the social conventions which, over a period of time, grow up around and become integral to the use of artefacts (for them this means the products of informational technology design). Their argument is complex, and I want to limit my use of it to their concept of 'border resources'. These are the 'socially constructed interpretive conventions that bridge the two sides of communication' (p. 10) about the value, meaning and use of an artefact, where the 'two sides' are most easily represented as the designers and the users. These resources are constituted socially and exist as conventions and traditions – the property of neither side, nor the artefact.

As conventions, border resources have implications for the use of artefacts – they circumscribe and constrain interpretations and lend support to particular social practices. More importantly, artefacts without borders are meaningless – meaning and artefact are interrelated through use. Borders also serve 'to embody, preserve, and represent authority' (p. 15). For example, academics know that their 'authority' rests with social conventions rather than with the artefact of a lecture theatre, or any other material aspect of the technologies of their role. Brown and Duguid introduce the notion of the social inertia of artifacts: 'the extent to which (artefacts) demand significant resources to get into circulation and resist changes once there' (p. 16). In doing so they draw attention to the way that some conventions are rather difficult to change, and to the strength of the association between the interpretive constraints offered by those conventions and the very materiality of the artefacts. Borders function to sustain, as well as to constrain, particular interpretations.

Border problems, particularly problems associated with the relative stability of artefacts and the communities that use them, challenge the successful implementation of all designs, and therefore changes. Brown and Duguid suggest that communities of users rely, in subtle but powerful ways, on the taken-for-granted continuity of an artefact's material properties. Traditional university pedagogical practices, considered as artefact, have a range of associated material properties, e.g. architectural features – lecture theatres, libraries, and refectories. The borderline perspective highlights the authority that social *inertia* lends to traditional pedagogies, irrespective of their actual educational value. By comparison, pedagogies associated with new roles and practices, irrespective of their potential educational value or economic efficiency, lack both borders and social inertia, as the initial anecdote suggests.

Tribalism and lone ranging

Finally, I want to look inward into these complex entities we call universities and introduce two concepts that I have developed in my previous work. The first is the concept of *tribalism*, the second the concept of *lone ranging*.

I use the concept of *tribalism* to capture a sense that there are a number of 'natural' constituencies within universities formed around the identities which staff derive from their roles and responsibilities (Taylor 1997a, 1997b). Using *tribalism* to characterize the consequences of occupational specializations within organizations is not novel. Peg Neuhauser, in her book *Tribal Warfare in Organizations*, writes that:

> Any organization with specialized functions and departments is made up of groups – which I call 'tribes' – that look at their work and at the organization in very different ways. Anthropologically, these groups in organizations act very much like 'real' tribes; they have their own dialects, ways of thinking, and rules for appropriate behavior.
>
> (Neuhauser 1988: 4–5)

She suggests that 'each tribe or culture has its own rules that govern its thinking and behavior and that these rules usually operate at the subconscious level' (p. 5). Her discussion explores both the value and potential negative outcomes of organizational tribalism.

Adoption of the concept of *tribalism* was based on commonalities which were identified through the analysis of interview data gathered as part of an investigation into the experiences of academics in changing their pedagogical practices, reported in Taylor *et al.* (1996). Other authors have drawn attention to the issue of tribes and cultures within universities. Tony Becher (1989) draws attention to discipline-based academic tribes. He points to the allegiance of academics to their disciplines rather than to the broader academic community, and the resulting cultural dislocations – the subcultures identified through their individual forms of knowledge and inquiry, and related beliefs and values – and territorial disputes. These allegiances were recognized and valued by his respondents. Bergquist (1992), on the other hand, points to broader institutional cultures, drawing attention to four types of academic culture – collegial, managerial, developmental, and negotiating – characterizing them, and exploring some of the implications for the way organizations respond to various issues, including the need to adapt to changing external contexts.

I use the concept of *lone ranging* to represent the principal mechanism through which change is achieved at the level of pedagogy, namely the initiative of individual staff members who are energetic, early adopters of new ideas or resources – the *lone rangers* (Taylor 1998). This individualistic and innovation-driven approach to the development of new teaching practices is consistent with the commitment of academics to the principle of professional autonomy. Lone ranging tends to produce innovation at the level of particular course offerings, but it also tends to be accompanied by a lack of institutional support and a failure to institutionalize the outcomes. In fact innovation often occurs in spite of this lack of institutional interest. Because of the lack of integration between their innovation and the institutional practices or the work of their colleagues, innovator-led approaches tend to produce pockets of isolated activity. Lone ranging is a concept that has resonated with the experience of many academics, and, in its name, captures something of the sense of romance (and isolation) associated with innovation and change.

Review

This chapter has introduced a set of ideas that are developed in the following chapters. One issue that I have not addressed fully is the 'global' applicability of my discussion. The literature on which I draw is international, but expressed in the English language. That literature tends to have most relevance to academics working in advanced Western economies. Yet I am aware that there are significant historical, economic, social and industrial differences between and within these economies. I leave the judgement of their relevance to any specific context to those who know those contexts best – the locals.

I have identified four themes for the discussion that follows:

- Engagement with change at the level of *individual academics* and their sense of *academic identity*.
- A *respect for ambivalence* and a *valuing of scepticism* – those who resist and/or express uncertainty, and those who question visions of certainty, should be listened to with care and interest.
- The characterization of my approach to the challenge of discussing academics' changing roles as *sensemaking* – developing a set of ideas with explanatory possibilities rather than as a body of knowledge.
- The need to acknowledge and deal with issues of *loss associated with change* together with the importance of the *non-rational* in the sensemaking process, and in any other engagement with change.

My approach acknowledges that the present sense of crisis associated with the nature, speed and scope of change in the roles of academics in changing universities has a history as well as a powerful sense of immediacy. Academics are already experiencing a sense of loss and anxiety as universities confront and are confronted by 'postmodern challenges' and discontinuous change. They should be better prepared to engage this future with thinking informed by these themes. Then they are less likely to forget that their stories are also 'made up, and therefore subject to change as well as blame' (Herron 1988: 103).

2

Visions of the Past and of the Future

In the 1790s increasing attention had been paid to higher education, especially to the topical issues of the organization of the universities and their proper purpose. The Uppsala philosopher Benjamin Höjer warned academics not to become dependent on the state when it came to finance and degrees. He envisioned a free market for academic knowledge, where competition between scholars would lead to the discovery of truth.

(Blomqvist 1997: 176)

Education is now firmly aligned with the broad social and economic agendas of the state in all advanced economies. In this chapter I explore how changes in the relationships between the state, society, and higher education have impacted on academics' roles and employment conditions historically. I also consider issues related to the purpose and future of higher education.

Your immediate task is to complete the following quiz. In each case indicate whether the arguments have a familiar ring to them, and then nominate the approximate historical period to which you think each is referring.

1. [Higher education should be based on] principles of wider access and the promotion of specialized knowledge and research, and geared toward meeting local demands for liberal education, practical professional training, and service to industry.

   (a) 1870s
   (b) 1930s
   (c) 1960s
   (d) 1990s

2. [T]he belief that too many graduates were being produced without adequate guarantees of being able to find jobs in industry was widespread . . . [as was] a feeling of economic and political insecurity which caused many students to concentrate entirely upon work for a degree . . .

   (a) 1870s
   (b) 1930s
   (c) 1960s
   (d) 1990s

3. Grounds for promotion should not include just scholarly accomplishment but also teaching competence – the professional teaching role and the duty of the universities to be teaching institutions were emphasized.

   (a) 1870s
   (b) 1900s
   (c) 1930s
   (d) 1990s

4. Politicians wanted the universities to provide degrees which would meet the needs of occupational life. They also wanted bureaucratic supervision of tuition and examining, and information about academic 'productivity'.

   (a) 1870s
   (b) 1900s
   (c) 1930s
   (d) 1990s

5. Most professors now accepted an organizational framework   (a) 1860s
   separating managerial and academic matters . . .   (b) 1910s
   administrative competence tended to be kept distinct from   (c) 1950s
   scholarly competence, and to be valued more highly. [They   (d) 1990s
   thought] that the new framework would be more efficient
   and rational than the old collegial determination.

The historical times to which each of the statements is referring are: 1: 1870s (Barnes 1996: 276); 2: 1930s (Barnes 1996: 279); 3: 1900s (Blomqvist 1997: 181); 4: 1900s (Blomqvist 1997: 181); and 5: 1910s (Blomqvist 1997: 182).

While you may have done very well on the quiz, I suspect that some academics might be a little surprised to find that the issues they confront today have such longevity. That these issues continue to be important suggests they are not going to be 'solved' in the near future.

Views of change in higher education

Others have written at length on the historical constancy of change in universities, often using the relatively recent past to document this phenomenon. Here I draw on the work of three authors – Guy Neave (1996), Thomas Bender (1997) and Terrence Morrison (1995) – to exemplify this phenomenon.

Guy Neave – a European view

In a special edition of the journal *Higher Education and Management* dedicated to reviewing developments in European university management over the previous 25 years, Neave (1996) suggests that 'the dominant perspective in Europe's higher education has been and still is today one of transition' (p. 17). In his view the 1960s involved a transition to the concept of the university as 'the force for radical reform in society', with values 'profoundly hostile to industry, trade, commerce and private gain' (p. 18). The 1980s transition involved the intervention by governments 'acting in the name of society – and fiscal rectitude – to check the way the university was apparently developing or had failed to develop' (p. 18). The intention involved 'the realization of greater social equality in which the university stood as an instrument for social mobility', that is, mass participation: 'a phenomenon without precedent in the whole eight hundred year history of the university in Europe' (p. 17).

The 1990s transition is to a market-driven system, and the associated attempt to 'uncouple the historic link between the university and the state' (p. 19). In fact the state may now be more accurately seen as a purchaser rather than a patron of higher education in former 'welfare states' such as Australia, Britain, Canada, New Zealand and Sweden. It reflects the view of higher education as a private rather than a public good. Neave regards this 'uncoupling' with great concern. It represents a 'utilitarian and frankly pessimistic vision' (p. 22), an abandonment of the '19th century Idealistic vision which cast the university as a cultural institution transcending time and State' (p. 21). He questions the moves to globalization and internationalization as responding 'too little to the specificities of a given nation' (p. 21), warning that 'society cannot survive intact in the absence of shared identity' (p. 23).

Thomas Bender – an American view

Bender (1997) provides an overview of the evolution of the American university during the fifty years since 1945 – its 'golden age'. During this period universities have adapted and grown in size, and in their research and graduate training capacity: 'It was a remarkable transformation, with both quantity and quality rising' (p. 1). He notes, however, that this success is relatively invisible to the American people, 'indeed, in a spirit of disappointment Americans may even be initiating its dismantling' (p. 3). His argument is that this success has led higher education 'into the center of . . . established institutions, including the government . . . but it has also made it vulnerable to a larger disaffection with those institutions' (p. 3). This is the ambivalent outcome of the expansion of access to higher education.

Another paradoxical outcome of the post-World War II period was that, as the system of higher education expanded, it became a more national (and nationalistic), and therefore homogeneous, system. Where universities had served local needs and values, they increasingly became the principal carriers of modern universalistic values. The associated claims of 'objectivity' and 'moral neutrality' served this sense of universalism. Increasingly, academics identified with their disciplines rather than their institutions, as measures of academic standards demanded comparisons of like-with-like. According to Bender, 'this pattern of change freed faculty for a stronger research orientation, and it enabled a firmer sense of academic autonomy and disciplinary professionalism' (p. 6).

In a powerful sense, the Cold War era marked the ascendancy of research – of the scholarship of discovery – over the former role of universities as the carriers of culture and the task of teaching that culture. As a consequence, 'it was assumed that the university would be held together by the ideal of inquiry' (p. 12). American foundations, the state, and the military–industrial complex invested in research. The concept of 'investment' in research implies more than an interest in enquiry, extending to an expectation of returns. Thus, universities which sought to develop their status as centres for research needed to 'produce the goods'. That requirement meant an increasing interest in developing the research capabilities of staff as well as their opportunities to engage in research. The knowledge developed within these research programmes became increasingly valuable and valued – it was treated as a commodity and sought by power brokers in the government and commercial sectors. The result was that as 'universities grew and moved to the center of American society, so did the professoriate and intellectuals generally' (p. 10). Elite researchers from elite institutions were employed as consultants in these sectors.

The relationship between academics and the broader community made universities increasingly vulnerable to the disaffection of that community. The powerful association between universities and 'the centers of power' meant that, as the American public began to lose faith in the grand plans of government (for example, the Head Start programme) and the military–industrial complex, faith in the value of the knowledge of universities also began to decline. After all, the design of those programmes had drawn heavily on the work of university researchers. The result was that academics, who were once identified with grand hopes, came to be seen as a part of the problem, rather than a part of the solution.

This loss of faith was accentuated by events within popular culture itself. The 1960s saw the rise of cultural developments underpinned by non-modernist values – precursors to what is sometimes referred to now as postmodernism. The impact of these cultural and social shifts on academics, according to Bender, was profound. As he describes it, a characteristic of the 1970s response to the cultural challenge of the 1960s was that many social scientists turned inward, becoming more focused on the development of their disciplines than upon describing or explaining the society around them. At the political level there was retreat also. Liberal and radical academics, who had to a greater or lesser extent become associated with political agendas, lost confidence in the conventional political process by the end of the 1970s. The result was that the political and cultural middle ground 'narrowed to the vanishing point' (p. 22) and academics retreated into their campus worlds.

The 1990s sees the emergence of academic postmodernism, which emphasizes the local, the particular, the fragmentary, but in ways unlike the pre-Cold War era. The new engagement questions rather than supports 'the local'. That questioning does little to bridge the gap between academic theory and the local politics of everyday life. Bender points to the additional possibility that, because postmodernism challenges the 'secularism' of the research university, it encourages the challenging of its teaching by religious fundamentalists. But within this fragmented world of scholarship, he notes the striking continuity in the structure of universities since the 1920s: 'the department remains the basic organizational unit' (p. 30).

Bender's conclusion calls for a rapprochement between the broader public and the academy: 'restoring a place for academic knowledge in the public culture and a role for public discussion in academic culture ought to be a high priority of both academic and public leaders' (p. 31). This mutual engagement should not seek an idealized, 'seamless web of discourse' because 'the university ought never be too comfortable in and with society – and vice versa' (p. 31). How this sort of positive disequilibrium might be achieved is a challenge that Bender leaves for the current and future generations of leaders to engage with.

Terrence Morrison – a 'global' view

Morrison (1995) provides a distinct analysis of the transformation that higher education is currently experiencing. Writing from a Canadian perspective he provides a historical perspective on more global challenges. Morrison's argument is that the current model of higher education is based on two features of a late nineteenth-century model. First, when higher education was provided for an elite it consumed a relatively small proportion of public investment in education. Consequently it was not an important policy issue for politicians or economic managers. The move from an elite to a mass system has seen higher education move from the periphery of public debate to a more central concern of states, and to much greater political involvement in the governance of higher education.

The second dysfunctional feature of the late nineteenth-century model is its focus on content – on what should be taught and how that knowledge should be organized. Morrison's argument is that, until now, the response of universities to social and economic change has been curricular change – changing what is legitimately taught. But this response is no longer adequate. The current challenges:

> increasingly face higher education not with issues of *what* to learn but of *how* to access learning, *how* to organize research, *how* to manage institutions and systems, *how* to link with technology, *how* to cope with social and ethical issues, *how* to distribute opportunity, and *how* to develop human resources.
>
> (Morrison 1995: 190 – his italics)

Thus, the transition implied here involves the displacement of a focus on content and the values of a professional elite by the social and economic priorities of the state.

While each of these authors refers to the recent move from an 'elite' to a mass system, it is useful to remember what did and did not characterize this 'elite'. Roderick West, in his Chairman's foreword to the report of the West Committee, makes this distinction with great clarity:

> We talk these days about going from an 'elite' to a 'mass' higher education system. There was nothing intellectually elite about the students of 50 years ago. A pass of five Bs was enough to gain entry to the faculty of medicine at the University of Sydney – the equivalent of a tertiary entrance rank no further than midway of the scale! What was elite about that cohort was that it had *opportunity*.
>
> (CRHEFP 1998: 5 – his italics)

And this opportunity was based primarily on the financial circumstances of their families. This is not to suggest that these students were intellectual dullards, but it is to suggest that access to higher education was based on issues other than an applicant's record of academic performance.

The discussion of the evolution of higher education provided by these three authors shows that, historically, academics' roles and employment conditions have changed. It seems ironic that a profession that is so frequently criticized for being too remote, too isolated in its 'ivory towers', is seen to be so consistently responsive to external challenges. Perhaps it is reasonable to speculate that the longevity of universities has been achieved only through academics' long-standing openness to and capacity for change.

Recent reviews of systems of higher education

Reviews of the national systems of higher education have recently been undertaken in Britain and in Australia. The reports of these Committees of Inquiry provide a snapshot of higher education in these two countries. Given that these reviews are of national systems, and were commissioned by their respective governments, it is hardly surprising that they take for granted an intimate relationship between state and higher education. The issue of the relationship between the state/s and higher education in a nation where there is no national system of higher education, such as the United States, is much more open to argument.

The Dearing Committee was commissioned by the British Government to develop recommendations 'on how the purposes, shape, structure, size and funding of higher education, including support for students, should develop to meet the needs of the United Kingdom over the next 20 years' (NCIHE 1997: Chairman's foreword, para. 1). Naturally, their report focuses on issues relevant to those terms of reference. But that focus did not exclude the interests of more 'local' players, as inferred by their reference to the 'growing interdependence between students, institutions, the economy, employers and the state' (Introduction, para. 9). Clearly, the Committee did not interpret 'interdependence' to mean 'mutual dependence', given their view that external changes will be even more influential on the development of higher education over the next 20 years (Introduction, para. 16).

This view of interdependence reflects the Committee's vision of a learning society, 'a society committed to learning throughout life' (NCIHE 1997: Introduction, para. 2). Such a vision is justified because 'the world of work is in continual change: individuals will increasingly need to develop new capabilities and to manage their own development and learning throughout life' (Introduction, para. 19). In the context of the current discussion, this sentence can be rephrased to read: 'universities will continue to experience discontinuous change primarily in response to external demands – therefore, individual academics will increasingly need to develop new capabilities, and to manage their own development and learning throughout their career, and beyond'.

The report provides an overview of the changes that have taken place in the higher education sector in the UK in the thirty-year period between the Robbins Committee review in the early 1960s and its own review. This overview forms Chapter 3 of the report, the introduction to which states:

UK higher education can take justifiable pride in what it has achieved over the last 30 years. It has expanded opportunities, changed and adapted as the needs of students and other clients have changed, maintained its international standing in research, introduced new approaches to learning and teaching and to quality assurance, and greatly improved its cost-effectiveness.

(NCIHE 1997: para. 3.2)

An impressive endorsement! Clearly the Committee was seeking to increase the confidence of employers and the state in graduate students and in the efforts that universities have made to meet their expectations, even though employers and the state have effectively decreased their levels of financial support for higher education.

The West Committee has recently reported to the Australian government (CRHEFP 1998). The central elements of the terms of reference for the review included:

- undertak[ing] a broad ranging review of the state of Australia's higher education sector, the effectiveness of the sector in meeting Australia's social, economic, scientific and cultural needs, and the developments which are likely to shape the provision of higher education in the next two decades;
- develop[ing] a comprehensive policy framework for higher education that will allow universities to respond creatively and flexibly to change, and will ensure that the sector meets the needs of students, industry and society in general as these are likely to develop over the next two decades.

(CRHEFP 1998: 1)

The strong similarity between the Dearing Committee's terms of reference and these are to be expected.

The West Committee's report pays scant attention to the first part of the first term of reference – reviewing the effectiveness of the sector – where the only significant acknowledgement is to growth. However, it is quite fixated on the second term of reference – the next two decades, and the changes that have to be made to meet Australia's social, economic, scientific and cultural needs in this period. Thus, it is change-focused, largely ignoring current achievements and issues such as uncertainty and loss associated with the changes it advocates. Its silence on these matters can be seen to imply an assumption that its audience only needs more information about the nature, speed and scope of the necessary changes.

This approach reminds me of the description of dysfunctional coping with change provided by Craib (1994):

We are pulled forward into the future and away from the past in such a way that it becomes very difficult to take things with us – internal things, an awareness and an understanding of our experiences; instead they often seem to lie jumbled up inside us, and we find we have an inner world like a rubbish bin . . . We might think that the rubbish bin can be sorted out, but it seems to me that the push is towards emptying it and starting afresh . . . So the debris of the day piles up, and it is easier to imagine that I can just leave the day behind, that each day I can become a new person.

(Craib 1994: 107)

The West Committee seems to have found it easier to share a preferred 'vision' than to make any systematic attempt to connect that vision with current achievements or realities. But it is with the 'debris' that academics, and those who work with them, must deal. I now turn to questions concerning the purpose of higher education at the beginning of the millennium.

Issues of purpose for and the future of higher education

There are no neat boundaries which separate higher education from other forms of post-compulsory education, nor features that can be used to distinguish in any fundamental way universities as institutions, from other providers. These separations and distinctions are the achievements of convention – legacies of history. The Dearing Committee accepted this position, while others, like Ronald Barnett (1996) argue the contrary position. While a conclusion to this debate is unlikely, my work with academics leads me to regard issues of purpose as fundamentally important to those who work in universities. The following comments offered by an EIP respondent illustrate this:

I think students have a great desire to rush to judgement, and I see my teaching as a sort of caution against this tendency . . . I mean for many teachers of ethics there is nothing to ethics but judgement, whereas I am actually quite keen on getting students to think about the practical question of how they actually make judgements. Not so much to ponder the moral desirability of a particular thing, but given that you think something is morally desirable, how do you translate it into an institutional context, a reform, or a value, or whatever. So I have actually put a lot of emphasis in one of the ethics subjects I am teaching of a sort of practical exercise of negotiating across a field of different people often with conflicting obligations. So I have been trying to give students a sort of ethical training . . . I am saying that within the domain of moral training there is a lot of room for the exercise of intelligence – even deep critical intelligence.

Academics' roles are changing and a major part of the reason for those changes has to do with the changing roles and purposes of universities. Changes are achieved through contestation, as noted earlier. The issue then is not to 'fix' purpose, but to acknowledge the more permanent foci for contestation – the pivotal relationships between universities and the state, the broader society, and the economy – and to make sense of the changing balance of power in terms of those relationships.

Given that higher education has become the focus of political decision making in many countries, it comes as no surprise to see speculation in many public forums about how it might be conducted in the future. The questions that appear central to this discussion include:

- What purposes should higher education serve?
- How should universities be organized to serve these purposes?
- What form should those services take? and
- Who should pay for them?

The current literature on leadership and management (and politics) exhibits a fascination with 'visions'. Another religious metaphor – mission – has also gained great popularity, and inordinate amounts of energy seem to go into developing institutional and/or departmental vision and/or mission statements. That popularity is also reflected in most of the literature on educational leadership and management. Indeed, it seems that any university that has not articulated a clear mission is doomed (damned?) to mediocrity, anyone who hasn't got a vision is deemed unsuitable to lead, and anyone who doesn't identify with the institutional mission and subscribe to the vision of their current leader is an unfaithful employee. Thus, faith seems an important competence for potential employees, although 'faith' might be represented less directly. For example, a recent review of employer expectations indicates that:

> Higher education should play a more direct role in shaping the personality of students. Graduates are expected to be more loyal to their employing organizations and companies, more entrepreneurial in their attitudes, better prepared for cooperation, ready to accept less demanding tasks as part of a job role, motivated for problem solving and able to cope quickly with unprecedented tasks.
>
> (Teichler and Kehm 1995: 124)

This version might not travel under the banner of 'faith', but it certainly does imply a form of non-rational commitment to a set of ideals.

The report of the Dearing Committee includes a chapter (Chapter 5) on the 'ideal' aims and purpose of higher education. Theirs is a broad view, emphasizing the need for graduates to be committed to lifelong learning, and for Britain to become a learning society. Achievement of the latter was so important in the mission of the Committee that the title of their report includes it: *Higher Education in the Learning Society*. The Committee's set of aims and purposes reflects their attempt to update the earlier report of the Robbins Committee (1963). That report identified the role of higher education in terms of: instruction in skills for employment; promoting the general powers of the mind; advancing learning; and transmitting a common culture and common standards of citizenship (NCIHE 1997: para. 5.7). The 'updated' set of ideals is:

5.10 The aim of higher education is to enable society to make progress through an understanding of itself and its world: in short, to sustain a learning society. There are numerous ways in which we could classify and describe what we see as the main components of this aim, but, in the interests of clarity we have summarized four broad purposes. They all overlap and interlink in important ways . . .

5.11 The four main purposes of higher education are:
• to inspire and enable individuals to develop their capabilities to the highest potential levels throughout life, so that they grow intellectually, are well-equipped for work, can contribute effectively to society and achieve personal fulfilment;
• to increase knowledge and understanding for their own sake and to foster their application to the benefit of the economy and society;
• to serve the needs of an adaptable, sustainable, knowledge-based economy at local, regional and national levels;
• to play a major role in shaping a democratic, civilized, inclusive society.

Compared with these abstract ideals, many find more 'problem-focused' ideals such as those referred to by Teichler and Kehm very appealing. They offer a version of higher education that is responsive to 'client needs' and to public demand. Many students would prefer to have an education that would actually provide the nominated skills, than one which left them with half-remembered ideas from lectures that were over-stuffed with information. The traditional discipline focus of higher education certainly doesn't guarantee high-quality teaching or learning. In an age of mass participation, and high levels of unemployment, a commitment to provide an education focused on employment-relevant competencies has great appeal, especially to those who speak on behalf of the commercial sector. This is neither a 'local', nor an unexpected, phenomenon. But is this vision consistent with the ideals of a learning society?

There are reasons for thinking that it is not. It implies limited engagement with the fourth of the Dearing Committee's ideals – playing a major role in shaping a democratic, civilized, inclusive society – and with the capacity for critical and ethically based thinking and reasoning. Ronald Barnett (1996) speaks of this version as 'precisely one which is oriented towards producing human capital which will reproduce itself in the interests of the learning society faced with global economic competition' (p. 18). And he argues against this 'closed' version of the learning society. I need to point out that in the conclusion to their article, Teichler and Kehm state a position very similar to Barnett's. They argue a version of 'positive disequilibrium' – that universities 'should not so much gear students to the presumed demands of the labour market, but instead use [their] given distance from the employment system for questioning and challenging the world of work' (1995: 129).

I too am yet to be converted by visions that focus on 'meeting client needs'. I view most talk of 'visions' with scepticism and suspicion. That talk usually ignores the past and it is too often mistaken for 'leadership'. Too much time is given to its articulation (often in the service of quality assurance activities), while too little time is given to the exploration of its possible implications – to if and how it might be enacted. That is, this talk too often fails to make connections between what has been, what is, and what might be.

So with these prejudices declared, I want to explore briefly some other views on the future of higher education. I present a series of views, beginning with responses to the first question – that is, issues of purpose – then moving to views which are focused more on how universities might actually operate, with a particular focus on the use of communication and information technologies. I discuss work by Clark Kerr, Michael Shattock, and John Seely Brown and Paul Duguid respectively, relating their work to issues that I have raised earlier, or will raise later. I then discuss two 'local' models that might be seen as anticipating the future.

Clark Kerr – an activist and civic future

The public debates and the reports of both the Dearing and the West Committees make it clear that universities will have to address more, rather than fewer, purposes. Clark Kerr sees higher education as 'more a responding than an originating segment of society', and it must respond to expectations and demands which it sometimes finds uncomfortable (1994: 225). As a senior officer of a university Kerr is very conscious of the challenges that responding, and then maintaining both organizational and educational integrity, pose. He identifies (pp. 223–5) three purposes (although he refers to them as 'functions') which are currently being added in the United States:

- advancement of social justice – universal access and affirmative action;
- advancement of the quality of life – providing opportunities for lifelong learning, and contributing to the quality of the social and cultural life of the community;
- advancement of political reform – acting as a centre of political thinking and dissent – where once universities were 'the citadel of conservatism', they are increasingly expected to be 'a critical aspect of society' – 'so society has moved in on higher education [as reflected in the first two new purposes], and higher education has moved out into society, more or less simultaneously' (p. 230).

Identification of this final, emergent, purpose sits uncomfortably with the review of the recent development of American universities provided by Thomas Bender, as discussed earlier. Bender's argument is that, since the late 1970s, academics have retreated, turning inward to the academy, rather than engaging with broader social agendas. Perhaps Kerr is pointing to a legacy of that era, a legacy that now includes a much broader range of political activism – gender politics, ecological politics, local politics and economic politics amongst others. Irrespective of its basis, he sees this as a central purpose for the future, as he makes clear in the sentiments that conclude his book:

> Higher education is now the greatest single source of new ideas, of higher skills, of the spread of culture, of the raising and satisfying of individual aspirations, of the expression of dissent, of the creation of leadership. It is more a part of society than ever before and less, as a consequence, apart from it, and this is likely to be ever truer in the future.
>
> (Kerr 1994: 231)

Given this enthusiasm for activism, Kerr suggests (p. 223) two additional purposes that may soon be added:

- residual responsibility for youth; and
- organized thought about the future of society.

In relation to the first addition, he suggests that higher education is one of the few social structures established to serve the needs of youth and others in a 'structureless' labour market. I note that it is not uncommon for commentators or academics to regard universities as 'holding camps' for the unemployed, and to suggest that the move by the state to mass participation was motivated by a political desire to decrease rates of 'youth unemployment' in particular. Kerr is raising the possibility of a new approach to this issue, based on a better integration of education with employment and civic action.

The second additional purpose reflects his belief in the need for curriculum structures that require engagement with large and complex problems. In Chapter 11 of his book Kerr exemplifies this suggestion, drawing on the ideas of the Spanish philosopher of education José Ortega y Gasset. Based on this purpose, he suggests a number of 'great issues for the twenty-first century', including:

> Gender, race and class
> The roles of religion and nationality in modern life
> The pathologies of industrial civilization
> The implications of the 'information revolution'
> The prospects for third world nations
> Competition in the global economy

He includes the suggestion that about one-third of the four years of an undergraduate curriculum should be devoted to liberal education of this type.

Kerr's perspective focuses on the relationship between the broader society and higher education. His activist position invites universities to exercise leadership both in developing this relationship, and in enacting what the Dearing Committee refers to as 'a major role in shaping a democratic, civilized, inclusive society'.

Michael Shattock – a struggle for institutional autonomy

Shattock (1995: 158), Registrar of the University of Warwick in Britain, identifies four trends (my term rather than his) whose nature reflects the state-focused system of higher education in the UK:

- greater accountability to the state – as the state's financial contributions to higher education increase, 'demands for greater accountability naturally increase and bureaucratic intervention rises almost exponentially';
- institution identity is weakened – while the report of the Dearing Committee refers to declining morale, Shattock suggests that, as the number of staff and students increase and per-student funding falls, universities have less energy and fewer resources to maintain their institutional identity;
- higher education is losing its distinctiveness, its status – it is now seen as a right rather than a privilege; increasingly all institutions are treated 'equally' by governments, funding agencies and students; the 'positional' value of any credential is declining as the proportion of the workforce which holds it is increasing; and,
- institutional diversity is declining – government funding policies, the operation of internal competitive markets, the operation of national professional bodies (in terms of accreditation of awards) and the current fetish for establishing international benchmarks and performance indicators – all work against diversity.

Shattock's view of the future draws attention to the state of the relationship between the state and institutions of higher education. He argues that Britain is putting at risk the most important contributions universities make to society, namely their capacity to initiate new ways of thinking, which results from their independence from the state. Thus, he argues the need to 'find ways to re-balance the relationship between universities and the state [lest] we . . . find that universities' dependency, and compliance, increases' (p. 159). Further, 'If the state becomes the only source of structural change in higher education, the revolutions that will have to sweep through higher education every decade or so to meet revised national perceptions of need will be that much more comprehensive and monolithic.' This is a scenario that is in the interests of neither the state, nor the institutions.

His suggestions for change focus on the development of institutional identity and autonomy. Shattock identifies three steps universities can take to emphasize their differentiation within the higher education market:

- decide clearly and quite ruthlessly where their real strengths lie; having decided on these they should try to build their long-term strategy around them rather than seek to be all things to all people;
- communicate their strategy confidently, both within the university and to the outside world, so that it becomes widely recognized; and,

- set about building a resource base to reinforce their strengths, if necessary, at the expense of areas that are less strong or distinctive.

These strategies recognize that, while universities can do little to challenge the strategies of the state directly, there is a great deal that they can do to govern their responses to agendas of the state. In so doing, they can influence those agendas.

John Seely Brown and Paul Duguid – a networked future

Unlike both Kerr and Shattock, the writing of Brown and Duguid is not informed by the recent exercise of high office in a university. The biographical information accompanying their work indicates that Brown is Vice-President and Chief Scientist of the Xerox Corporation, and Director of the Xerox Palo Alto Research Center, while Duguid is a research specialist at the University of California. The work on which I draw here is entitled *Universities in the Digital Age* (1996). It is a speculation on the possible impact of communication and information technologies (CITs) on pedagogical roles and operational structures of universities in the future.

Brown and Duguid spend some time reviewing the 'state of play' of universities with respect to the use of CITs. They comment on institutional inertia and campus schizophrenia, noting that 'institutions that were able to accumulate the resources (financial, intellectual, social) to develop computer-intensive infrastructures were most likely to be large, wealthy, and above all else . . . profoundly stable'. I hear echoes of Michael Shattock's comments on the lack of energy, here militating against the adoption of CITs. But they point to the fact that digital technologies sit alongside very traditional practices – reasoning that 'people who have paid a lot for a chunk of tradition usually will resist attempts to dismember it'. So, while campuses are changing:

> It's probably less helpful . . . to say simply that higher education will change because of changing technologies than to say the emerging computational infrastructure will be crucially important in shaping an already changing system.
>
> (Brown and Duguid 1996: 11)

This is an important distinction. It acknowledges that change is always *from* something, and that universities have very considerable institutional inertia, largely because of the *social inertia* associated with traditional practices. Those who speculate on the future of universities by starting with a blank page can delude themselves.

Brown and Duguid reject the media-view of future universities, i.e., virtual universities. They regard that view as flawed because it:

> both underestimates how universities as institutions work and overestimates what communication technologies can do. Learning, at all

levels, relies ultimately on personal interactions and, in particular, on a range of implicit and peripheral forms of communication, some of which technology is still very far from being able to handle proficiently.
(Brown and Duguid 1996: 12)

They note that, for the majority of American higher education students, participation represents 'an investment – a down payment on a career, social status, or, more immediately, just a job'(p. 12). In this sense, their scenario is more that of 'the investing society' than 'the learning society'.

Theirs is also a networked society. Of course issues of networking and investment are not separate – decisions about 'which university' one should pay to attend are often linked to the value of opportunities to network with other students that might be made possible. But Brown and Duguid look to networks as involving more than students. In particular, they discuss how knowledge is developed and shared within 'communities of practice' – in the case of universities, communities of scholars, reflected in the claim that 'the core competency of universities is not transforming knowledge, but developing it, and that's done within intricate and robust networks and communities'. They point to participation as the only way to access the cultural peculiarities – the implicit and peripheral information – that underlie authentic participation in any community. This is not the information in textbooks, the information that can be 'delivered' via the Internet. It is what privileges participation over 'packaged' information.

Their analysis leads them to suggest that students need three things from a university:

- access to authentic communities of learning, exploration and knowledge creation;
- resources to help them work in both distal [virtual] and local communities; and
- widely accepted representation for work done [i.e., credentials].

Beyond these, a university would need academic staff, facilities, and an administrative structure that could award credentials.

Having established these requirements as the only prerequisites, Brown and Duguid then share their thinking about a new design. They begin with the final requirement, suggesting that this function could be undertaken by a separate degree granting body (DGB) – much in the way that Cambridge University awards degrees, based on work undertaken by students in the relatively autonomous colleges. A DGB would be 'essentially administrative, with little need to own much beyond its administrative competency and a building to house its . . . staff'. Unencumbered by overhead and infrastructure costs, DGBs would be highly flexible, therefore able to adapt to meet the changing needs of students. DGBs would enrol students in accredited programmes of study, and receive fees from those students.

The model of academic staffing seems to be based on practices in medicine, where practitioners contract to provide services to hospitals, clinics and the like. In their scenario, academic staff would act as independent agents, contracting to provide services, individually or in teams, to one or more DGBs. Fees-for-service would be paid by the DGBs to the academics, with the fee varying according to service provided. In this scenario, academic staff could be required to provide facilities for the required service. This could involve renting space in complexes 'very much like the campus of today'.

Brown and Duguid present such a radically different version of higher education that it is difficult to identify any particular relationship (involving the state, the broader community, or the business community) that might be strengthened by it. Replacing existing conceptions of a university with a DGB and academics as service providers erases the 'university' in the sense that it is currently understood. At first glance it is very difficult to see a DGB achieving the purposes of higher education enunciated by the Dearing Committee, or Clark Kerr. It looks like a radically individualized and privatized form of education, particularly in terms of its structure.

But I think this 'reading' overlooks the three 'needs' that Brown and Duguid establish for students, and the possibility that a focus on the satisfaction of those needs would do much to achieve the Dearing and Kerr purposes. Let me explore this possibility more carefully, drawing on two 'local' examples.

The OLA model

The first example involves the Open Learning Agency (OLA) of Australia. It mirrors some aspects of the Brown and Duguid scenario. It is a brokerage agency, established to contract with universities, rather than individual academics, to provide courses of study. Universities provide services primarily in the form of study materials (print and audio-visual for broadcast via radio or television), specified levels of tutorial support for students, and assessment of and feedback on completed student work. However, the OLA is not a DGB – that task is left with individual universities which award credentials to students who have completed particular OLA programmes, even though those programmes might be 'taught' by staff from a number of other universities. But it is the collector of fees, and it does pay the contributing universities for both the resource materials prepared, and the tutorial and assessment work undertaken, by academics. The OLA is now an independent company owned by a consortium of seven universities.

The cost of studying through the OLA is less than the minimum fee requirements at any of the public universities in Australia – its fees are set below the level of the Higher Education Contribution Scheme (HECS) fees that are paid by students. In 1998, as HECS fees rose, enrolments in OLA courses plummeted – by about 30 per cent. It seems that Australian students have not found a cheaper education sufficiently attractive.

Evaluated in terms of the Brown and Duguid scenario, the OLA model is flawed. It is a model that is based on a broadcast model of distance education, a model which Brown and Duguid argue is ineffective because it fails to provide access to authentic communities of learning, exploration and knowledge creation. Students are supplied with study resources, but instead of working in both distal and local communities, they work mainly in isolation, and that work involves the study of an extant set of resources, i.e., materials stripped of their 'border resources'. Missing is the necessary opportunity to access implicit and peripheral information, the information that would enable them to become members of those communities of practice, an achievement to which their credential should attest. Finally, degrees are awarded by a recognized university, and should have no less acceptance than an identical credential awarded by that institution to a student whose programme of study is completed in an entirely traditional manner.

The Logan Campus model

I have referred to my current work in supporting staff in adapting their teaching to a technology-rich on-campus learning environment on the Logan Campus. As a model it is incomplete, even speculative, yet I think it offers a substantive enactment of technology-augmented higher education that has some degree of consistency with the three 'needs' that Brown and Duguid identified for students. It is part scenario, part description.

This is a new Australian campus, with the initial building complex nearing completion as I write (June, 1998). It opened this year, with an intake of approximately 600 students into 12 degree programmes. It is intended to have a student population in excess of 2000 students within three years. At present no academic staff are permanently located on the campus, but this will change through time. The vast majority of staff who have developed resources for the campus, and who are teaching on the campus, are based on the main (Nathan) campus of the university (approximately twenty kilometers to the north), where they teach in traditional environments. Others are employed on a part-time basis.

In terms of its CIT infrastructure it is a very impressive site: there is one advanced PC for every six students; all PCs are networked to a local server and Internet capable; all teaching spaces are networked; there is a high-capacity wide-band microwave link to the main university network. In fact the CIT infrastructure for students is far better than that of the majority of academic staff on the other university campuses. The largest 'spaces' are designated as 'student learning areas', which include a range of types of furniture, individual carrels, carrels with PCs, tables for group work, tables + PCs for group work. In addition there is a range of specialist facilities: PC laboratories, science laboratories, photography areas, and so on. The collection of print and other resources is housed in the largest of the 'student learning areas'. Thus it is both a library and a student learning area.

There are no lectures – students access the vast majority of the primary source information through WWW sites, print resources, and other multi/ audio/visual resources, e.g., CD-ROMs, audio cassettes, and video cassettes.

There are face-to-face discussions, where academics lead discussions, provide additional information, demonstrate the function of particular pieces of equipment, engage students in various activities, and so on. While much assessment follows more traditional patterns, there is extensive use of the CIT capacities to allow for automated and independent diagnostic testing and feedback, on-line submission of student work, and feedback from academics via bulletin boards and individual email. This collection of pedagogical practices is referred to in this university as 'flexible learning'.

For reasons entirely beyond the control of the university (i.e., reasons of state), detailed planning for the campus, including finalization of its academic profile, began less than 12 months before it was occupied. This meant that the timeframe for designing and developing courses and resources was very tight. The process of development involved extensive collaboration between academics (individually or in small teams) and a relatively small group of support staff with considerable expertise in the areas of multimedia design and development.

Preceding that collaboration I coordinated a programme of staff development activities to provide an orientation to issues involved in flexible learning – including options they might explore in developing their specific practices, examples of flexible learning practices already used within the university, and strategies for managing the development process. Participation in these activities was voluntary – in many cases we did not know which academics would actually be involved in the Logan Campus work. Reactions to the possibility of teaching at Logan varied enormously among those who did participate, from those who were delighted by the possibilities to those who were appalled that anyone could associate technology and/or flexible learning with higher education. While those extremes, particularly the latter, were obvious, they were also the minority. Most staff initially expressed considerable uncertainty, even reluctance about their involvement – as evidenced in the anecdote shared in Chapter 1. And most reactions focused on the issue of the use of CITs – technologizing teaching.

However, I do not want to focus on the issue of academics' reactions to change here. I want to describe some promising features of the flexible learning practices I see developing on this campus. My comments are relatively speculative – the courses have been in operation for less than a year, and the final outcomes can't be known. But academics have shared examples of patterns of engagement and emergent outcomes that are educationally exciting. Nevertheless, I share this thinking here without any strong sense of optimism. The possibility of their maintenance is anything but assured.

The design of the most promising courses and resources for the Logan campus share several features. First, while all academics gave considerable thought to the resources that students would need to access, the most promising designs involve lateral thinking about resources. Specifically, some courses have deliberately sought to draw on resources additional to those that they might prepare in some 'package'. Examples of these additional resources tend to focus on the people who are in or near to the campus

– the students themselves, the staff and the local community. These are 'non-instructional' resources in that students access them largely through their own initiative, even though they may be required to do so in order to complete assigned tasks.

Second, academics report that students are coming to the face-to-face activities after having used those resources. The face-to-face work is not providing a set of 'safety-net' activities for those who need a lecturer to summarize the major points of the readings. The best use of face-to-face time involves orientation to and/or clarification, extension, augmentation of tasks that students complete at some other time. These tasks are mapped out in advance by the lecturer, or may be undertaken outside formal contact time. In some instances academics have 'weaned' students off instruction in a relatively controlled fashion, while others simply refused to lecture from the outset.

Third, promising outcomes also resulted from thinking which gave a lot of attention to the question of how those resources would be used – structuring their use. Two strategies were particularly important: orientation of students, and small group work (including problem solving). In these instances students were given careful introductions to the resources and their use. In addition, the learning tasks tend to be based on small group activities – tasks that require and/or reward collaborative effort. Here reward is largely in the nature of the tasks in which students engage, and the opportunity to collaborate in their completion. That is, students have been encouraged to engage in tasks that actually require a team for their achievement.

Fourth, the most promising small group learning tasks involve both complexity and significant elements of community-based activity. These are authentic tasks, in that they invite students to go into the local community and to work on problems that are negotiated with members of that community. These are not the more traditional first-year undergraduate tasks involving relatively routine problem solving, or rehearsal of relatively well-trodden paths. The students appear excited by the challenge, and by the importance the people they are working with attach to their work.

Fifth, the students have distinguished between more and less promising uses of the Web. The following (edited) comments are from a colleague who shares some of these.

One of the most interesting experiences I have had this week was when I asked 'who was using the WWW subject content'. From *both* my Nathan and Logan classes, only a few people (less than 5 per cent) admitted to using the 'WWW subject content' for learning. Most students just printed the material out and took the material home.

Most students *do* however use the Web for assessment items (because that's where I put the assessment), interactive tools, and downloadable resources (very pleasing!).

Also interesting, not a single student has used the 'Forum' tool. Email (when it works) seems to be the most popular form of interaction, second only to 'wheelie' chairs.

Students seem to have quickly converted Web-based instructional material into 'print resources'. On the other hand, Web-based interactive resources and information searching have proved very motivating for students. Several academics have reported the development of research skills in these first-year students which exceed their expectations of second- or third-year students. The use of the Web has contributed positively to that achievement.

Sixth, the activities involve deliberate attempts to maximize consistency and cohesion between individual subjects, and within any course of study. This reduces the learning that each student has to undertake in order to participate in each subject. This is possible because all subjects are taught in flexible mode, and all involve the use of home-pages that have common 'front-ends', navigational systems and 'tools' within them.

Finally, the most promising activities seem less a result of the information that the academics have shared, and more to do with the opportunities they have provided for students to locate, evaluate, integrate and communicate information. I've mentioned the importance of authenticity and challenge, but the issue of undertaking these activities in a relatively supportive and non-judgmental environment seems extremely important to these first-year students.

While each of these features can individually be evidenced in the more traditional setting on the Nathan Campus, their centrality to, and orchestration in, the learning environment on the Logan Campus stands in great contrast to those traditions. I am suggesting that the learning experience of students on this campus is *very* different to that of their peers. Those discontinuities focus on the new learning environments as being:

- structure-rich – through the learning tasks, activities and resources provided to students;
- information-rich – as a result of the resources developed to support their learning, and ready access to the global resources of the WWW; and,
- conversation-rich – as formal on-campus contact time is used for discussion rather than instruction.

These features are facilitated by the CIT infrastructure, aligned with an intention to promote forms of student-centered learning. If the experience is different, then I have every reason to believe that the learning outcomes will also be different. So how do these practices equate with student needs as identified by Brown and Duguid?

Despite the fact that it is 'early days', my sense is that these practices do rather well in terms of these criteria. Students are getting access to authentic communities of learning, even though these are largely communities of peers rather than communities of multiple and varying levels of expertise. The pressure to 'get the information' has been taken off the face-to-face discussions, freeing them for more learning-oriented purposes. The very authenticity of the tasks has led to higher quality discussions, and to a greater sense of awareness amongst students of the value of both the tasks and their learning.

The nature of both the resources and the learning tasks has supported their engagement in small group interactions, class discussions and interactions with the wider community. To date there is not a lot of evidence of the use of the potential of virtual communities, through the use of on-line chat sites, bulletin boards and the like. This is probably more to do with academics' confidence in using those types of facilities, and the need to develop learning tasks which authentically invite/require their use. This experience is consistent with the observations of Brown and Duguid (1996: 17), that 'though Net interactions offer profoundly useful means to support and develop existing communities, they are not so good at helping a community to form or a new-comer to join'.

Little can be known of the acceptance of the work done or credentials that will result. We have data on student withdrawals, and it confirms that some students found these technology-rich environments unsatisfactory. But those rates are not troubling. On the other hand, we know of the increasing enthusiasm of these students for the structured independence and intellectual challenges they are experiencing. They regard this approach to learning as requiring more of themselves, but see that as an added investment in their learning. They are very aware of the valuable networks they are forming. A number have gained employment, or changed careers, entirely as a result of their engagement in their university work. The extensive links with it have contributed to the 'visibility' of the campus and its programmes within the local community.

The Logan Campus provides a scenario for the future that, at this stage, suggests ways to change significantly the nature of the university experience for undergraduates, and for those who teach them. The embryonic practices provide examples of ways in which CITs can be used to add value to the educational experience, and to act as a catalyst for the restructuring of institutional pedagogies. From the outset, academics were repeatedly told that this was not to be a 'virtual campus'. Yet they were also told that they had to use technology, and that they were not to give lectures. Their initial reluctance and anxiety reflected their uncertainties about how they would teach, how their pedagogic intentions could be achieved without utilizing their well-rehearsed strategies. The issue of technology dominated their thinking and discussions. Would it work? Would students accept its use? Would it be reliable? Increasingly those who are teaching on the campus are suggesting that 'technology is not the issue' – designing and developing environments in which high-quality learning is likely to eventuate *is* the issue.

But I believe that without this provocation, without having to 'think the unthinkable', these outcomes would not have been achieved. The introduction of the technology-rich learning environments meant that these academics were forced to step back from their traditional practices, to reflect if and/or how those practices should or could be used in this setting. The recognition that 'technology is not the issue' reflects the continuity between their more traditional practices and those they are developing. They found that students didn't just want to download information from the WWW and go home. They expected, and demanded, the 'border resources' that give meaning to that information. Academics have been able to draw on the social inertia of some traditional practices, and are investing considerable energy in orienting students to these new practices. Interestingly, reaction from staff and students on the other campuses has become one of envy – value is being given from the reactions of those outside the campus, including international visitors. Perhaps the future of my university is being reinvented through this process of campus-focused technologically oriented change.

Thoughts about change

In concluding this chapter, I want to state, rather bluntly, a number of beliefs about change at this relatively broad level – to nominate some 'big picture' issues that have been prompted by the development of this text.

Discussion of the purpose of higher education for the beginning of the next millennium, and the changes that are signalled by those purposes, is less a matter of conceptual rigour or empirical description than it is a matter of speculation. Some refer to these speculations as visions, others as dreams. Any innovation involves a step into the unknown. But that step is always *from* somewhere. We can only make sense of the present, and anticipate the future, in terms of the past. But we often mistake our experience of that past as known rather than felt, as shared rather than idiosyncratic.

Engaging in that speculation is not a neutral activity. Visions come wrapped in prejudgments. The future has to be constructed, imagined, worked for, and speculation is a very significant step in that process. That is, speculation is a creative process – imaginative, constructive and selective. Because it is speculative and creative, change is not a linear process. We need to be prepared to look for the unexpected – to be surprised.

Change does not 'happen'. Its achievement is a constant process involving both progress and regress. But those too do not just happen – they are recognized and they are brought into being. Recognition requires that we pay attention to experience, and the direction of change is very much determined by the issues to which we attend. Recognition also involves naming – experiences don't come with subtitles. We give form to an emergent change by noticing it, by naming it, by discussing it, by celebrating it. It is through this type of work, rather than through plans, that we create change.

The development of purpose involves context-specific accommodations between what should be, what can be, and what must be. The processes of noticing, naming, discussing and celebrating wrap change in values. Whatever else they might be, the outcomes of change are not going to be perfect. Planning for change always involves compromises, and we need to pay very careful attention to the values underlying both visions of the future, and the plans for their achievement. This helps us to know what values to wrap the outcomes in. Change is not a rational process – it is a process of expressing values in new ways, under new conditions.

Purposeful change can be understood as a political response, a means of improvement, and a survival strategy. All have their value. All involve the redeployment of resources. Change tends to be multidimensional in terms of the purposes it serves, and to be discontinuous. I have noted that Kerr argues that the range of purposes for universities will expand, while Shattock argues that the opposite should happen. But I suspect they are exploring change in different dimensions of the operation of higher education. We need to pay attention to the relationships between these multiple dimensions and any proposal for change, or process of discontinuous change. Changes that are valued on one level may be very destructive on another.

When change happens, power may be conserved or strengthened, improvement may be achieved, and survival may be ensured. While these are possibilities, and may be achieved through work, loss is guaranteed. Speculation comes with no guarantee of success. But whenever we decide to change roles, we will lose aspects of the security of knowing how to perform our existing role, and of knowing what to pay attention to in order to get our intrinsic rewards in that role – the things that keep us going. We 'know' what we are changing from, but there is always uncertainty about what our new role will be. Significant learning is a risky business, full of surprises, and it is best undertaken in situations which provide a range of forms of both encouragement and support. Then both academics and students can be players rather than pawns in the process of change.

3

Academics' Work and Working

Culture shock is the effect that immersion in a strange culture has on the unprepared visitor . . . It is what happens when the familiar psychological cues that can help an individual function in society are suddenly withdrawn and replaced by new ones that are strange or incomprehensible.

(Toffler 1970: 19)

The following comments from one of the academic respondents to the EIP project interviews, shared without endorsing or criticizing the position adopted, exemplifies thinking about the challenges academics are facing.

> I believe in universities that we have stagnated. We found our niche, we have been comfortable in it and we have stayed there. Now because of the tremendous change since 1988 and the demands that have been put on us by the Federal Government in terms of quality and account-ability, I believe we have to make the change.
>
> Whilst I understand that people feel stress and pressure, I think that we are a very protective bunch . . .
>
> I mean it is a hard profession, being in universities at the moment. You know we used just to teach. Now we are teaching, doing research, doing continuing education, doing community service. Well, so be it. I do not have to be here, I choose to be here . . . I am working longer hours. I am feeling the stress of it, but I believe this is my commitment to the profession and I choose to be here to do it.

Universities are changing to address multiple purposes and, as a result, are becoming fragmented. They want to be all things to all people: to have centres of international excellence in research; to be globally competitive in marketing their courses; to have established collaborative networks with local industry; to have attracted the 'best and brightest' scholars; to have integrated CITs within all aspects of their operations; to have achieved inter-national 'best practice' in all aspects of their operations; to have a vision and mission which energize and mobilize the efforts of all staff; and on, and on, *ad infinitum.* And they expect their academic staff to commit to the achieve-ment of all these things, without missing a beat!

While 'there is no such thing as a standard career pattern which spans the range of intellectual activity' (Becher 1989: 110), there is, for most aca-demics, a sense of career. This includes a continuity in terms of the pursuit of particular lines of research, the development of expertise in teaching, and the development of a reputation and capacity to engage with – and contribute to – the community through various service activities. It is through this essentially linear progression that contributions to their institution will be recognized and rewarded, that an academic's career will advance. Indeed, interruptions to these continuities are almost universally seen as 'setting back', at least in the short-term, a career. The advice is: 'Don't change your research programme', if you have one; 'develop a research programme, and fast' if you don't; and, 'don't get distracted from developing your research profile'. The academic career path is marked out by advice such as this. At least it used to be!

Academics are experiencing a form of 'future shock' that is linked to the institutional fragmentation, and to the resulting disruption of expectations and continuities. But their shock is always experienced in relation to specific locations and identities – their own. It is also linked to a sense that they, like others in their communities, are increasingly seen as 'disposable, rootless workers' by their institutions. Institutional structures are becoming more fluid and this is spilling, or rather it is being poured, into academics' work settings. Some are resisting, others are flowing with it, others are confused by it, and some seem to be drowning. Others are displaying their own version of emergent fragmentation, as they do all of these things. This is the 'big picture' that I want to examine more closely in this chapter.

I undertake this exploration through using the following 'frames':

- academic identities – as multi-level, as achievements, and as discipline-focused;
- changing roles – competence is an emergent phenomenon which requires the evolution of identities, and the management of this evolution;
- changing responses – focusing on the extension of expertise (particularly in teaching) and cross-tribal communication within the academy; and
- emergent roles – relationships between changing work and changes in roles.

Academic identities

The concept of identity is broader than that of role, given that 'identity' refers to aspects that characterize a person generally, and 'role' refers to the part played by an individual in a particular social setting. While it is not unusual to regard identity as meanings given to the self, that is, as part of self-concept, I use the term here to refer to '*indexes of the self*': 'signs that refer to qualities of the identity claimant. An identity . . . is not a meaning but *a sign that evokes meaning*, in the form of a response aroused in the person who interprets it' (Schwalbe and Mason-Schrock 1996: 115). These signs are necessarily public rather than personal properties. In this sense, identities are attributes used to characterize a person, rather than intrinsic features of the person. Thus, identities and roles are related to each other and to the surrounding cultural and social milieu, which acts both to constrain and to enable the formation of particular identities and roles in a range of ways.

Indexes of the self lend coherence and continuity to academics' practices. Within fragmenting universities a sense of coherence and continuity is an important resource for enhancing academics' ability to function. But *indexes of the self* work in a double way. They also serve to constrain academic practices in ways that extend beyond the individual. In this sense, they make those practices recognizable as 'academic', for better *and* worse. It is for this reason that *indexes of the* 'academic' *self* demand scrutiny. They take us beyond the specifics of an academic as a person – temperament, personality, family and social history, and so on – to a consideration of the situated academic who shapes and is shaped by his or her individual workplace.

Academic identities are not unitary

It is possible to distinguish at least three 'levels' of academic identity: signs linked to the site of one's work; signs linked to the discipline of one's work; and more universal signs of 'being an academic'. The first level involves relationships with employer and work. Universities aren't identical. In the UK there are, for instance, the traditional and the 'new' universities. In the United States there are the elite research universities, the liberal-arts and technical colleges, the second-tier doctoral-granting universities, and the community colleges and two-year technical schools. These differences impact on the way the public, and therefore those who work within them, view them and are viewed. That is, I am suggesting there is a level of 'the index of self' that is signalled by the type of institution and of work by, and with, which academics are involved: 'I'm from Harvard.'

The second level of identity involves identification with an academic discipline. Tony Becher (1989) advances the very significant claim that academics identify more strongly with the 'characteristics and structures of the knowledge domains' of their disciplines (p. 20) than with their institution. David Damrosch (1995) provides an account of some mechanisms by which this disciplinary identity is forged:

> Academic work is institutionally arranged in a patterned isolation of disciplines, and then of specialized fields within disciplines. This patterning is not something inherent in the material; it shapes the questions we ask and the ways in which we ask them. These scholarly values in turn foster – and reward – alienation and aggression at all levels of academic life.
>
> (Damrosch 1995: 6)

Here the identity is signalled through reference to the discipline: 'I'm a biologist.'

But there is another version of self-shaping going on as well. Academics have to learn to work with two 'publics': the general community, and the disciplinary community. Thus, very early in their careers, academics learn to live by two sets of rules; one involves discipline-focused rules, while the second involves a more publicly recognizable set.

This public set of rules and values is the third 'level' of signage. This is the more universal image of the academic identity which overlaps disciplinary boundaries – *a cosmopolitan identity*. This aspect of academic identity is centred around two values: 'academic autonomy' – the symbolic claim of and for disinterested inquiry; and 'academic freedom' – the symbolic claim for 'the faculty as a *collectivity* to retain sovereignty over the educational process' (Aronowitz 1997: 202). This is the identification with the career: 'I'm an academic.'

This cosmopolitan ideal is portrayed through treatments of academics in the global media, particularly in film. In fact the universal nature of this identity is what makes it 'work' as a character anchor for international films. Here the academic identity is overwhelmingly male, post-middle age, intellectual and eccentric. The characters played by Michael Caine in *Educating Rita*, and Anthony Hopkins in *Shadowlands*, reveal privileged lifestyles and an inadequacy in dealing with life. Harrison Ford's character in *Mosquito Coast* leaves the unworldliness of academic life to become the resourceful hero. These media 'signs' situate the academic as impractical and unworldly, as someone in flight from a 'real world' rather than one who thrives on being tested within it. A more sympathetic interpretation of the cosmopolitan identity would emphasize enactment of the concept of positive disequilibrium discussed in Chapter 2.

My point is that the 'academic identity' is not a unitary construct, and can be thought of in terms of levels or layers of symbols. The picture I am wanting to create is one which recognizes both the diversity in the meanings attached to the term 'academic', *and* the relative uniformity that the term captures at the cosmopolitan level. Those are the global symbols of disinterested, individual inquiry and collective educational sovereignty. These traits stand in contrast to those that seem to be required of employees in modern universities – commitment to the corporate mission.

These symbols express folkloric myths, taken as accurate and important representations of how academic culture came into being, and, perhaps more importantly, how it *ought* to be. The behaviours that support them are learned: 'apprentice scholars learn to select out from their overall personality those qualities that create a successful scholarly personality' (Damrosch 1995: 85). And they have a sense of accuracy and continuity, as the discussion of the historical development of the Uppsala and Lund universities provided by Göran Blomqvist (1997) indicates. However, in that setting contestation between the state and the universities tended to focus on issues related to corporate rather than individual autonomy. But this qualification is, in the main, unknown to the majority of those who claim the academic identity. They are stories told in defence of idealized practices, rather than stories that motivate actual practices. They are exaggerations, inventions – used to create a sense of unity among academics when in fact the practices of the academy have always been diverse and open to change.

Academic identities are achievements

Identities attain significance over time, as particular qualities are linked with particular signs of identity – they are achievements. They are *social* achievements, and a requirement of social life. They give a sense of belonging, a feeling of personal significance and a sense of continuity and coherence. Successful identity work is, therefore, anxiety reducing – a different version of boundary formation and maintenance. Identities provide the basis for expectations in social interactions – we know what to expect from others, and what/who it is that we are expected to be.

The view of identity as a social (and cultural) achievement is consistent with the work of a number of researchers. In commenting on professional cultures in organizational contexts, Geoffrey Bloor and Patrick Dawson (1994: 276) define organizational culture as: *'a patterned system of perceptions, meanings, and beliefs about the organization which facilitates sense-making amongst a group of people sharing common experiences and guides individual behaviour at work* (original italics). Thus, culture is an outcome of group work 'act[ing] to enable, constrain and guide action at the level of the individual' (p. 276). Consistent with the discussion of sensemaking in Chapter 1, Bloor and Dawson suggest that the achievement of culture is always a retrospective activity – focused on what has already happened – and it relies on individual knowledge of stories, myths and experiences. Importantly, these form the basis for deciding present actions, and anticipating the future.

The earlier discussion of sensemaking may have implied that it is an isolated, individual activity. However, Bloor and Dawson argue that:

> individuals in organizations do not 'sense-make' in isolation, but rather, rely heavily upon observing the behaviour of others in social settings, and upon the shared meanings others give to that behaviour. Moreover, whilst people may act in new ways in response to new interpretations of events, there is a bias towards those patterns of interacting which have been successful in the past (for both individuals and groups).
>
> (Bloor and Dawson 1994: 278)

This is the very power of shared information, of culturally produced stories and myths – they work. Indeed, these patterns and shared meanings must work in order to defend the interests of one organizational group against hostile actions by other groups. In unsettled times, culture serves to shape actions. Groups under challenge are likely to rely on 'tradition' to legitimate their preferred position, representing their particular interests as universal and the natural state of affairs (p. 289). Bloor and Dawson's research suggests that professionals only articulate their values at these times. This supports the idea that the cosmopolitan ideals of academic work tend to be claimed primarily in times of external threat.

Michael Schwalbe and Douglas Mason-Schrock (1996) provide a very similar story to that of Bloor and Dawson in that they regard identity making as 'simultaneously a making of culture' (p. 121). Both pairs of researchers note that group identity or group culture, respectively, are not 'finished constructions' – they involve constant interplay and negotiation between the group/culture and the social context, which is itself always in a state of flux. Thus, identity and culture are *accomplishments*. The constancy of this process can encourage people to forget that these stories are made up, and that their ongoing achievement requires constant work. Thus, the way things are can be mistaken for 'the natural order' – the way things should be.

These propositions have important implications for this examination of academic identity. I have suggested that academics' notions of identity are multi-level, and, in the case of the central notions of identity, are problematic in terms of congruence with organizational priorities. However, problems arise largely in the context of contestation and confrontation associated with change. Because the cosmopolitan values have the widest recognition and appeal, and therefore the greatest value-as-defence, academics tend to rely on them in situations of uncertainty. That is, academics' rational sensemaking relies on these values in these situations. This response is in keeping with the suggestions of Bloor and Dawson (1994), who note the importance of culture in 'shaping action' in response to challenges. Resisting change often involves representing sectional interests 'as being universal' and reifying the status quo as being 'the natural state of affairs' (p. 289). But of what benefit to academics are responses based on cosmopolitan values? Do they work?

In responding to this question, it is important to acknowledge that academics undertake a number of roles. Those include what might be termed the roles of knower, teacher, and researcher-of-the-discipline, as well as colleague and employee. The reliance on cosmopolitan values privileges the roles of knower and researcher-of-the-discipline. However, these are but two among many, and this privileging tends to diminish the importance and values of the other roles. In addition, if the 'cosmopolitan response' is enacted in situations that focus on those other roles, it is likely to be seen as inappropriate, even self-indulgent.

Let me exemplify this possibility. In preparing the courses to be taught on the Logan Campus, academics found themselves collaborating in relatively stressful circumstances with senior academic managers, and with multimedia 'experts'. When the academics sought to resist pressures from these two groups to adopt new practices, some tended to resist through claiming that their academic freedom – the collective sovereignty of the faculty in terms of the design of the educational process – was being undermined. The resistance and protests of the academics were, in my opinion, justified in terms of the specific circumstances of the demands.

Nevertheless, their protest against what was perceived as the undermining of their academic freedom – their 'collective sovereignty' – was problematic for several reasons. First, there had been no real attempt to organize any collective response. For this reason it looked very much like the protest of isolated individuals, who, as a result, tended to be regarded as 'difficult'. Second, what they wanted to protest about was the perceived value (to them) of the traditional teaching practices they were being asked to revise, and the very ambiguous nature, and therefore value, of the practices which they were being asked to develop and adopt. That is, the issues being contested had more to do with their roles as teachers and with pedagogical values than the values associated with their cosmopolitan identities. At no time did I hear any of 'the resisters' address pedagogical issues with real authority or conviction. I am aware of their reasoning now because of more recent and extended conversations I have had with some of those individuals. Their resistance had relied on the rhetoric of academic freedom, rather than any explicit expertise related to the implied values.

Thus, where they might have chosen to resist in terms of their existing and anticipated roles as teachers-of-the-discipline, they initially resisted in terms of their roles as knowers. Where they might have become very helpful advocates of a more considered approach to the redevelopment of their educational practices, their protests were ignored (appropriately in my opinion – they could not justify their resistance, nor could they offer any useful alternative). Regardless of the reason, the consequence was that they missed an opportunity to influence the course of change. And their actions further cemented in the minds of the multimedia staff and several academic managers an ongoing and unhelpful view that 'academics need to be more carefully and closely managed in future'.

Changing roles

The preceding discussion has suggested that academics' traditional cosmopolitan values are of little value in situations of individual conflict involving roles other than research. Before discussing the development of alternatives to these values I want to discuss issues related to the organizational context of changes in academics' work.

As the purposes of higher education change, universities are changing. So, in turn, are the roles of academics. The work of Richard Boyatzis (1982) provides a useful model to represent this relationship. His work is focused on the concept of a 'competent' manager. His position is that:

> *effective performance of a job is the attainment of specific results (i.e., outcomes) required by the job through specific actions while maintaining or being consistent with policies, procedures, and conditions of the organizational environment.*
> (Boyatzis 1982: 12, original italics)

Figure 3.1   A model of effective performance

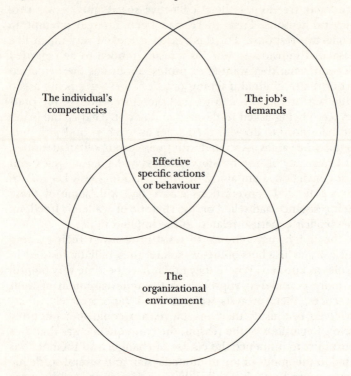

Source: Boyatzis 1982: 13, Figure 2.1

This statement suggests that his model is germane to the more general theme of 'competent' academic workers, and I use it in this way.

Boyatzis' (1982) model involves three elements: the job's demands; the individual's competencies; and the organizational environment. The job's demands refers to those specific results which, when combined with the results from other jobs, 'yield the organization's product or service' (p. 12). These demands include the specific actions that are necessary to the achievement of the desired outcomes. The individual's competencies 'represent the capability that he or she brings to the job situation'. Finally, the 'organizational environment' includes its direction, stated through its 'mission, purpose, or corporate strategy', and the policies and procedures which are 'reflected in the internal structure and systems of the organization'. The thesis underlying Boyatzis' work is that competent performance occurs only when all three of the critical components of the model overlap. The areas outside this overlap represent incompetent or ineffective behaviour or inaction. He uses a diagram of his model to represent this argument (Figure 3.1).

There are several reasons for drawing attention to Boyatzis' work, even though it presents a picture whose clarity and simplicity belie the complexities with which I want to engage. It is a reminder that roles are themselves contextualized, located within sets of expectations and organizational affordances. More importantly, as universities change, the former area of overlap between the three components inevitably changes, and this change is experienced at an individual level. One of the academics involved in the Logan Campus wrote that:

> In traditional settings I have thought of myself as a facilitator of the learning process, but I now think that this facilitation only worked because there was already a fair level of structure.

While some staff find that there is congruence between their competencies, the job demands and the new organizational environment, others experience the opposite. In either case, the degree of congruence will be reflected in evaluations of the individual's behaviour – the former being seen as more 'productive', while the latter risks being labelled as 'inactive'.

Evolving identities

The reality is that for a majority of academics, the emergent job demands are not the demands described or implied in the 'job descriptions' of the positions for which they were originally employed. Nor are they the demands that attracted them to enter an academic career. Trowler (1998) includes the following statement from one of his respondents: 'I love my job, I love [my discipline], I love teaching. I get a terrific amount of stimulation and satisfaction out of the job but what I want is the job as we used to know it, not as it is now. That's why I would like to get out' (Trowler 1998: 115). Elaine Martin (1999) provides considerable evidence that this feeling, despite pockets of optimism, is representative of academics in the UK, US and Australia. She concludes that academics appear to be overwhelmed by the enormity of the challenges they face, and to feel undervalued and overworked.

The demands of the emergent 'jobs' are increasingly diverging from those of the traditional 'academic job', i.e., the job most academics were employed to undertake, and in which they may have been highly competent. Francis Oakley (1997) provides some sobering statistics on the demographics of US academics. He reports that in 1977, nearly half of the faculty were under 40 years old. By 1988, this proportion had fallen to slightly less than a quarter. The trend has been projected to the year 2000, by which time: 'if the projection made by the Carnegie Council in 1980 proves to be correct, there will be "far more faculty members [aged] 66 and over than there are faculty members 35 and younger"' (p. 52). My point is that most academics began their career quite some time ago. Therefore many risk experiencing both a sense of loss and a lack of commitment to the new demands.

The relationships between commitment, career and ageing have been explored by several authors. William Firestone (1996: 215), in commenting on teachers in the schooling sector, speaks of commitment in terms of 'partisan attachment to the goals and values of an organization'. This attachment is a form of psychological bond between the individual and the school, a bond that takes on special meaning and importance for that teacher. He notes that, as people age, the costs of changing careers become higher even though their commitment to their existing work may decrease. This:

> loss of commitment can have a substantial effect on teachers' plans to leave teaching for another occupation *but almost no effect on actual quitting behavior.* As a result, many teachers feel trapped in their work and are no longer committed to providing the skill and effort they did earlier.
>
> (Firestone 1996: 216 – emphasis added)

Oakley (1997) and Altbach (1997) provide additional evidence that academics are facing particular demands to change their roles as they age, and that many are feeling 'trapped' (in the sense that Firestone uses this term). One EIP respondent commented thus:

> We have got an ageing lecturing population here. I mean, I was interested the other day to hear that the average age of teachers in schools was forty-five. Well it must be more than that in the lecturing staff, at least in this Faculty. So, in a sense it is not surprising that they are reluctant. I mean you will often get people saying, 'Oh, yes, we have got to get into these new technologies.' But, when it comes down to actually committing time and effort to do it then, it is an option, and they will more likely than not opt out.

On the other hand, Becher (1989) observed that academics' careers tend to involve an internal evolution, with commitments to active research giving way to other involvement, including administration, service and teaching, as individuals age. However, there are limited opportunities to undertake administrative roles, while the rewards for teaching tend to make it an unattractive option for those who have experienced earlier success in research.

But there are also 'winners' in any process of change. Some academics might have capabilities which were underutilized in earlier times, capabilities such as a capacity for entrepreneurialism, or an interest in information and communication technologies. These can be regarded as accidental, but not undeserving, beneficiaries. Other individuals might have developed these capabilities, perhaps because they recognized what was being expected of them, perhaps because of their enjoyment of novelty, perhaps because they were provided with intensive developmental support. These are the more intentional beneficiaries – those whose personal development leads to their increasing effectiveness in the emergent environment – the *lone rangers*.

The capabilities of the 'losers' tend to be increasingly underutilized. For example, the capacity to deliver very effective lectures is of decreasing importance to academics whose teaching 'job' is now located on the Logan Campus. Similarly, academics whose teaching practices are less amenable to 'multimedia packaging' are facing demands to reinvent themselves – to develop new approaches and capacities. Without wanting to 'naturalize' this process, it is salutary to remember that most models of evolution are based on the assumption that 'losers' are eliminated. Even the process of identity formation, as noted earlier, leads to the 'weeding out' of those least suited to the existing conditions. That is, in nature evolution is not a uniformly benign process, something that is most often overlooked by those who speak of the evolution of the roles of academics, or of the higher education sector more generally. They only speak of 'meeting the challenge', i.e., of winners.

However, competence itself is constantly evolving. Therefore the effectiveness of individuals is an ongoing adaptive outcome of their own capacities, the specific demands of their roles, and the directions, policies and procedures of their institution. In addition, Boyatzis' (1982) model suggests the possibility that the evolution of the components themselves, or of aspects of a particular component, may decrease the overall coherence of the system. For example, as universities struggle to respond to changing external demands, there is a risk that their corporate strategies may come to sit uneasily beside their mission statements, while policies and procedures may become inconsistent with actual job demands.

Managing this evolution

If change is evolutionary, are universities able to be managed so that dysfunctions can be minimized, if not avoided? I have noted that the Dearing and West Committees have pointed to accelerating rates of change in higher education. Toffler's work is also based on the premise that it is the rate of change that is creating 'future shock'. The term 'shock' is important because of the implications it carries in relation to an experience. The 'shocking' experience was not expected, so there is surprise – synonyms include 'a bolt from the blue', a 'bombshell', an 'eye-opener'. But this surprise is of an unpleasant, even violent kind. The experience may be physically and emotionally traumatic.

Externally generated challenges are increasing, and the timeframe within which universities need to respond appears to be decreasing. But who is noticing these trends? Phillip Altbach (1997) suggests that, in the main, US academics are oblivious to these external trends:

> In general, there is little sense of crisis among academics; most seem unaware of the magnitude of the problem facing American higher education . . . The average full-time American professor remains largely insulated from the broad trends taking place in higher education. Not only that, the professoriate seems to have little understanding of these trends.
>
> (Altbach 1997: 330–2)

He suggests that this is because 'the professoriate' has largely been unaffected by the changes until now. Martin's (1999) work suggests that this view is likely to be held by most academic managers. Those changes have differentially impacted on part-time and non-tenured staff – the rapidly growing academic underclass – a phenomenon that I will discuss more fully in Chapter 5.

Altbach also found that American academics were 'remarkably content with their careers' (p. 330). Their contentment was linked to professional autonomy, to job security, and to respect from campus colleagues. This finding of 'general satisfaction' is consistent with a 1991 Carnegie Foundation survey into the attitudes, values and work patterns of the academic profession in an OECD survey (Sheehan and Welch 1996). That survey found similar reasons for satisfaction, and for dissatisfaction, with the latter focusing on the ways the institution was being managed. More detailed studies, such as that of James Everett and Leland Entrekin (1994), suggest that the levels of satisfaction vary between institutions, and between disciplines.

The earlier discussion of the formation and nature of academic identity suggests that academics are 'programmed' to ignore 'external' trends and issues related to higher education more generally. Their focus is the discipline, as Becher (1989) found. A career depends on evidence of a growing reputation with one's disciplinary peers, and an awareness of trends in the development of the discipline and its research agendas. To be distracted by broader trends would be to invite career stagnation. Indeed, Becher's work is widely interpreted to imply that academics' loyalty to their discipline is much stronger than their loyalty to their institution, at least in the case of those academics who have a strong commitment to research.

However, my research suggests that academic managers are noticing these trends – as discussed in Taylor *et al.* (1996) and Taylor (1997a). The academic managers who were interviewed as part of the Evaluations and Investigations Program (EIP) investigation were very aware of 'external' trends. More importantly they had, in a range of ways, initiated responses to those trends, responses which were discussed in terms of institutional needs and priorities. These included issues like funding, competitive pressures, market share and the like. These managers weren't experiencing 'future shock' – they were showing entrepreneurial flair. While I have no strong evidence that suggests they are typical of the larger group of academic managers, the overwhelming majority of the academic managers with whom I have had contact over the last five years have shown similar levels of awareness.

The academics interviewed during the EIP investigation were very interested in teaching – this was why we interviewed them. Unlike Altbach's 'professoriate', these academics had a strong sense of external trends, and were able to relate their work to a number of those trends. They are, as noted in the EIP report, perhaps atypical of the wider academic community. However, and this is a very important qualification, they did not think of these trends in the same ways as the academic managers. Their thinking focused primarily on two issues – access and equity: issues related to their core pedagogical values. That is, they sought to make their teaching practices more accessible to those for whom on-campus participation was difficult, and to ensure that these new forms of teaching retained the qualities that they regarded as characterizing their traditional on-campus teaching. In fact they found managers' concerns with funding, competitive pressures, market share and the like entirely inappropriate, even offensive. Their negative view of the motives they attributed to academic managers is consistent with Martin's (1999) findings and Altbach's professoriate: 'Unhappiness with the academic administration is a near-universal phenomenon' (1997: 331). This is an issue I will explore more fully in the next chapter.

While my focus is on academics, I need to emphasize that the changes in roles that I am discussing here necessarily involve changes in the roles and work of others – they are social achievements. As work becomes more team-based, then general staff tend to become more involved, as noted in the EIP report. One of the resulting challenges involves collaboration across old boundaries. The following comments from two EIP respondents reflect the need to manage this process.

> There is a sense of a culture of dependency among students. That they feel somehow that if the lecturer is not there explaining the information and sorting it out for them, then they are not going to cope, or they are being short-changed, or both. Now the new teaching environments require them to become a little more autonomous as learners. But students are coming to these courses with their own expectations of 'open learning' . . . It is not as if we are not explaining our approach to them. I think we explained it all to them. But it was different to what they had experienced previously, and that was not what they expected. It took them some time to take advantage of the resources we had created, and the support we provided.

> As librarians we feel our work is undervalued, and that lecturers do not understand our real or potential contributions . . . This may be because we do not have a doctorate. There certainly are barriers to interaction and communication. We are not involved in most curriculum planning processes, and we find out about plans far too late to help in making those decisions, and even to act on them sometimes. We are probably more knowledgeable about the new technologies than many academics, yet our advice is not sought.

Changing responses

I want to discuss two alternatives to the limitations of the cosmopolitan academic identity. The first response involves the development of expertise and capacities to articulate values beyond those of academic freedom and autonomy, particularly values that are associated with academics' roles as teacher-of-the-discipline. The second involves the possibility, or, as I would prefer to argue, the need, to develop what I have referred to elsewhere as cross-tribal communication (Taylor *et al.* 1996; Taylor 1997a).

Extending expertise

Academics' teaching expertise is underpinned by explicit educational values in very few instances. Becher (1989: 17) includes a quotation from Sanford (1971) that 'professors, when they assemble informally or formally, almost never discuss teaching; this is not the "shop" they talk'. One of the consequences is that academics can be relatively inarticulate when asked to comment on the value of their teaching practices – when asked very directly 'What does your teaching add to the learning of your students?' and 'How do you know that you do this?', they can describe how they go about their teaching, and, in some cases, they can also explain why they go about it in the way they do. But those explanations tend to refer to feedback from students in terms of what they liked, rather than any coherent understanding of how students learn. The report of the Dearing Committee (NCIHE 1997) reaches similar conclusions, while Ramsden (1992) offers an entire (and highly recommended) book on the subject.

The values of academic freedom and autonomy arose in a very different context to that in which academics currently work. Blomqvist's (1997) discussion of the contestations surrounding the universities of Uppsala and Lund suggests that autonomy was a legal issue – universities, as communities (of scholars and teachers) pre-existed nation states. Resisting the intrusion of 'statist agendas' had considerable significance for those communities of scholars – their long-standing traditions (in some cases, traditions that stretched over hundreds of years) and their identities as self-governing corporations were threatened. Autonomy and freedom related to the right of the scholars and teachers to teach the ideas that they held as most valuable to society, irrespective of the particular demands of the state.

It was also a time when 'teaching' really was 'a cottage industry'. That is, a time when the knowledge base underlying effective teaching was scant, and could be acquired through an apprenticeship model – through being a student of other teachers (Hargreaves 1997). There were three disciplines: theology, philosophy and law. The craft of university teaching was seen as requiring certain skills in oration, in rhetoric, and in organization, but little more than these. None of the major works on university education before this century have given any attention to *how* education might be conducted beyond those issues. Certainly, there is little sense of theories of learning being important for primary education at this time, let alone for 'higher education'.

We are now in a very different 'pedagogical' era. Research findings and their applications from the area of compulsory education have developed concepts and practices like self-directed learning, group work, problem-based learning, while theories of learning known broadly as behaviourism, humanism and constructivism have led to the development of quite specific teaching practices. Research in higher education is rapidly expanding, taking up ideas developed in the compulsory sectors as well as ideas developed primarily within the context of its own practices. Concepts like 'surface' and 'deep' approaches to learning have been available in higher education for over 20 years. Those concepts have given impetus to a very significant body of research into the approaches of students to learning, and of academics to teaching. Ramsden's (1992) text is one of the most comprehensive syntheses of that research. Thus, there is now a discipline of educational understandings and research practices.

While it would be foolish to suggest that these understandings could guarantee learning for all students, or effectiveness for all teachers, there is a profound sense that teaching in higher education is well placed to make extensive use of understandings derived from research into its own teaching practices, and to be based on values that are explicitly associated with those understandings. That is, teachers-of-a-discipline have available to them a set of understandings that can assist in the design and evaluation of environments for learning, and value positions associated with those understandings. Academics could contest issues related to the practices and conditions of their teaching more cogently and credibly if they were to utilize this information quite systematically to develop their expertise as teachers-of-a-discipline.

Tribalism and communication

The second response – cross-tribal communication – draws on the notions of tribalism introduced in Chapter 1. I want to build on those notions rather than repeat them. They were derived through the analysis of interview data collected during the EIP research project (Taylor *et al.* 1996).

The earlier discussion in this chapter indicates several 'internal' trends, and 'tribal' responses. One trend involves the ignorance, if not indifference, of academics to the external threats to universities. This is most characteristic of the tenured research-focused academics who embody the cosmopolitan ideals – the traditional tribe of academics. This group is likely to be confronted by these external threats as 'a bolt from the blue' – to be surprised. A second trend involves the very important minority tribe of *lone ranging* academics who are developing the teaching practices that are likely to form the basis of some of the necessary responses to the external threats. They are monitoring aspects of the external changes, but considering responses only in terms of opportunities to innovate in ways that are likely to provide them with professional satisfaction. Another tribe is made up of the academic managers, who are aware of and leading the institutional response to these threats. Their environmental scanning has a strong sense of corporate self-interest attached to it, and may lead to initiatives that are not valued by either of the two other groups. Indeed, it is likely that the first tribe will see the response of both the lone rangers and the academic managers in terms of disappointment, even grief. (The EIP work, and more recent experience in relation to the Logan Campus, suggests the importance of a fourth tribe – general staff.)

These trends suggest that, rather than a process of managed and cohesive evolution in universities there is more evidence of intertribal warfare, or, at the very least, a lack of an intertribal language born of trust. The EIP investigation found the multiplicity of tribal interpretations and cross-tribal tensions could be disruptive and unproductive. The latter may have arisen because of the high levels of cross-tribal communication that any innovation requires, and the suspicion with which those communications were interpreted. On the other hand, the investigation suggests that there is little reason to fear that *tribalism* is itself a barrier to the development of specific innovative practices. What tribal values and beliefs do represent is a barrier to intertribal communication about the need for, and the nature and value of, those practices. For example, messages from academic managers about the reasons for initiatives can be rendered problematic for academics and support staff if those messages are focused on the value/s of 'market share' or 'market growth'.

This view is supported by research undertaken in the UK by Keith Randle and Norman Brady (1997). Their research, along with that of others, including Becher (1989), suggests that the identity work undertaken to form groups and tribes leads to very little understanding of the values or motivations of other groups or tribes. Becher comments on the impressions shared by his respondents of colleagues in other disciplines, thus:

> I found most of the answers to be surprisingly hazy: the stereotypes which emerged of both subjects and practitioners – most of them shared among people from quite diverse backgrounds – seemed to me neither particularly perceptive nor particularly illuminating.
>
> (Becher 1989: 28)

There are two points I want to emphasize here. First, individuals construct stereotypes of other groups, stereotypes that are 'surprisingly hazy'. Second, these stereotypes tend to be consistent between otherwise diverse groups. They govern interpretations of communications from members of those groups, and they tend to be rather self-serving (just as the image of the 'unwordly' academic serves anti-intellectual rhetoric).

However, once representatives of the tribes come together in the context of a joint project, differences in perspective can become assets, as can differences in expertise. Genuine attempts to communicate across tribal differences require a stretching of an individual's understandings if he or she is to make sense of the position of a member of another tribe, or wants to make his or her own position known to that person. That is, in conversation individuals can come to recognize the nature and limitations of their own assumptions and values. As a result they become more literate about their own and others' understandings and values and more open to new possibilities – to change. Throughout our EIP investigation we found this opportunity for conversation to be a most powerful context for learning. Thus diversity, represented here in terms of tribal allegiances, is a crucial learning resource. However, its successful use requires respectful sharing, challenging and/or probing of values and assumptions.

If the message is to make use of cross-tribal conversations, with participants speaking with and through their diverse perspectives, how might this be achieved? Neuhauser (1988) refers to the value to cross-tribal communication and collaboration of migrating skills – 'the communication skills need to link what you are saying with the other person's point of view in a way that is likely to produce a negotiated agreement' (p. 106). She also writes of the value, in collaborative activities, of members who have multi-tribe experiences. This is highly consistent with the comments of a number of EIP respondents who spoke of the positive contributions of colleagues who had, over time, been members of more than one so-called tribe.

Finally, Neuhauser refers to the necessity to establish 'cross-tribal innovation teams' (p. 145), to ensure that innovative work draws on the perspectives of all relevant tribes. Again, the EIP and Logan Campus work supports this assertion, but extends it through emphasizing the need to establish cross-tribal collaboration at the outset of projects rather than later, when the absence of expertise or suspicion of motives can become a problem.

Interestingly, while most academic managers had prior experience in the academic tribe, the EIP investigation suggests that few explicitly seem to take advantage of this experience to help them anticipate or interpret the views of academics. This is frequently noted by academics involved in the Logan Campus work. This observation is also consistent with the findings of Randle and Brady (1997), Elliot and Crossley (1997) and Hort (1997).

Universities must also make better use of the *lone rangers* through maximizing the opportunities for learning based on their explorations. Two forms of learning seem necessary – tribal and organizational. Tribal learning involves change in dialects, ways of thinking and rules for appropriate behaviour. This is expedited by the development of more literate tribal cultures. Literate cultural practices are more likely to support development of innovation because they allow evaluation of existing values, beliefs and practices. I have commented earlier on the potential value to academics of developing their educational understandings. Here that idea is extended to the development of a capacity to engage in conversation about educational issues. While cross-tribal communication depends on the development of capacities to discuss issues, the appropriate time to develop that capacity is before intertribal contestation occurs, and the appropriate context is intratribal.

This process is likely to lead to very heterogeneous learning within a university unless it is accompanied by the second form of learning

– organizational learning. This is because it depends largely upon the actions of individuals working within quite specific contexts. The EIP investigation highlighted the ways that these local environments both enable and constrain innovations, acting to shape the processes of both innovation and learning in profound, yet largely invisible ways. Just as tribal learning can be facilitated, organizational learning can be facilitated by a deliberate process of critical scrutiny, one which explores, amongst other things, the impact of local circumstances in order to identify broader ramifications. The EIP investigation found little evidence of this happening, a finding consistent with the Canadian study of Riffel and Levin (1997). One of the challenges for organizational learning is to evaluate systematically the work of the lone rangers. Another is to develop policies and practices which institutionalize that work, and the associated ways of working which are seen as most valuable (e.g., cross-tribal collaboration). A further challenge is to distinguish between practices that are important because they are innovative, and practices that are educationally and organizationally sustainable. I return to the issue of organizational learning in the following chapter.

There are other pressing reasons for focusing on both tribal and organizational learning. One relates to the sense of professional isolation from colleagues, particularly for the lone rangers. This was most evident in feedback on the value of opportunities to share experiences, where EIP respondents spoke of the value of finding out how others were addressing the same problems they were facing. Lone rangers spoke of the value of knowing about the work of others primarily as an affirmation of their own investments. A second reason involves inter-tribal scepticism and/or cynicism, represented by the opinion of some members of the non-teaching tribes that 'academics are dragging their feet' in relation to change. In a context where so little is done to share or critically review rationales for, or evaluations of, innovations, it is not surprising that members of the non-teaching tribes formed this opinion. Our data suggests that this view is false – we found much evidence of innovation and reason for optimism (see Taylor *et al.* 1996: 90–2).

The discontinuity in perspectives is accentuated by a related difference in contributions to agendas for change – based on roles and responsibilities. It is clear that academic managers have priority in defining those agendas, while the academic tribe has more responsibility in relation to their implementation. The general staff tribe, by comparison, seems to feel least able to influence the process of development, and looks to 'policy frameworks' to provide leverage, particularly in terms of the allocation of resources. The EIP work suggests that they want managers to provide those frameworks while managers indicated a sense of powerlessness in relation to 'directing' the allocation of resources, particularly academic staff time. Thus, the capacity of individual managers to direct change is limited. While this diminishes the potential of rational decision making, it points to an increased role for leadership which focuses on the formation of multitribal coalitions around particular projects.

Emergent roles

I want to turn here to a more specific consideration of the emergent roles that are associated with the challenges universities are currently facing. I also discuss examples of emergent response to those challenges, focusing on the role of teaching. In Chapter 2 I noted that the constancy of change represents a significant challenge. I reiterate the view expressed in the report of the Dearing Committee: 'there are strains resulting from the pace of change, especially in the last few years, which must be addressed if higher education is to continue to be able to develop and serve the nation well' (NCIHE 1997: para. 3.3).

It is useful to note that changing career patterns were seen to have implications for the roles that academics might undertake.

> Such changes [in career patterns] will offer academic staff the opportunity to re-interpret their traditional role if they wish to do so. The likelihood is that there will be a greater range of opportunities, with staff undertaking different combinations of functions at different stages of their careers, depending on the development of institutional missions and their personal career aspirations.
>
> (NCIHE 1997: para. 14.13)

The phrase 'if they wish to do so' implies an option that seems increasingly unavailable to academics. Job security is one of their major concerns, as universities everywhere move to redefine tenure and other conditions of employment. There are also particular concerns around the increasing use of communication and information technologies (CITs) as illustrated in the Brown and Duguid scenario discussed briefly in Chapter 2.

Paul Trowler (1997) provides a very useful example of how external changes are being experienced, and responded to, at an institutional level. He suggests that the model of academics presented in the literature is one of passive and unwilling participation in events largely outside their control. He contrasts this with the view of teachers in the compulsory sector, where they are seen to be actively negotiating and changing policy. While there is evidence (see Goodman 1995; Elmore 1996) to support his contention that the literature on 'reform' in the compulsory education sector suggests that 'top-down' approaches are actively resisted and show little evidence of success, other evidence suggests this resistance is not without its costs.

For example, Sharon Gerwitz (1997) explores the impact of reforms designed to increase the control of UK teachers' work by the state. She notes that 'teachers feel under growing pressure to perform and conform' (p. 224). At an emotional level they express a sense of being 'squeezed dry' because of the 'manic grind' and 'frenetic pace' of work. As a result, 'teachers become repositories of accumulated stress' (Gerwitz 1997: 225). While teachers are meeting more often, and for longer periods of times, the agendas they are addressing are those set above them, decreasing opportunities for collaboration and their sense of collegiality. In fact, teachers report a 'growing inter-departmental competitiveness of school life' (p. 226). The impacts on their teaching are significant, including 'a general decline in the vitality and creativity of their teaching' (p. 226), and a 'narrowing of focus in their work' (p. 227), along with a sense that they are unable to protect what they value – their real work – from these intrusions:

> These clear lines of accountability coupled with appraisal systems effectively regulate the work of teachers, ensuring that the values of the performance-driven market are institutionalized to the extent that they penetrate classroom practice.
>
> (Gerwitz 1997: 225)

Thus these teachers increasingly look like the pawns that many see academics to be.

But Trowler (1997) disagrees with the implied uniformity in academics' responses. In commenting on the response of academics in his study, Trowler points to the active response of academics in contesting the interpretation and implementation of a national 'credit framework'. He characterizes those responses in terms of four broad strategies: sinking; using coping strategies; policy reconstruction; and swimming. He suggests that the literature tends to paint an overly uniform picture consistent with the passive, 'sinking' response. His argument is that this literature relies too much on the 'essentialist positions', particularly epistemological positions, adopted by other researchers, including Becher. He suggests that other factors are important in allowing for a greater range of responses. Those factors include educational ideology; 'organizational, professional, gender and other cultural "traffic" found in the unique configuration of the site'; the 'profitability of the change' for the academics; and 'the extent and nature of other aspects of the "framing" of a discipline' (Trowler 1997: 312). His work points to the openness of the process of change, and the rejection of suggestions that academics' responses can be predicted on the basis of the nature of the change itself, or any single pre-existing aspect of their academic identity.

The 'Dearing trap' – using CITs

While I readily concur with Trowler's warning I want to return to the challenges that universities are currently facing. The introduction of CITs is seen by the Dearing Committee to pose the greatest challenge to traditional roles in the next 20 years. Trowler (1997) refers to the 'Robbins trap': 'the paradox presented by a simultaneous and incompatible commitment to higher education expansion and a model of higher education founded on élitist principles' (p. 302). Because of this trap UK academics are argued to have experienced great difficulties in 'reinterpreting their traditional role' throughout the period of rapid expansion of higher education, i.e., since the early 1960s.

If the 'Robbins trap' resulted from the move to mass, if not universal, higher education, then the 'Dearing trap' involves the paradox presented by a simultaneous and incompatible commitment to the 'local' and to the 'global'. Thus, universities are under pressure to engage more effectively with their local communities, in both cooperative research and service functions, and through providing students with work experience within their undergraduate courses. Students want courses that are more relevant to their capacities and intentions. At the same time, universities are expected to internationalize their courses (and student bodies), including the establishment of links with universities in other countries; respond in many instances to national professional accreditation requirements for graduates; and increase the international profile of their research programmes and achievements. This is more than 'thinking globally, and acting locally'. It is thinking and acting both globally and locally. And it is likely to challenge academics as they redevelop their roles over the next 20 years.

However, to 'trap' can also mean to 'trick' – to deceive. I have argued earlier that the discussion of change tends to highlight issues of discontinuity, rather than issues of continuity. This can be deceptive, and result in 'anticipated entrapment', which may itself be far more intrusive than the outcomes of the change. Let me illustrate this possibility. I noted earlier that, in relation to the introduction of technology-rich learning environments at my university's new campus – the Logan Campus – I was involved in an extensive round of staff development workshops and discussions in April–May 1997. Reactions of staff to the possibility of teaching in these new environments varied – from outright and hostile rejection to enthusiastic anticipation. In April 1998, I was involved in a day-long workshop attended by over 60 academics, the purpose of which was to share 'lessons learnt' by those who had been teaching on this campus with those who were soon to start teaching on it. Most of those who attended were in the latter group, and their concerns dominated the discussion. They raised almost all of the negative expectations – their anticipation of entrapment – raised some 12 months earlier. These included:

- *Impossible workloads*: We are being expected to prepare these materials while we are doing our normal work. But there is no recognition for this. You want me to carry my regular teaching load, be a productive researcher, and do this?
- *Vague expectations*: You seem to be saying what we can't do – we can't lecture, we have to use the Web – but I don't know what you expect me to do. And what is worse, I still don't know how what you seem to be wanting me to do will actually be an improvement on what I already do.
- *But we can't teach that way*: Almost any variation on the theme that 'our course' needs to be taught in the way that it has always been taught, often referring to the need to develop particular professional skill sets, from counselling to chemistry.

- *Use of 'the Web'*: I really know very little about how to do that, and what little I do know tells me that it is not a very student-friendly place. I know some students love it, but I really have my doubts about whether the majority of students feel that way. We know that they just go and print off the notes. So why not just print them off? Why are we forcing them to use the Web?
- *A lack of funding*: You say we should try to buy in multimedia resources, but where do we get the funds from to do that? My School is already functioning in the red. You tell us how important this is to the future of the university, but when is the centre going to put some of its money into it?

Several days later the senior academic manager associated with the campus expressed his disappointment with the tenor of the discussion, not all of which he had attended. He felt it misrepresented the many positive achievements of those who were teaching on the campus. However, it seemed that the extent of anticipated change in their teaching roles made it very difficult for those who had not yet experienced that change to see it as other than threatening and negative. After all, this same manager has consistently argued that the learning environments to be developed had to be 'at the cutting edge'. Working on a 'cutting edge' is bound to be dangerous – too many 'sharp' practices can mean someone ends up bleeding!

The reaction of those who had experienced teaching on the Logan Campus contrasts with this 'anticipated entrapment' scenario. Indeed, they had given their experience of the new campus a four- (out of five-) star rating in a survey conducted in April 1998. In that survey they had also been invited to identify the metaphors they would 'use to describe [their] teaching in more traditional settings, e.g., guru, comedian, news presenter, interpreter' and to nominate any changes in the new settings. Interestingly, the overwhelming majority reported 'much the same', with some only noting additional tasks. As one respondent said:

> What I have come to see is that technology is not the issue. I spent so much time worrying about it, and feeling inadequate. But when you get down to it, it's really the relationships you form with the students, and that you help them to form with each other that makes a difference. I'm still a mix of Mother Hen and Attila the Hun.

This is not to say that other aspects of their roles didn't change. They did, particularly in terms of the relationships with academic colleagues and other members of staff, especially the staff in the multimedia unit. In written responses, and in the discussion, the academics highlighted changes including:

- A much higher level of teamwork, with their Heads of School, with peers, with the multimedia staff who contributed to their subject, and with a range of general staff whose work became more integral to the achievement of subject implementation.

- A perception that not all of this teamwork was 'collaborative'. In particular the relationship with the multimedia staff involved considerable loss of academic autonomy, and they wanted control to revert to them, i.e., to academics.
- A sense of uncertainty about their teaching role, as expressed by one respondent:

  > At first it seemed my role was to teach students how to use technology. I didn't like this. I think in retrospect that I unwittingly encouraged a situation where students took material off the Web. I deliberately re-focused my role on content, being more directive than I normally would, in order to 'force' them into getting into the content of the subject [rather than the technology]. Now, weeks later, I want to withdraw from this lecturing role and I am questioning what my role is.

- A much greater need to deal with student anxiety – with the lack of confidence, competence, and comfort of students in this new learning environment, as implied by the previous quotation.
- Competition for students – on a small campus, with the need to maximize the use of resources, while minimizing the cost of their development, students become 'the currency' for exchange. One Head of School argued that while she could arrange for the sharing of resources between Schools, the funding formula did not allow for any flow of funds to compensate the source School for its resources: 'That is why we will also fight to avoid any cross-School teaching.'

Some implications

There are three points I want to make about the above discussion. First, the anxieties of those who are 'about to enter the water' are understandable, particularly in the context of genuine innovation – settings where practices cannot be specified ahead of time, or outcomes predicted with any sense of certainty. This calls for new approaches to management and to staff development. The approaches need to be much more sensitive to 'anticipated entrapment' and/or 'precocious loss' in university cultures which are both conservative and sceptical of change for the sake of change. (These are issues I address more fully in the following chapters.)

Second, the changes that do result are consistent with the broader phenomenon of 'the end of enclosure' – the boundaries between roles are increasingly blurring. Where once teaching was the province of the academic, in technology-rich environments it is increasingly a task shared between academics, multimedia experts, IT specialists, librarians and others, including the students. There are real risks in this process, however, in that the importance of expertise in IT or multimedia may be overstated. This overstatement can invite transfer of control of the process of subject development or implementation from the academic who designs and/or teaches the subject to those who have much greater expertise in the development of teaching resources (also known as 'educational product') by those who wish to diminish symbolically the importance of teaching and teachers within the learning environment.

Academics tend to have little sense of how to manage the process of IT resource development, or of the timescales that have to be observed in order to produce the necessary resources before teaching begins. Their traditional practices require only a relatively formalized sense of what the course is to achieve, and the resources that are available before teaching begins. The detail is worked out 'on the fly' – specification occurs in the teaching context. Indeed, students tend to criticize teaching which fails to engage with their interests and/or responses – teaching that is overly structured and unresponsive. On the other hand, multimedia designers tend to have very little sense of how the resources might be used in a specific teaching context, and of the need for adaptability in that context. Theirs are generic skills – applicable to any 'product' – rather than understandings that are based on extensive experience with students in a particular course or programme of studies. Indeed, they are employed to ensure that planning is generic, as well as meticulous, especially if one of the purposes is to generate 'educational product' that can be commercialized.

The views and experiences of academics who have prior experience in distance education teaching are of relevance here. In the EIP research our academic respondents expressed great dissatisfaction with traditional distance education practices. In fact, most attributed the development of their more innovative practices to a desire to avoid the non-interactive nature of 'broadcast' or 'correspondence' versions of distance education. The Logan Campus experience suggests that those with distance education experience were better prepared for the collaboration with the multimedia staff – they were experienced in cross-tribal communication. But they experienced other difficulties. In particular, they tended to prepare too much material – to reproduce a largely 'transmissive' pedagogy through the new media. They experienced a related problem, in that their familiarity with the production of 'educational product' tended to invite them to ignore the consideration of how they would use those resources to augment their face-to-face teaching practices. The academics who most readily adapted to the new environment were those who had experienced some variation of resource-based face-to-face teaching. Of course, they still faced the challenge of helping students to use the computers.

I mentioned earlier the inability of the Logan-bound academics to articulate sound reasons for their resistance to the procedures put in place by multimedia staff and academic managers. Academics too often lack a convincing rationale for their practices, and the capacity to discuss those practices and to evaluate alternatives. Traditionally their teaching roles have been enacted in the privacy of their lecture halls and tutorial rooms. Discussion of practices with peers has been atypical. As a result, few academics have access to language which represents the complexity of their thinking in ways which are intelligible (and compelling) to either peers or the general staff who might be required to work with them. Where academics need to be able to engage in cross-tribal contestations with clarity and confidence, they can appear to be inarticulate, and therefore seen as self-indulgent, even unreasonable.

On the other hand, one of the unanticipated messages that emerges from our experience on the Logan Campus is that it is general staff rather than academics who may need to become much more 'customer oriented'. Academics have a long tradition of engaging with students, while IT staff in particular have tended to see themselves as having a 'back room' job. As the distinction between roles decreases, and supporting students becomes a shared responsibility, 'back room' attitudes need to be revised. There is enormous pressure on IT staff to acknowledge students' learning needs and to provide appropriate and timely responses to failures in the IT infrastructure when that infrastructure is central to the learning environment. Keeping the system 'up' and fully functional must be more than wishful thinking.

A third implication of the discussion of 'anticipated entrapment by CITs' is that, while the actual experience of the new teaching environments may not ultimately lead to significant changes in academics' roles, it may call into question the purposes that those roles are serving. A consistent theme in comments from the academics involved in the Logan Campus is a decline in their role as motivator. Where much of the energy of traditional practices has an implicit motivational function – keeping students awake, keeping them going – the new learning environments are intended to focus on lifelong learning for the learning society. There is a fundamental sense that this places a priority on individualization and privatization of control and responsibility for learning, and that successful practices do lead to a much more active student participation in the learning environment. If this motivational aspect of the role is to diminish, it should offer an opportunity for a more creative role, one more focused on *what* students are thinking, than on ensuring that they *are* thinking.

Looking to the future

This brings me back to the 'Dearing trap' – the incompatible commitment to respond to both local and global challenges. CITs can serve a number of purposes, as can the work of academics. One version of the future of higher education privileges the needs and capacities of the individual. This is the just-in-time, whenever you need it, wherever you need it, whatever you need (as long as you can afford it) version. It is consistent with Terrence Morrison's (1995) vision. The fascination with technologies is typical of many stories on higher education offered in Australian popular print media. One publication included the following sentiments, attributed to the Chair of the Australian Government's Information Policy Advisory Council, Dr Terry Cutler:

Rather than faculty curricula and courseware being 'bespoken' by each institution, the economics of distribution meant the competitive advantage was with universities that could 'productise' the labour and skill-intensive components.

Networked business systems provide the infrastructure for the distribution of curricula and courseware as commodity products.

(*Campus Review*, July 23, 1997: 11)

In this vision the global reach and standards of CITs, and the portability of their products, are used to maximize accessibility – a distance learning version. Rita Johnston (1997: 118) characterized this as: 'the ultimate commodification of education, offering a standardized material product, pre-processed, quality controlled and packaged for maximum appeal to the widest market'. Here the academic's role as instructional author comes to involve a significant extension of the more traditional authoring role – that of discipline expert. This role requires additional educational expertise – the sort of expertise discussed by Diana Laurillard (1993) and Alistair MacFarlane (1995). In addition to this expertise, it requires significant re-allocation of resources within the institution, and the establishment of quite extensive infrastructures to support student learning, as also discussed by both these authors. In this sense, its achievement depends on far more than simply changing academics' roles, as is the case with any substantive change.

A second version of the future involves a concern with the development of learning communities as a step towards a learning society. These are the learning communities that Brown and Duguid (1996) advocate as universities engage more effectively with their local communities. It is the version of the future which the Logan Campus foreshadows. Here the global reach and standards of CITs, along with the specific experiences and understandings of students and their teachers, are used to maximize opportunities to access information, and engagement in conversations which attempt to make sense of those experiences and that information, and their implications. Importantly, the use of CITs to support the development of communities of practice will require academics to become familiar with, and competent in the use of, a range of Web tools to support synchronous and asynchronous discussions, e.g., email and bulletin boards. In this scenario the roles of academics include instructional authoring, but extend to the capacity to share experiences and understandings, to challenge understandings, to generate and focus analytic and sceptical conversation, and to insist on the sensemaking that looks to implications and applications, rather than the attainment of credentials. This requires the student-centred, learning-oriented approach to teaching described by Kember (1997).

This second version of the future is the more ambitious, but both require forms of organizational discipline that are unlikely to be achieved. I noted earlier the view of managers interviewed as part of the EIP work. They saw themselves as relatively powerless to develop effective policies to coordinate the use of resources and/or to direct the work of academics. Alistair

MacFarlane (1995: 65) may be right in predicting that the 'more probable outcome will be a set of piecemeal, disjointed, *ad hoc* responses to increasing economic and political pressures'. Most universities will need to work to achieve elements of both versions. What this means is that most academics will continue to face multiple, and contesting, expectations. The range of roles is therefore likely to increase, rather than be maintained as traditional roles undergoing some form of radical pruning. In particular, the future is likely to place greater importance on an academic's role as teacher, as a professional educator and as a leader in the development of communities of practice which involve both face-to-face and virtual conversations.

4

Issues of Leadership and Management

Naming the intolerable is what must pre-exist change.

(Shapiro 1994: 63)

This is a book about academics' work, not 'how to manage academics'. However, the issue of management cannot be overlooked because the work of academics and the work of academic managers are mutually constructed. What distinguishes this chapter from the previous one is that it focuses on issues related to *the creation of the conditions within which academics work*. While it is both fashionable and appropriate to suggest that 'all workers are managers', there is a very significant difference between self-managing and managing the work of others. The latter involves responsibilities for creating the conditions within which others work. Nevertheless, I do not seek to underplay the role of all academics as leaders and managers, including managing 'up' the hierarchy in their institutional setting.

It is for these reasons that I want to address a limited range of issues related to leadership and management. They are:

- a model of change, applicable to both individuals and organizations;
- several challenges for those who have a managerial role; and
- several issues and opportunities related to self-managing roles.

Change through leadership and management is a theme which dominates a plethora of writing about organizations. Bookshop shelves are crammed with the work of those who are given guru status – Deming, Drucker, Peters, Senge, and so on – and those numerous others who have piggy-backed on a belief in change as a necessity, and management as a solution. There is a populist air of expectancy surrounding these possibilities, whose focus is increasingly on management-of-the-self as a principal strategy for enterprising, autonomous individuals in these troubling times.

However, in seeking to enlist readers in management-of-self projects these writers tend to treat the achievement of change as relatively unproblematic. They rely on an assumption that, to change, people primarily need to understand the reasons for and the value of change – they need information, i.e., their book. The main ingredient that needs to be added to this information is motivation – that is why there is also a lucrative market for motivational speakers. The task of leadership is to capture this information in a vision which will serve to gain commitment and to energize enterprising action at the organizational level – 'vision is about change' (Ramsden 1998: 141). The vision is transformed into goals, to be achieved through processes of strategic planning, prioritizing and, finally, through personal planning and commitment. In this process, change becomes an outcome of planning.

I have several reservations about this view of change. First, it suggests that change is essentially a rational process – if we can plan for it, we can achieve it. This treats humans as unidimensional, ignoring their capacities for and commitments to the plans, and the relational nature of most actions. It ignores the fact that it is sometimes easier to give uncommitted acquiescence than to argue for alternatives. It also ignores the inevitability and unpredictability of the response of others to those actions. Second, it prioritizes and privileges action over purpose. The sequence of vision–strategy–plan–action allows for plans to be infused with values and purpose, but its linearity insists that it ends with action. There is no suggestion that this should be a recursive process. Third, it conflates change with learning. This implies that, while there might be a need for some training in specific new practices, the learning necessary to achieve the actions is also an outcome of planning.

A model of personal change

This model is based on thinking initially developed during my doctoral research into the achievement of change in teaching practices (Taylor 1991). I suggest there are two very different approaches to learning-for-change; one focuses on actions, the other on beliefs. That is, while achievement of personal change ultimately requires modifications in both thinking and acting, it can be initiated either through changing behaviour, i.e., simply adopting new teaching practices or monitoring existing practices, *or* through changing beliefs underlying thinking about teaching. Irrespective of the approach, change is difficult to achieve and sustain, particularly if it requires revision of beliefs. In spite of that difficulty, the provision of information is *the* common 'educational' strategy for belief-revision in most educational activities, an issue I have explored more fully elsewhere (Taylor 1997b, 1998).

Learning-for-change, at the individual and organizational levels, is achieved through processes that interrupt the usual, the taken for granted. At the individual level, 'mental management' operates primarily at a level below conscious-awareness – we function on 'autopilot' to achieve the vast majority of our behaviour. The autopilot is programmed by past experience, and the strength of programming reflects the significance and repetitiveness of experience. Programming requires effort, and time, but once achieved, autopiloting requires little conscious attention – this is its value. If autopilot is interrupted, actions become much less fluid, and much more demanding – we become less competent. Learning to use a pen/biro/pencil to write is an example. We spend considerable time – years in fact – learning how to hold the implement, and then learning to create smooth lines, and particular shapes. When we now turn to write with a biro, we no longer have to think about how to hold it, how to make the individual shapes. We can actually give our conscious attention to what we want to say through writing. But if we try to write with the other hand, we quickly realize how much mental management of our actions is being done without us needing to 'think about it'. Try it!

Reprogramming an autopilot is not easy. The first step is to interrupt automaticity, and I have already implied two ways of achieving this. One involves deliberate self-monitoring – noticing that we act and think in a particular way. This allows continued action, but involves an attempt to reflect on the action, and therefore its consequences. For example, the instruction to notice how you are holding your shoulders, and the angle of your back, as you type can initiate a change in your typing posture. Maintaining that change requires additional effort, and ongoing monitoring. A second approach involves changing actions without necessarily paying a lot of attention to them. For example, simply changing the height of the keyboard, or the height of your chair, will change your typing posture – your adjustment will be automatic.

Cognitive views of learning use the term *metacognition* to refer to the deliberate monitoring of the self-management of mental processes. A deal of scholarly effort has gone into arguing the need for, and efficacy of, such a concept. That research has explored its implications in terms of the development of new teaching strategies – exemplified in the 1998 'special issue' on metacognition of *Instructional Science* (Vol. 26 (1–2)). This research points to the value of the adoption of metacognitively based teaching strategies where learning involves the development of new learning strategies, i.e., when programming or reprogramming of autopilot is required. Importantly, the intention behind these teaching strategies is to make the new learning strategies so familiar that students come to use them automatically. The intention is to programme or reprogramme rather than disable the autopilot. Unfortunately, the concept of metacognition has been given little attention in the literature on learning in higher education. For example, neither Ramsden (1992) nor Kember (1997) call on it in their analysis.

The relative value of self-monitoring, compared with change in behaviour, as a strategy for reprogramming is most evident in socially complex contexts, or where the change itself cannot be pre-specified. The latter situation rules out any possibility of 'simply changing behaviour', because the 'new' behaviour is unknown. In more complex social situations, a change in the behaviour of one person is likely to be questioned and possibly resisted by other social actors unless it is accompanied by a change in the expectations of those other individuals. That is, their autopilots also have to undergo some form of reprogramming. Thus, in situations which involve either genuine innovation or significant social constraints, a process of change which involves the development of the capacity for self-monitoring of outcomes is essential to the achievement of change.

This conclusion is unhelpful unless the requirements for self-monitoring are also understood. No action is ever planned on the basis of all that we know about any situation or the complete range of options which we could consider. If we were to take the time to do that it would effectively paralyse our capacity for action – we would become incompetent. We plan using quite simple models of a situation and consider only a small range of well-rehearsed options. The models are based on beliefs about the situation – what it involves, what is expected of us, and so on, and the options for action – what this might require of us (i.e., what might 'work' here), how effective we are in terms of those actions in situations we expect, and so on. Those beliefs represent the 'distilled wisdom' of prior experiences. Because they function below explicit awareness many, if not most, of these beliefs are not available to be 'thought about' in any deliberate way. They cast their shadows over our actions, but their nature and value remain unknown, and unchallenged in the ongoing need to act competently.

There are strategies which directly address the task of belief revision. They focus on the identification of existing beliefs, largely through reflective conversations (with ourself or with others), using specific aspects of our belief system as the object of that conversation. These conversations are most helpful when we trust the other/s to be respectful of the significance of those beliefs, when the other/s help us explore the strength, coherence and value of those beliefs, and when they invite us to consider alternatives to them. These are the sorts of conversations to which I referred in the discussion of the value of cross-cultural communication in Chapter 3, and which I explore further in Chapter 6.

Autopiloting cuts the mental load of living in two senses. It reduces the complexity of planning. And it reduces the need to attend to consequences – we know what should happen, so we are able to function without paying much attention to the world around us. I sometimes amaze myself by driving along a busy freeway, while paying very little attention to the traffic around me. I know I do this because I 'wake up' at some point in the drive. This is not an issue of tiredness, just 'driving with undue care' as a police officer might say. But the reality is that I can do it, and without causing accidents. Some students would argue that their lecturers deliver their lectures in much the same way, while some lecturers hold very similar views, but in relation to the participation of students – present in body but not mind. Autopiloting frees us from both having to think before we act, and having to reflect on those actions before we do anything else – it makes competent living possible. The autopilot is also self-contained, in that it only requires a stream of information from the external environment to trigger and maintain its functioning. Interruptions are minimized for very good reasons – they decrease competence.

Let me review what I have said about the learning necessary for the achievement of change. It involves the achievement of modifications in both thinking and acting. It can be initiated through changing either practices, or the beliefs that guide our subconscious processes of action-planning

– reprogramming our autopilot. As adults, the overwhelming majority of our actions are planned subconsciously, with minimal, if any, conscious deliberation. In fact, deliberation represents an interruption of an otherwise automatic and ongoing planning process. Thus, interruption provides the possibility of sensemaking. My point is that learning in complex situations requires more than just deliberation on, or information about, plans. It extends to a critical awareness of the basis for otherwise automated planning (i.e., mental models and beliefs), and an equally critical consideration of alternatives.

This is a model of change at the personal level, but it could be readily adapted to change at an institutional level. That adaptation would involve certain substitutions. Rather than personal knowledge, it would refer to cultural knowledge. Rather than 'beliefs', it would refer to 'traditions'. Rather than 'deliberation', it would possibly refer to 'strategic planning'. Thus, the idea that most planning proceeds automatically in response to 'internal' expectations, and that little attention is given to the evaluation of its consequences beyond meeting those expectations, 'tells it like it is'. Organizational learning requires a critical awareness of the basis for planning (i.e., the traditions that underlie it), and an equally critical consideration of alternative practices and strategies.

Some challenges for those who have a managerial role

The challenges facing academic managers are, in many senses, framed by the broader challenges facing higher education. I have in mind issues such as 'doing more with less', maintaining the quality of what is done, responding to the expanding range of student expectations and needs. Then there are challenges that are more role-specific: leading and managing in the context of rapid change in the expectations of universities; balancing the role of leader and manager with the roles of researcher and teacher; and budgeting. There is the added issue that all of these challenges are concurrent and interactive. And the role may not have been coveted, let alone sought.

Leading and managing in universities is undertaken within constraints that, while not unique, certainly provide challenges which are not necessarily common to all settings. One of the Deans interviewed as part of the EIP project described his situation thus:

> It is wrong thinking to imagine that I am in control here. Yes, I am held accountable, but while I can influence the agenda, in fact I have very little power to make it happen. Universities have very devolved decision-making processes. Some of them do not make for efficiency. In this university we have Course Coordinators who are responsible for the development of courses of study. But those courses of study are taught by staff located in Schools, which are run by Heads of School. In

other words, the resources are under the control of the Heads, not the Coordinators, and certainly not me. If a course becomes too expensive to run, Heads become concerned, while Coordinators can ignore that issue. On the other hand, Heads can make life very difficult for Co-ordinators by not providing the staff they need. The whole system works in mysterious ways. But this recognizes that I do not have all the answers, that there is an enormous pool of talent and expertise located in those Schools. It reflects the value of collegiality, and it is very dependent on goodwill.

Perhaps Lewis Elton is right when he suggests that collegiality is 'too cumber-some for these fast moving times, but this should apply only to policy execution, not policy making' (Elton 1995, quoted in Imrie 1996: 90). But this statement needs to be read carefully. Collegiality may not be helpful in policy execution, but, as this Dean implies, it can be very helpful in policy development.

A Pro-Vice-Chancellor made the following comments in relation to the value of policy as a means of 'leading and managing':

It is difficult changing things in a university. People who are frustrated by the speed at which things are not moving say 'What the hell is going on, what is the Dean doing, what is the Vice-Chancellor doing', and that is fair comment. The reason why it is not moving is because the Vice-Chancellor, after having allowed one-line budgeting for Faculties, is quite powerless. Deans are quite powerless . . . There is only so much you can do in terms of policy. You have still got to police the thing, and basically in a university it will only work if you leave it to the good sense of one's colleagues. If you say 'Everything that is submitted in this new open learning format must be vetted by a university committee' it would clog up the system. And even if I have the expertise to go through the stuff, there is only 24 hours in a day. So I think we must have in place a policy which is sensible and that means basically for the vetting to be done at the individual team level.

In this section I want to discuss a number of issues which tend to be associated with the role of management. These include:

- approaches to change within discussions of leading and managing;
- locating the importance of academic culture within discussions of univer-sities as evolving organizations;
- the need for organizational learning;
- managing border issues.

Leading and managing in an age of uncertainty

The broad cultural conditions we are experiencing have been referred to as 'the postmodern condition'. Some of the challenges associated with this 'condition' include a sense of anxiety and loss of direction for individuals, and fragmentation, inconsistency, and a mix of organizational structures, policies and procedures for organizations. Organizational boundaries are failing, while managers face increasing difficulties in concentrating resources, distributing space, establishing and achieving timeframes, achieving productivity. This is 'a new era of flexible, lateral forms of organizing' (Rousseau 1997: 516).

While these conditions are particularly challenging for some forms of organizations, universities have for some time been characterized as 'organized anarchies' (Weick 1976). Indeed, Weick's paper tends to provoke a sense of *déjà vu* in relation to these characterizations, suggesting that, yet again, the present looks more like the past than we care to acknowledge. This possibility highlights the role of academics and academic managers in constructing 'the challenges' that confront universities.

In a very real sense the work of individuals like Bergquist and Deleuze, and groups like the Dearing and West Committees, *form* these challenges through the processes of naming and describing them. For example, some critical commentaries on university management practices characterize those practices in terms of 'managerialism'. The term has come to represent not just a convenient characterization, a concrete and coherent set of managerial practices and a set of experiences (alienation, falling morale, and so on) associated with an assumed world-view. While close scrutiny, such as the work of Craig Prichard and Hugh Willmott (1997), shows that this is an exaggeration, once named and described 'managerialism' has a life of its own.

My point is that use of terms like 'managerialism' or 'challenge' are no more neutral than any other act of naming. These are claims in 'games of truth' (Foucault 1985), games which involve the self-interested exercise of power. We create reality through the processes of naming and describing. Naming is a selective process – it draws attention to some issues, while simultaneously drawing attention away from others. It is a constructive process, 'forming' objects for thought, e.g., 'managerialism', and a political process in terms of allocating significance to those objects, e.g., strategic planning.

Use of the term 'leadership' is itself a political act. Its use signifies the priority given to producing change over creating or maintaining order, i.e., managing (Kotter 1990). Kotter's argument is that uncertain times place a priority on the use of processes associated with leadership – direction setting, aligning people, motivating and inspiring staff – rather than the use of management processes, such as planning and budgeting, and organizing and controlling staff.

However, those in managerial positions have to provide leadership in relation to specific challenges, while concurrently administering other aspects of their organization. Challenges have to be 'named' and described so that they can be discussed and prioritized. Thus, innovations are initiated through processes of planning which are very much associated with managerial or bureaucratic processes. It is only after this planning that innovations can be developed – when projected outcomes have been 'taken as an established fact and integrated into the planning system' (Spender and Kessler 1995: 46). Then processes associated with leadership come to the fore. Later, as the specific strategies necessary to achieve those projected outcomes are identified and proved, leadership processes give way to managerial processes, as the innovation is institutionalized. Thus, uncertain times call for an interplay between leadership and management skills.

There is a question as to where 'uncertainty' originates. Spender and Kessler (1995) argue that uncertainty is created within rather than outside an organization. They suggest that both uncertainty and innovation are created, at least in part, through the very processes of planning for change, including the naming of external threats. Thus, an essential prerequisite for change is the fostering of uncertainty by managers, an issue which I explore more fully in the later section on *organizational learning* (p. 80). That requirement sits very uneasily with the more common view that academic leaders, at least at the level of Head of Department, see their jobs as involving two tasks – administration, and protection of 'the academic autonomy and independence of academic staff and duties' (Sarros *et al.* 1997: 10). Uncertainty is seen primarily as a problem by such managers.

Where would change 'fit' in terms of these two tasks? I suggest that it can only be seen as part of the administrative task. If so, these managers are attempting to 'administer change' – to treat change as an essentially rational process, and to rely on others to pre-specify not only the outcomes of change, but also the strategies by which those outcomes will be achieved. This suggestion is consistent with the situation where particular 'solutions' are designed elsewhere and imposed on academic managers and their Departments through bureaucratic fiat. These are circumstances that cause great stress among academic managers as noted by Sarros *et al.* (1997) (and academics!), but seem unavoidable as long as those managers see their task only in terms of administering or protecting.

Deans, at least in Australian universities, are much more focused on leadership for change than are the Heads of Department. In a follow-up study, Sarros *et al.* (1998: 73) found that 'the leader aspect of the role of academic dean takes precedence over all other roles'. This is consistent with the view expressed by these Deans that they were chosen because of their ability to facilitate change. Thus, they seem to be occupying a role which is quite change-focused, even if they feel poorly prepared for the management side of their role, and especially for 'conflict resolution' (p. 86).

Change in the management literature on higher education

The literature on organizational change tends to privilege one or other of the two approaches to change noted earlier: change actions; or change assumptions and beliefs. Some do both. Examples of each of these approaches are not difficult to find.

Most of the literature on leadership and management in higher education sets out to promote (or resist) change through informing the reader. Henry Miller's book, *The Management of Change in Universities: Universities, State and Economy in Australia, Canada and the United Kingdom* (1995), examines the changing culture of universities in these countries, changes wrought against the dominance of 'established forms of collegiality, professionalism and bureaucratic administration' by 'managerialism and market forces' (p. 1). Thus, its approach is not only partisan, but defensively so. The books of Clark Kerr (1994) and William Bergquist (1995), on the other hand, set out to promote particular forms of change.

It is relatively rare to find books which provide practical instructions on how to lead and manage in higher education, i.e., which approach change from the action perspective. A notable exception is the work of Peter Ford and his colleagues: *Managing Change in Higher Education: A Learning Environment Architecture* (1996). It provides a systems-view of change, a view which the authors take considerable care to locate within the context of higher education. They represent the functioning of universities in terms of three related systems: a business system, a social system and a technical system. Their architecture represents these systems as responding to changes in the external socio-economic and technological environments. Their view of managing change involves a four-stage process – *direction* setting, *organization* of resources, development of core *processes* to make use of those resources, and establishing and aligning *infrastructure* to operationalize those processes (pp. 20–1). They add a fifth stage in the change process: *evaluation and review* – producing a cyclic rather than linear process of change management. Their methodology invokes a planning approach to change.

One of the most recent, and perhaps the most ambitious, book on leadership and management in higher education is Paul Ramsden's *Learning to Lead in Higher Education* (1998). Ramsden (pp. 9–10) declares an intention to 'establish principles' for academic leadership and management rather than to produce a set of 'how to do it' techniques, yet later in that paragraph he states that he is attempting to produce 'a manual for the future'. Thus, he instructs readers on both how 'to think about' leadership and management, and how 'to do' leadership. Ramsden provides this advice in a three-stage journey from principles to practices, although the amount of discussion given to each stage decreases as the journey progresses. He concludes the first part by identifying six principles of academic leadership (pp. 126–8):

- academic leadership is a dynamic process;
- it is properly focused on an outcomes-agenda;
- it operates at multiple levels within the organization;
- it is situational and relational, depending on both circumstances and social conditions;

- leadership involves learning (to lead); and
- it is transformative in a number of senses – it involves value-adding and change.

Ramsden adopts the position that leadership is essentially 'for change'. Not only is he 'for change', but he is decidedly upbeat about it – motivation of the leaders seems to be his intention. To him the role of leadership is to embody 'vigour, energy and optimism' so as to 'revitalize and energize their colleagues to meet the tough times with eagerness and with passion' (p. 3). The message is that the current game plan isn't working, and the coming matches are going to be even tougher. But he wants managers to 'play within the rules' of academic culture. He continually stresses the importance of academic traditions, and of the need to know what motivates academics. In this sense, Ramsden's book works to motivate, even to inspire, change.

Given that this literature is written for academic managers, it is hardly surprising that it is based, implicitly if not explicitly, on a rationalist, top-down model of change. While authors like Ramsden are sensitive to the need to know what motivates academics, that sensitivity is seen as a prerequisite for anticipating reactions in order to ensure that opposition to management intentions can be minimized. That is, to ensure that the visions and policies of the managers are implemented as intended. This is a view that ignores the reality of policy implementation as necessarily distinct from policy development (by management). Paul Trowler's (1998) study illustrates the way that policy necessarily changes during implementation. Implementation is a mutually adaptive process – both intentions and practices change. Thus, cultures and traditions are also changed, and always at the local level.

Managing academic culture in times of change

In preparing this manuscript I have been confronted by several ironies that relate to managing in academic cultures and the messages of the management 'gurus' (Deming, Drucker, Peters *et al.*). One involves conditions of employment. The gurus are advocating the creation of a 'flexible workforce' – workers who are independent, who think of a career in terms of a portfolio of projects rather than a career path involving increasing responsibility and remuneration, and, most importantly, who are self-managing. In many senses, these are the attributes of the cosmopolitan academic. The irony is that academics are experiencing conditions which diminish their autonomy, including increasing demands for accountability through mechanisms like 'performance appraisal' (see McDaniel 1996), at the very same time as workers in other industries are experiencing conditions which require them to act more autonomously.

A second irony involves the very notion of organizational culture. The organizational 'gurus' are calling for organizations to be held together by visions rather than bureaucratic 'red tape'; to be values-focused rather than profit-driven; to rely more on the knowledge, skills and attitudes of staff than on the knowledge, skills and attitudes of management. The irony is that in universities the direction of cultural change appears to be contrary to this. Collegiality is being displaced by bureaucratic control, academic values are consistently challenged by the values of commercialism, and management has become a new career path – the one most rewarded in terms of the symbolism of office, title and remuneration.

There is a strong sense within the literature that academic culture is seen as resistant to change – conservative, inward-looking, bound by tradition. It is seldom acknowledged that the intellectual skills of academics make them less amenable to change strategies that rely on instruction. Their intellectual skills and attitudes make them sceptical of emotion-charged exhortations to excellence, or warnings of grim consequences if the status quo is retained (Trowler 1998; Martin 1999). For these reasons, approaches to managing change which are explicitly or implicitly paternalistic (or naively optimistic) tend to generate dissent and result in alienation rather than contribute to the achievement of commitment to some new order.

But most approaches to management in higher education are based on leadership as patriarchy and paternalism, of leader–follower relationships. Patriarchy locates primary responsibility for decision making with the leaders, while paternalism involves the belief that leaders are responsible for the success of the organization and the well-being of its members. These positions stand in sharp contrast with the academic traditions of collegiality (shared decision making) and autonomy. They are seen as alien to that culture, and are resisted. The response of resistance is evidenced in the literature, with the work of Simon Marginson in Australia and David Hartley in the UK exemplifying this scholarly engagement with the alien and the unwelcome.

I want to turn to the work of Ian McNay (1995) because of his representation of these cultural tensions. He typifies possible university cultures in terms of two dimensions: policy definition and control of implementation. Each dimension becomes a continuum based on the degree of managerial control, from 'loose' to 'tight'. His options are represented in Figure 4.1.

Type A, with its loose policy definition and loose control over implementation, is the traditional collegial culture. The emphasis is on academic freedom and autonomy, with staff organized in terms of discipline-based departments. Decision making is consensual and often located with committees, with an emphasis on peer review as the primary form of evaluation.

Type B, with its loose policy definition but tight control of implementation, is a bureaucratic culture. With a focus on control, consistency and predictability, this is a management-focused version of 'managerialism'. Power is located with those who audit compliance, while policy definition is diffuse, allowing strong influence for external regulators, professional associations and the like.

Type C, with its tight control over both policy formation and implementation, is a corporate culture. Here both leadership and management are important attributes of the culture – a culture in which leading and follow-

Figure 4.1 Four options for university culture (after McNay 1995)

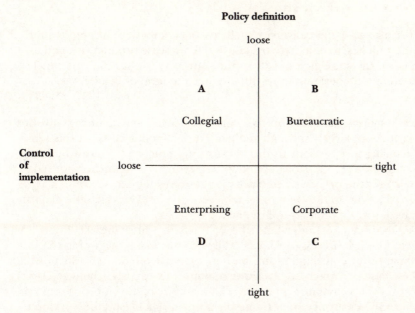

ing have great importance. A high priority is placed on detailed policy and financial planning, and robust institutional evaluation, all directed by central administrators. Power is centralized.

Type D, with its tight control over policy definition and loose control over implementation, is the enterprising culture. The emphasis is on leadership – mission statements and direction setting – with the details of implementation left to those nearer to 'the coalface'. The assumption is that individuals and Departments need freedom to be able to identify and respond to local opportunities. In this culture power tends to be located with the entrepreneurs and 'the clients'.

Universities are not monocultural in terms of these options. All include elements of each, but there is a sense that the balance between them is shifting. Ramsden (1998: 32–3) reports the 1996 views of Australian academic managers in relation to these cultures. Respondents were asked to distribute one hundred points between the four options to represent their institutional culture/s in 1991 and 1996. Their responses suggest a rapid decline in the academic culture (from 55 to 25 points) accompanied by a rapid increase in the importance of the corporate culture (from 5 to 25 points) in that period. It is as though these respondents have experienced a displacement of academic culture by corporate culture. However, what is less clear from his discussion is the attitude of his respondents to these trends.

Experience would suggest that these responses would be expressed more with disappointment than acclamation, and are likely to be exaggerations.

The ascendancy of corporate culture is represented in institutional moves to 'restructure' – characterized by:

> a reshaping of the university to focus on competitive strengths and market niches, to eliminate weaknesses, to increase productivity, and to enhance the strategic capacity of the university whilst devolving much autonomy to operating units often below the level of faculty.
>
> (Davies 1997: 132–3)

Davies suggests that the primary motivation for restructuring involves cost reduction, largely through reducing direct labour costs. In this sense, restructuring is equivalent to the 'downsizing' practices of industry. In the corporate culture, decisions about strategies for cost reduction are taken centrally, yet the process of restructuring devolves the burden of managing those reductions to the Departmental level – the level at which the majority of Ramsden's respondents are managing.

It is important to understand the contexts in which these cultures are likely to be most successful. Davies addresses this issue, suggesting that the combination of a strong culture and an external orientation will provide the best basis for quick and positive responses to external change (Davies 1997: 137). This combination is most characteristic of the enterprise culture, which combines strong policy frameworks with a reliance on the workforce's professional capabilities. Similarly, Rousseau (1997) suggests that the new organizational era calls for the promotion of freedom of action in dynamic environments, and 'do-your-best' goals where tasks are novel and complex. One of the Deans interviewed during the EIP work expressed his view thus:

> Let me put my position fairly strongly. Any Dean or any educational leader who did not leave the detailed decision making to academics these days would have to be stark, staring mad. There is no one who can come into this office and tell me the best way to offer open learning courses. Most of the people who are working in the area are saying that it is just too early to work out what is the best way – is it by video conference, is it by satellite, is it by residential schools? I think it is far better to set a whole range of practices that use all different ways of delivering and entering into a learning experience with students. However, I am hoping that over a number of years we may be able to find out which ways are more authentic, which are the better ways of doing it. But at the moment you could not direct me to any literature that would give any definitive response to this.

The irony is that the current cultural shift is from collegial to corporate when the optimal shift would be from collegial to enterprise – a shift sideways. This shift would require the reframing rather than the abandoning of the strengths of the academic culture. Reframing would entail the development of loyalties to the institution in addition to the loyalties to the discipline – a sense of 'dual citizenship'.

Craig Prichard and Hugh Willmott (1997) explore the ways that the broader phenomenon of 'managerialism' interacts with the more traditional practices of university management, i.e., those that might be consistent with the collegial culture. Consistent with the views of Ramsden's respondents, they suggest that 'each university is a mix of organizing practices, which are historically located and variably resilient and resistant to being whole-heartedly overthrown by the "new" managers' (p. 289). They elaborate:

> Many of our respondents' comments can be read as a confirmation that universities are being reconstituted as knowledge factories organized by managers, whose aim is to intensify and commodify the production and distribution of knowledge and skills to whomsoever has the wherewithal to purchase them . . . [B]ut, equally, our data suggests that this reconstitution is partial and is likely to remain so . . . We suggest that a recurrent managerial problem and challenge . . . for these (at times reluctant) 'managers' is to enrol the support of 'the managed' by contriving to reconcile embedded, largely localized and tacit discourses with the imperializing discourses associated with the new performance measures.
>
> (Prichard and Willmott 1997: 300–1)

They note that some senior managers see managerialism as broadly congruent with existing cultural practices. But staff are suspicious of the hierarchical and rhetorical nature of much 'new management'. Prichard and Willmott conclude: 'whatever "transition" may be occurring, it is likely to be patchy, extended, and incomplete' (p. 311). Rather than introducing new work practices, 'new management' is tending to lead staff to work harder, especially in situations where teaching and research values are high. Now there is an invitation for scepticism!

One way to make sense of this 'patchy, extended, and incomplete' transition is to draw on the concept of 'sedimentation', as used by Cooper *et al.* (1996). This concept represents organizational change in terms of a layering of one set of practices, or culture, on top of another, rather than the displacement of one by another: 'sedimentation points to the persistence of values, ideas and practices, even when the formal structures and processes seem to change, and even when there may be incoherence' (p. 624). This allows for a reading of Ramsden's findings in terms of multiple layers of culturally identified meanings, where each layer is recognizable, yet all coexist. Seen this way, a university, as an organization, involves multiple layers of culturally interrelated ideas, values and practices that coexist, as is illustrated in Trowler's (1998) study. Specific events bring one or more layers to the surface, while individual members of staff are able to interpret events according to the logic of one or more of those layers.

This provides another way of thinking about the organizational fragmentation noted in Chapter 3. The concept of sedimentation recognizes organizations as multicultural, without implying an imperative for cultural assimilation or homogenization. As external pressures change, the relative value of each layer changes, yet none need be actively removed. Thus, increasing the cultural coherence within an organization may achieve short-term benefits, but make that organization less adaptable in the medium to long term. And in times of rapid change, the 'short term' has a very short shelf-life.

Cultures are social achievements, not inanimate layers of sediment. Individual cultures renew or decay through use or disuse. Cooper *et al.* (1996: 634) argue that 'organizational structures, processes and practices are produced, reproduced and changed through interpretation and action'. The corporate culture is growing in universities as new vocabularies and practices are added. Collegial culture, on the other hand, while represented most often in terms of 'tradition', is itself evolving, as is exemplified in Chapter 2. Rather than regard these cultures as competing-to-the-death, they are better understood as adaptively coexisting. Their coexistence allows the adoption by staff of multiple and conflicting perspectives. Irrespective of the value of other cultures, this section points to the ongoing potential of the capacities and perspectives associated with the academic culture.

Managing organizational learning

The principal source of innovation in academic practices is *lone ranging*. While this may be a very effective way to develop innovative practices, the challenge is to achieve innovation at the institutional level – the reinvention of cultures. Until this happens, the very innovative practices that need support may be inconsistent with – even at odds with – broader institutional priorities and practices. Lone ranging is a radically bottom-up approach to innovation. It is consistent with the loose control of implementation of both the collegial and the enterprising cultures. One of the Deans interviewed during the EIP investigation illustrates this approach.

> I can be influential in a longer term, cultural way. It is not an intervention of any specific kind at any one time, so it may be more of directing – a bit like the captain of an oil tanker, you can go a bit to the left and a bit to the right, but nothing is going to change quickly. You can have a commitment and that might entice people to go along with you. They think it is a good idea, 'so I'll put my hand up and go along with that'. Or it can simply be a path that is resourced, so that the group of people who are in place and working on that path get a sign that it is okay to keep on going. How many people join them and how far it goes takes many years to see. So it would not make sense for a manager to sit down and say, 'right, this is an important agenda and we will drive hard to make this happen'.

However, historical studies of education, such as those of Elmore (1996) and Goodman (1995), suggest the weight of tradition will not be moved in any profound way by this romantic, even heroic, approach. There is a need to recognize that the challenge is not limited to the development of innovation, but extends to the institutionalization of the outcomes of innovation – to organizational learning. This represents a significant challenge for managers, as this Dean later elaborates:

> I like the idea of the Faculty continuing to be a learning organization in its own right. My role is to ask questions about whether we are still learning and whether there are opportunities to learn in research as well as in teaching, to keep both issues on the agenda without being too directive about the particular things that have to occur underneath them. I must say that you have to get the right balance, and that by asking too many questions nobody gets a chance to bed down anything.

However, extrapolation from the work of lone rangers to the general academic community needs to be done with great care. That community is a very broad and multicultural church. To push the congregational metaphor a little further, the very singularity and strength of the faith of some of 'the believers' can be as much an impediment as an asset in any process of 'conversion'. The 'certainty' of their knowledge can heighten the scepticism of the 'unconverted'. Bill Karle (University of Manitoba) shares a similar view:

> User input is the best determiner of what a design will need. The problem is the users are naive about technology and many are naive about teaching and learning . . . We find that most professors are having difficulty determining if they should employ any technology more sophisticated than slides. There are innovators who are doing wonderful work. But crossing what Geoghegan calls the 'chasm' to get mainline faculty to use moderately advanced technology seems to call for different faculty development techniques than used with innovators.
> (11 November 1997: AAHESGIT email list, post #213)

Genuine interdenominational communication needs to occur, and that communication must encourage discussion of the local traditions, preferences and prejudices, values and beliefs – not as an aside, but as *the* point of departure for any attempt to fundamentally rethink any aspect of the way in which universities provide their services.

Research on the importance of uncertainty, doubt and conviction in organizational learning complements and extends this discussion of lone ranging. Earlier I noted that uncertainty is a prerequisite for change, and that it can be generated through the process of planning. Param Srikantia and William Pasmore (1996) supplement this interpretation, providing a model of organizational learning that includes doubt and conviction as necessary elements. Their model involves a cyclic relationship between individual doubt and collective conviction. Doubt is associated with individual reflection on the status quo and/or active experimentation with alternatives – lone ranging. Doubt and the individual actions that result can inspire:

> interaction and dialogue between group members as they attempt to grapple with doubt and ambiguity and move toward group awareness

and consensus. The resultant interaction and dialogue produces ideally, a 'paradigm shift' which, finally, culminates in a new state of collective conviction.

(Srikantia and Pasmore 1996: 45)

They argue that doubt is necessary to the initiation of change. Without questioning of the status quo, there is no reason to change. However, doubt is difficult to achieve: 'Doubt is tied directly to fear, loss of security and threats to self esteem, which make establishing . . . [it] difficult. Conviction, on the other hand, is tied to curiosity, inspiration and our eternal hope for a better future' (p. 43). It is not difficult to predict which of these two emotions most managers would want to nurture. In terms of the organization, doubt is reduced through acts of organizing, because it generates consensual compliance, if not agreement. Individuals do not readily lose faith in the practices of the status quo.

And there are other reasons why doubt is difficult to achieve. It is one thing to doubt the status quo, another to commit to the unknown. Organizations tend to reward individuals for performing, rather than doubting – to 'tinker' with alternatives is to decrease one's performance, i.e., interrupt competence. Therefore doubt is likely to be ignored in the interests of the achievement of accepted objectives in known ways, particularly in settings which involve strategic planning and performance management measures. Doubting tends to be associated with those at the margins, or those who have a flair for independence – the lone rangers. In both cases, their doubting is unlikely to be motivated by expectations of rewards.

The failure of most systematic attempts at change is a failure to achieve doubt, and to achieve conviction in the value of the exploration of alternatives (Srikantia and Pasmore 1996). The literature suggests that academic culture is replete with both a variety of interpretations of the status quo, and considerable doubt about it. However, to express doubt publicly about one's own situation can be seen as an act of disloyalty. Discussion is more likely to be focused on the achievement of conviction and conversion – on eternal hope for a better future. As a result, alienation is achieved more frequently than is 'collective conviction' focused on the achievement of change. And management becomes more directive, the culture more corporate.

Managing border issues

The concept of 'border' is used to refer to institutional boundaries, and the related concept of 'the end of enclosure' (Deleuze 1992). Here, managing has to do with the establishment, maintenance and redevelopment of institutional identity. This is a particularly important challenge for academic managers, as universities are faced with increases in the complexity and diversity of expectations, and demands to respond more rapidly to those expectations. I have noted how well universities have adapted over their very long history as a form of institution. But the majority of that evolution involved a series of slow changes at the margins, changes that have nudged rather than shocked the system. The current demands are being experienced in a context where internal fragmentation – cultural and disciplinary – challenges even the notion of a unified core, let alone a relatively clear or continuous border.

This may be why the term 'gatekeeping' has given way in some of the literature to references to borders. The metaphors suggest that it is increasingly difficult to predict the actual points of 'incursion' or 'defection'. In more chivalrous times, there were agreements about when and where battle would occur. Now warfare is more likely to involve guerilla tactics where the enemy can't be distinguished from the civilian population, and the term 'collateral damage' is used to naturalize mistakes. Thus, instead of passively watching over a gate, managers now actively have to patrol a more extensive, less defined, border.

The lack of internal coherence is perhaps most evident when institutions are viewed as a whole. At the level of individual Departments, there is good news, and bad news. The degree of coherence tends to be greater, but intercultural and intertribal disputation may be both more evident and more intrusive in terms of the process of managing. Irrespective of their location within the organization, one of the most important roles of managers is to achieve an internal and ongoing sense of collective conviction about 'who we are, and what we do', and to champion that conviction in the external environment. Thus, like identities and cultures, borders are social achievements, and require constant maintenance. This is a task whose achievement is, like cultural domination, also likely to be partial, patchy and incomplete.

One challenge involves managing flows of resources and information across these borders. Mitchell (1997: 269) argues that 'openness to the environment cannot mean surrender to it'. Management of these flows tends to rely on two broad strategies: buffering and bridging.

Buffering includes attempts to absorb or deflect the demands of the external environment without altering the organization's fundamental structure or processes. Internal fragmentation can be seen as a form of buffering, allowing some enclaves to ignore external pressures, while others engage those same pressures with great openness. Buffering is usually focused on protecting the core values and processes – those associated with research, and to a lesser extent teaching – from intentional and unintentional external demands. This strategy requires monitoring of the external environment, but places a premium on managers' sensitivities to those core values and processes, issues that would be unique to their 'element' of the institution.

One form of buffering involves explicit 'decoupling' of structure from behaviour by adopting policies as symbolic responses to external expectations, with little effort or intention to implement the policies, especially if they are at odds with other internal sets of beliefs (Montgomery and Oliver 1996: 667). This is a strategy related to sedimentation – adding another layer of policy – but here the purpose of the policies is to absorb and deflect external expectations. Check with your local politician if you are unsure about how this might be done. Less developed forms of decoupling involve the relabelling of existing internal processes with the language of the external demands. Some managers, whether knowingly or unknowingly, use the language of managerialism in this way. The result, as noted by Prichard and Willmott (1997: 302), is that 'the new managerialism is acknowledged but is seen as something of a puzzle precisely because it is deemed to be broadly congruent with an established ethos'.

However, not all demands can be absorbed or deflected without altering parts of the organization in quite significant ways. Bridging strategies attempt to absorb the effect of external demand by creating limited accommodations while maintaining the core processes or values (Mitchell 1997: 271). The word 'bridging' suggests the nature of these strategies – they are border-spanning strategies. Teaching hospitals, demonstration schools, research parks, institutes and research centres are examples. In these activities the intellectual resources of a university are developed as joint ventures, allowing the university to retain its resources, yet respond to broader community expectations. A more recent phenomenon, at least in Australia, involves the establishment of commercial subsidiaries which are wholly owned by universities, but which engage in commercializing some of the core work, particularly teaching. In this case, this response is largely an attempt to respond to the funding policies of the Federal Government.

While most of these examples are relevant to those who are senior managers, the underlying ideas can be adapted to more local conditions. For example, consultancies are a local form of bridging. Another form of border management that has particular importance at the Department level involves managing tribal and cultural borders. Here management has more to do with capacities to engage in cross-border conversations than with buffering or bridging, although these are also important. Examples of this form of bridging include the establishment of multitribal or multicultural working groups.

The importance of the protection of core values and processes as a managerial responsibility should not be underestimated for managers who want to build credibility with those who identify most strongly with that core. Of course the corollary applies with equal significance. Having offered these suggestions, my sense is that the most powerful, and the most useful, strategy for managing borders remains the word 'no'. It is also, in many senses, the most dangerous in terms of its implications for can-do approaches to management and visions of excellence.

Managing tribal issues

Tribalism must be managed. In Chapter 6 I discuss the conditions under which tribal differences can become assets, as well as the conditions under which they can be counterproductive. Here I want to focus on several specific issues related to intertribal communication, and the emergent conditions of employment.

The major source of disappointment expressed by academics with respect to their emergent working conditions is academic management. In a profound sense, much of the dissatisfaction stems from the lack of attention given by academic managers to communicating in ways that demonstrate an awareness of and respect for the values and motivations of academics.

Geoffrey Elliott and Michael Crossley (1997) provide a case study of this failure in a large urban college in the UK. They report that:

> the lecturers in this study appeared to be in sympathy with educational reform which is directed towards increasing lecturer accountability, but out of sympathy with the manner and style of policy implementation by senior college managers.
>
> (Elliott and Crossley 1997: 88)

A failure to engage in conversation about deeply held (and contested) values gave rise to 'an ongoing state of mutual hostility, characterized by miscommunication, noncompliance, misunderstanding of practice and lack of consensus' (p. 89). The result was a general withdrawal of goodwill.

This type of mutual hostility becomes particularly significant in contexts that rely on self-management. The new organizational settings call for greater trust in employment relationships as new forms of loyalty emerge. Bradford Imrie (1996: 89) suggests that systems of performance appraisal depend on the improvement of the interpersonal relationships between appraiser and appraisee, and extend to issues of confidentiality. Rousseau (1997) refers to the importance of 'interactional justice' as a criterion of managerial effectiveness. She refers to the importance of 'politeness and respect', and 'credible explanations' in situations of conflict. Perhaps these are the capacities that the Australian Deans are seeking to develop.

Some issues and opportunities related to self-managing

The introductory comments of this chapter highlight the continuity of the agenda of management from the institution to the individual. This is an era where self-shaping works to fit particular expectations – empowered, active, enterprising and self-managing individuals. As external guides for work are withdrawn (because they are proving ineffective), self-governance becomes imperative (Rousseau 1997). Performance appraisal is one strategy that is intended to emphasize personal, rather than managerial, goal setting and monitoring of progress. The current financial stringencies and need for a flexible workforce combine to suggest that the future is going to require academics to develop considerable self-management skills.

The broad picture is of individual complexity as an adaptive aspect of all individuals, an aspect that is dynamic and evolving. Self-managing in challenging times requires a deliberate approach – identities are produced and changed through reflection, conversation and action. In this section I discuss three issues related to that task:

- issues related to the 'web of rules' that define work settings;
- opportunities in a context of change;
- planning and uncertainty.

Living in a 'web of rules'

I have illustrated the inventedness of organizations, of practices, of cultures, and of identities. That sense of inventedness conveys, amongst other things, the message that these are effortful achievements, and they operate as technologies because they both enable and constrain. Frederick Gamst (1995) uses the term 'web of rules' to refer to the socio-cultural technologies within which such work is undertaken. His position is that 'the web is more than just the formal regulations and logic; it is also the social interactions of persons' (p. 149). He traces the evolution of the conditions of work, pointing to the increasing reliance on formal rules for work and related corrective disciplines, especially management.

In universities the academic managers make the rules. There may be Councils or Boards of Directors sitting as the ultimate authority, but, in reality, those groups react to quite specific proposals brought to them by senior managers, who are likely to be acting in consultation with administrative advisers and more junior managers. But rule making is not a one-way process for the managers. It speaks to the maker as well as the subject. The documentation by Linda Hort (1997) of the establishment of a system of performance appraisal in one university, discussed in Chapter 5, shows how managers come to operate as a 'corrective discipline' and are, in turn, disciplined by the need to 'correct' their staff.

But the relational functioning of rules seems little acknowledged in discussions of management or policy implementation in higher education. Processes of performance appraisal, for example, can be used by academics to increase the certainty of expectations about their work, as is implied by the description by Bradford Imrie (1996) of one system of appraisal. They can also be used as a basis for declining invitations to 'work harder'. That is, they can be treated as agreements, and the conditions of their operation clarified. In particular, they can be treated as opportunities to clarify the conditions under which work is to be accomplished, including the resources that will be made available to support that work. A colleague, Professor Nancy Viviani, passed on the valuable wisdom that any rule/agreement-making process should involve two components: the agreements themselves *and* rules for changing the agreements. The second component needs to be agreed in any formal process of performance appraisal.

One of the more important challenges for self-managing is to identify conditions which govern an individual's work – his or her 'web of rules'.

Many of those rules will be tacit, based on tradition or untested belief. Some 'rules' are likely to be assumptions. Here the importance of doubt becomes important, inviting consideration of the degree to which compliance is actually expected, along with a degree of alignment between those rules which constrain most tightly, and considerations of purpose. It is important to remember the wisdom of Sherry Shapiro's challenging assertion (1994: 63) that 'naming the intolerable is what must pre-exist change'. It is through naming that practices come to be recognized, to become specific objects of thought, and open to the possibility of change – either changing them to make them more tolerable, or changing the way they are thought about so that tolerating them becomes a possibility.

Opportunities in a context of change

The Chinese proverb speaks of problems as both threats and opportunities. Self-managers have to be open to both possibilities, but here I want to address some quite specific examples of opportunities. The Dearing Committee suggests that integration of communication and information technologies (CITs) will pose the greatest challenge for academic work in the immediate future. Most attempts to restructure universities as organizations reflect attempts to reduce costs, largely through reducing direct labour costs. It is hardly surprising, given this priority, and the possibility of extensive use of CITs, that many academics believe that CITs will be used to substitute for academic workers. One consequence of this belief is a *principled reticence* on the part of many academics to engage with CITs. Of course there is a range of additional reasons for this reluctance, including anxiety, lack of time, lack of resources, and lack of support.

It is creative potential of engagement with CITs that I am most interested in here. Marietta Baba (1995) discusses the relationship between work and technology, tracing the evolution of that relationship, and acknowledging that technology is used as a substitute for human work. But Baba's work offers a reason for seeing the introduction of CITs as an opportunity, as well as a threat. She argues that work and technology act upon one another as mutually shaping causal forces. She notes that new technologies depend on spontaneous and creative enhancements by human workers who 'creatively solve problems that were not soluble within the formal domain of technological knowledge' (p. 137). Thus, work activity can create, through mutual shaping, a creative frontier with new technology:

> At the frontier, workers discover the actual capabilities and limitations of the technology, and they spontaneously generate coping strategies and tactics that maximize technology's . . . capabilities and compensate for its limitations. This frontier is only penetrable by the work force, since the actual capabilities and limitations of technology can be discovered only under real conditions of work.
>
> (Baba 1995: 137)

The value of 'coal-face worker' involvement in the development of CITs is evident in the comments of Ann Kovalchick (University of Virginia):

> We have just completed a formative assessment of a technology support effort at our university and one important finding was that prototyping and modification activities happen throughout the semester when new technologies are integrated into the classroom. The classroom functions as a testbed for both technical feasibility regarding service and support, as well as for proof-of-concept for new instructional methods or strategies. Clearly, this violates the more prescriptive approaches to instructional design that have traditionally been used to define how instructional materials should be developed.
>
> (3 February 1998: AAHESGIT email list, post #27)

This of course risks the development of technologies that will be even more effective, and will risk displacing even more workers from employment.

However Baba (1995) argues that debates around technology inevitably become political, given that issues of power are involved. The challenge she presents for self-managing is very clear: 'To the extent that work groups learn to exercise political clout in the workplace, they will gain greater opportunities to choose technological configurations that enable work activity to make creative contributions' (p. 138). In the case of CITs, this is an important possibility. Martin Trow (1997: 294) observes that 'during the computer's brief history, very little has been accurately predicted about its future development, either technological or social'. Combining these possibilities with the earlier position on mutual shaping suggests that academics should become involved with CITs in order to ensure that their development reflects academic values, and better serves the interests of both staff and students. In terms of the latter, academic involvement could help to ensure that the introduction of CITs will augment rather than replace direct and personal relations between teachers and students.

The most obvious area of involvement for academics is in 'courseware' development. This tends to follow one of two paths. The first is the *lone ranger* path, where individual academics take the initiative. Here the process tends to ignore commercial issues, and even the costs of development. The second path involves extensive involvement of IT technicians, including instructional designers, while academic expertise is used primarily as a source of content. This path tends to prioritize commercial and cost efficiency issues. But who should control the process? The second path leaves control, particularly in relation to the overall design, and subsequent improvement in the hands of the designers rather than the teachers or other staff who may contribute to its development.

The second path tends to shift professional status, and educational expertise, away from academics. In effect, it gives rise to a new tribe – an elite responsible for the development of courseware for use by others, most of whom are likely to be members of the academic underclass. This path generates a number of risks for academics. It risks contributing to a general devaluing of the educational status of academics, and an exacerbation of the marginalization of the part-time, casualized pool of teaching academics. It risks increasing 'the power of institutional administration and especially the administrators of technical services to coordinate and manage, if not initiate, the variety of activities taking place on campus' (Trow: 309). It also risks an increasing intrusion of market values into the pedagogical work of universities.

Academic involvement could shape decisions not only about courseware, but also broader technological configurations, including the version of education that is being developed. In Chapter 2 I shared some of the educational possibilities that the use of CITs makes possible, including reference to my experience with academics on the Logan Campus. I note here that those academics are confronting the risks that Trow identifies, but, while the contestation with the local IT tribe is giving greater emphasis to academic control on that campus, back at the main campus the situation is far less clear. This is partly because the two tribes are tending to work independently in this more traditional setting. However, my sense is that the academic administrators are likely to side with the IT specialists if that independence poses difficulties.

Academics should also contribute to the choice between seeing CITs as tools to augment traditional practices – an 'add-on' approach – and seeing them as an opportunity to reconfigure the educational process. The latter involves the possibility of teaching and learning being transformed by technology (Riffel and Levin 1997: 61). The IT specialists tend to see only the first possibility – after all, their agenda is to develop IT as a more powerful and effective tool. Only those who use the CITs in the context of teaching are in a position to experiment and identify new educational capabilities – that is, only academics. Riffel and Levin suggest that 'it may be that technology is not living up to its promise because it has been seen as an answer, rather than a reason to ask questions about the purposes of schools and the nature of teaching and learning' (p. 62). They argue the need for experimentation – to 'learn as we go' – but observe that the capacity to learn from all that experience is sadly lacking. It seems that neither schools nor universities are particularly capable in the area of organizational learning.

There is a third opportunity for academics. Trow suggests that there is a risk to academics of the development of a new elite of IT specialists. Once that elite has colonized this area, it will be extremely difficult for academics to win back authority or credibility in what is going to be an increasingly important aspect of university work. But, a new elite of academic educators who are teachers-of-disciplines, and also capable of utilizing the potential of technology-rich learning environments to serve new educational ends, could also develop. There is evidence that some Logan-based academics are recognizing this possibility, but there are few official opportunities for them to exercise this leadership role.

These issues should be of importance to all academic managers. The role of CITs in university teaching is being constructed right now, and that construction is being little influenced by academics, other than through the piecemeal and uncoordinated work of lone rangers and resisters. There could be no more important challenge for academic managers than to ensure that this construction is based on educational values and understandings.

Planning and uncertainty

Taken-for-granted planning occurs through 'autopiloting'. It requires very little effort or attention, and is an essential marker of expertise. However, careful studies of the behaviour of experts suggest that when they are confronted with ambiguity or uncertainty, most of their attention is given over to making sense of the situation they are encountering. The development of a response, by comparison, is given very little time or attention. That is, they engage in a sensemaking process which converts 'the strange' into 'the familiar', and this may take some time. Once they have done this, they proceed quickly to respond to their diagnosis, using well-rehearsed strategies which reflect the imposed, yet provisional, familiarity. Novices, by comparison, spend little time trying to make sense of the problem, tending to move quickly to generate 'solutions'. They spend more time than experts in problem solving, and they spend it differently.

What is not addressed by this version of expert problem solving is how experts deal with novel problems – problems for which their well-rehearsed strategies do not work. While the research is unclear on this issue, experts treat their selected strategies as 'provisional'. This suggests that they engage in a process of self-monitoring until the value of those strategies is clearer. Their initial (sensemaking) response means that their principal strategy involves attempting to understand the problem. Thus, in these situations, they are less likely than novices to engage in a trial-and-error approach to problem solving. Their priority is problem definition, not the generation of a response. This is a very important message for managers, including self-managers.

Putting doubt to work

I want briefly to revisit ideas related to these observations, and earlier comments. Sensemaking is a deliberate process. It arises because of doubt – it is an appropriate, even wise, precursor to action in situations of uncertainty. But sensemaking is not the same as planning. It is based on experience rather than an understanding of the future. However, if it allows for the adjustment of beliefs, it creates the basis for planning, and thus, for shaping the future.

The formal research programmes that engage so much of academics' time are versions of a sensemaking process. The training for research is training in the use of particular strategies and resources that underpin a disciplined approach to sensemaking. That is, research involves a very disciplined approach to sensemaking, disciplined in terms of both the strategies and the ideas – the conceptual resources. These disciplined capacities are available to be used for formative as well as reactive purposes. This suggests the value of an equivalent programme of training for managerial sensemaking, whether for organizational or for self-management purposes.

While academics tend to find many managerialist strategies distasteful, strategic planning strategies can be useful to those who want to engage in deliberate sensemaking processes. They can assist in the exploration of options once the assumption that the future will be the same as the past is called into doubt. In particular, they can help individuals identify their personal priorities, and achieve a sense of personal direction in relation to that doubt. At a different level, they can help in the exploration of the 'web of rules' that govern the conditions of work. This clarification can help to distinguish issues over which the individual has some influence or autonomy from those where there is really very little ground for negotiation. The age of self-management will also place a premium on being able to identify the precise resources individuals need to accomplish their work tasks, and strategic planning can help with this.

I have found open-ended questions very useful to help academics engage in challenge-focused sensemaking. They seem to invite a 'problem definition' response, and a realization that 'solutions' are better generated after basic understandings have been clarified. Examples of these questions include:

- Describe the students who you will be teaching in 10 years' time. What understandings, capacities, resources will they bring with them, or have ready access to outside of your contributions? What will you be able to add to their understandings and capacities (that they will not be able to readily access elsewhere)?
- What educational goals do you have for your teaching, and what uses of CITs would be consistent with them?
- What do you want to achieve through increasing the flexibility/openness of your existing teaching practices?
  - for yourself
  - for your students
  - for your Department
- What do you cherish most about your existing teaching practices, and not want to lose?
  - for yourself
  - for your students
  - for your Department

Some implications of this discussion

At the broad level this discussion offers an argument against the tight policy and implementation frameworks that many universities are now putting in place. Close governing of the work of academics is likely to inhibit the development of truly innovative practices, the sorts of practices that could be of great value to universities. An analogy from research is helpful here. Research teams are always given considerable freedom to pursue their research. Bureaucratic controls are an anathema to freedom. Yet these are the very forms of control that are currently being imposed indiscriminately on and within universities. They express a corporate culture that is oppositional to the collegial, academic culture. Their use will change the roles of academics, but I see little reason to believe that they will assist in the improvement of higher education.

But the news is not all bad in terms of the displacement of academic culture by this more 'managerial' culture. Rather than displacement, the evidence suggests uneasy coexistence, although the precedence of academic culture is being eroded. That is not entirely surprising, given that the proportion of staff who are academics is less than 45 per cent in Australian universities. There is an urgent need for academics to revisit their sense of identity and cultural values, with a view to adapting these to the existing and prospective circumstances of their conditions of work, and to differentiating these values and their culture from the range of other values and cultures within these places of work. These outcomes will only be possible if academics find *and* take the time to engage in extended conversation to achieve 'collective convictions' about the nature of their work, the values that they share, and the material and symbolic practices which are characteristic of academic work as this work changes.

The emergent workplaces are multicultural in the sense explored in this chapter. As the patterns of work change, new roles are created, while others become less important. These emergent roles are being constructed, and there is a strong sense that academics are slow to engage in this process. The risk is that 'academic' work will occupy a decreasing proportion of the total work of universities. There is a risk that universities will become less 'academic' in their nature, perhaps even to the point of ceasing to be recognizable as 'universities' as we know them, in a relatively brief period of time. The challenge is for academics to 'stake a claim', and to do so in terms of the contributions that only *they* can make to the shaping of those roles and the resulting practices, particularly through the use of CITs. Their use offers an opportunity to reshape educational practices fundamentally, while the control of this process by academics would ensure that educational rather than technological or commercial values would be prioritized. Indeed, the importance academics place on uncertainty and doubt make their involvement in these challenges essential.

At the level of individual academics, this chapter can be read as an argument for a more strategic awareness of the 'web of rules' within which they work, and an awareness of how that web 'works'. It is no longer appropriate to 'trust' the organization to be protective of the rights or interests of individuals – universities are less 'civil', more 'hard-nosed'. Conditions are being systematized, new forms of surveillance and control put in place. Yet those systems are not unidirectional in terms of their actual effects. They can be used in one's own interests, but only from a position of engaged understanding. Academics can use these rules to buffer themselves against the arbitrary and the irregular. Some of that buffering will certainly require collective action, but academics are going to have to pay attention to the conditions that govern their place of work, as well as to their discipline of scholarship.

Collectively these implications point to the need to reassert the role of academic managers and academics in ensuring that universities are places where doubt and uncertainty are welcomed, and risk taking in the interest of resolving that doubt and uncertainty is rewarded. These features cannot be provided if the conditions of work are overwhelmingly based on imperatives of control, predictability and accountability.

An important resource that academics can draw on in response to uncertainty are 'glimpses of the future'. They invite thinking outside an established vision that is already integrated into the planning system (to adapt Spender and Kessler's thinking). I offer the following email reflection, sent by a colleague, as an example of a glimpse of the future, knowing that for others it may represent a 'glimpse of the intolerable'.

Hi,

I had an interesting experience tonight that I felt compelled to write to you about . . . after all the 'suits' had gone (& I too had changed out of my work clothes), before I rode home, I went for a walk up into the [music] studios feeling somewhat camouflaged by my baggy shorts, T-shirt & sneakers. There were students everywhere, all engaged in sessions that would proceed into the night.

what I saw was a group of Jazzers, rehearsing/arranging a very hip version of 'A Night in Tunisia', completely controlled, very professional & sounding incredible . . . whilst this was going on in studio A, the control room was being run by a Y3 Mu-Tek [third year music-technology] Producer, teamed with Y2 Mu-Tek Engineers and Bachelor of Multimedia students: x[cross]-year, x-discipline . . . once again, very happening, very together: working on the same material, but from different perspectives. I peered down through the south windows & saw that in studio B, yet another group were editing material & rolling forward the project on another level . . . this is the FIRST time I have really seen this going on & at this level . . .

& I recall various rhetoric from the last few years, about 'creative musicians of the 21st century', 'interdisciplinary collaborative activities' . . . you know the drill . . . the stuff that tends to circulate at committees, or stay within the boundaries of subject outlines, or is directed at some imaginary point of light, somewhere in time . . .

well, I have to tell you: 'I've seen the future & it works' & I don't think it would be misdirected to say 'congrats' to all of us.

all the best

5

Academics' New Work

The thinking in question remains unassuming because its task is only of a preparatory, not of a founding character. It is content with awakening a readiness in man [sic] for a possibility whose contour remains obscure, whose coming remains uncertain.

(Heidegger 1977: 378–9)

Academics are already inventing the roles that will become more important in the next 20 years. Three academics involved on the Logan Campus provide reactions to the emergent work practices that their teaching involves.

I underestimated the impact of these new strategies on my workload and work habits, particularly the new assessment strategies. On the other hand, I have been delighted by the reactions of students to what I have attempted to achieve. Their enthusiasm, independence and motivation are truly inspiring. It is worrying to think what our more traditional practices did to deny them these opportunities.

For me the difficulties seem to be that I need more time to access the resources that are available. I do not have that time, so I tend to muddle on. The multimedia people seem to have more available time than the academic staff and this means they are frustrated because we can not always provide what they need, cooperate as fully as they would like, etc.

We need above all some strategies to build strong staff commitment and interest in IT as a dominant mode of course delivery, otherwise it will become an added-on feature of the course rather than the trailblazer it is hoped to be.

I think we need to get 'state of the art' models in from elsewhere and make time available for staff to meet to study these. The academic/IT split does not really work. The academic content needs to be conceptualized in the forms of the media which will present it or it will always be piecemeal.

It sounds as if the university wants to cut back on resources now, but this is exactly the moment when we need to take the risk and continue to invest in this approach, and in the development of academic staff who can create with it.

I think it will be unfortunate if IT is used to replace staff contact time. I think computers and technology can be used to make understanding easier. I am not sure that you can use it to replace staff time, but that depends on what staff do in the time they spend with students. If the academic is simply delivering material in static fashion, sure you can replace that with a computer. But when you are teaching them to problem solve you are not really just teaching them a technique. Inclusive in what you are teaching them are values, ethics, communication skills – a whole range of things which a computer, as far as I know, can not do.

Learning new work practices

In the traditional path to an academic career, the development of teaching expertise has been relatively unimportant. That places academics at a disadvantage in collaborations and contestations which focus on *how* teaching is to be augmented through the use of CITs. Academics' contributions are often restricted to issues of *what* should be taught. This limits their control over how these new learning environments might be structured or operated. However, the growing use of CITs (particularly the World Wide Web) is likely to increase the relative importance of the capacity to tailor global information to local needs. In addition, the pedagogic roles of mentor, modeller and monitor are likely to become more important, as academics support the development of authentic communities of practice. These new aspects of their work will require them to be more self-knowing of how they undertake their own learning, and of the function and operation of the community of learners to which they belong.

While I agree with Trowler's (1997) suggestion (Chapter 3) that some academics will respond to the challenges that confront them by learning to swim, and others by drowning, I think he underplays the challenges involved in the first possibility. He suggests, for example, that 'ideologies . . . represent sets of positions which individuals can take up or drop rather than ones to which they irrevocably and permanently subscribe' (p. 313). The idea that changing ideologies, or any of the other factors that influence an academic's response to change, is merely a matter of choice misconstrues the complexity here. I can not choose aspects of my identity in much the same way as I choose to wear a particular shirt. Developing new practices involves both unlearning as well as learning, and is likely to be a long-term process, requiring extensive support. To think otherwise is to engage in self-deception. It seems fitting to name this deceptive simplicity a 'trap' – the 'transformer trap', named after those strange toys which can be readily changed from one type to another through a series of relatively simple manipulations. This label also invites a reframing of some of the claims accompanying calls for 'transformational leadership'.

The 'transformer trap' arises, in part, from the paradox that some individuals seem to make change look easy. I well remember peers in my primary school who made learning look easy, peers who invited me into the trap of thinking that I could get by on native talent alone. As a consequence it took me some time (and effort) to restructure my identity to include the recognition that learning was hard work and required sustained effort. Most universities rely on *lone rangers* to be the pioneers of new teaching roles, and there is little reason to believe that this is not equally true for other innovations. In this context, lone rangers also appear, without help or apparent effort, to have learnt new ways to 'swim'. The fact is that the period, and the cost, of learning is as great for a lone ranger as it would be for any other academic. But their learning is undertaken as an individual project, and the time and effort involved is invisible to the organization, and to most of their peers. These lone rangers also tend to forget how much identity work they have done to establish their new capacities. Academic managers fall into the 'transformer trap' when they think that, if several can do it, then all can do it, and with the same (minimal) amount of support.

Thus, while academics' roles will change, that change will have more to do with the intentions that underlie them, and the tools that are used, than the development of entirely new roles, or the loss of existing roles. To use an analogy, the change will be similar to that which doctors are experiencing as their work evolves from restorative to preventative medicine. This does not mean that doctors no longer 'set' broken bones, or that they avoid providing intensive care for the very ill. But it does mean that their work is increasingly focused on keeping people healthy, rather than waiting for them to become unhealthy. Similarly, academics are facing a number of likely role shifts at this point in time. One involves a focus on the global opportunity: to focus more on networking with international colleagues for research; making extensive use of CITs to enable access to networked educational products; and provision of additional services to 'global' students.

A second change in academics' roles will involve more local opportunities, including the provision of research and consultancy services to local communities and industry, and the development of communities of practice as the principal conversational learning environment for students. These environments will be supported by extensive use of CITs to facilitate access to multiple sources of information, and to extend the possibility of participation to include both synchronous and asynchronous virtual conversations. This is more like the scenario advocated by Brown and Duguid (1996). However, I am not suggesting that academics need to become experts in multimedia authoring, or related multimedia skills. I believe that those skills are better accessed through teamwork. The development of capacities to teach in ways that they have not experienced as learners is sufficiently demanding as to preclude the desirability of concurrently attempting to develop expertise in multimedia authoring.

Academic careers

This discussion has treated academics' roles largely in isolation from the immediate organizational context. I want now to locate these possibilities within an organizational context, using the concept of a career to invite an examination of issues related to the conditions of work, especially the issue of employment conditions.

I am using the term 'career' to express a sense that, while academic work involves a 'job', most academics and aspiring academics desire more than a monthly salary. They expect their work to involve opportunities for advancement within the institution. This is the sense of career as a path rather than a position – to borrow from real estate advertisements, they seek a 'position with a view'. Thus, I am interested here in exploring issues related to the conditions of employment, and to opportunities for advancement. These derive from the relationship between academics and their institutions, particularly in terms of the relationship between academic and institutional values, priorities and practices. This aspiration, and investment, suggests a career-focused identity as a worker. Here I have a sense of a psychological connection with the work they perform, and the conditions under which that work is undertaken. This aspect of identity is largely taken for granted, because many of these connections and conditions lie outside the control of the individual. The investment is more in an expectation – a psychological contract.

The nature of an academic career is related to the overall environment of change in universities and this will continue to be so. The report of the Dearing Committee provides some suggestions on likely career patterns – a snapshot of the view from and for the position:

> In the long term, we believe future career patterns might be expected to show some of the following characteristics:
>
> • more staff transfers and secondments between higher education institutions and other organizations, with individual staff developing and managing their own career portfolios, combining teaching, research, scholarship, and public service as appropriate, at different periods in their lives;
> • a smaller proportion of an institution's staff remaining as core employees, but a need to ensure continuity in management, administration and learning;
> • the erosion of historic staff categories and pay structures and also the distinction between academic and support staff;
> • more flexible criteria for promotion which reflect the wider range of relevant skills that staff can offer . . . ;
> • increased institutional collaboration, offering staff more opportunities to develop their skills and widen their experiences.
>
> (NCIHE 1997: para. 14.12)

This snapshot, like many commentaries on the future, tends to accentuate the discontinuities within the current situation. Nevertheless, these suggestions are in keeping with trends discussed elsewhere in this book. The Committee's recognition that academic morale is declining has been noted elsewhere. In Chapter 3 I referred to the findings of other researchers which suggest that, while academics are relatively content with their work, there are considerably lower levels of satisfaction with their relationship with their conditions of employment and the management practices associated with those conditions. Two issues seem to dominate the dissatisfaction: recognition and reward; and loads associated with non-core work.

Recognition and reward

Taken as a whole, academics regard management practices as failing to provide appropriate mechanisms for the recognition and reward of their work, particularly non-research work. As the roles of academics expand, and new roles are added, it is clear that old forms of recognition and reward that focus on scholarly output, often defined in very narrow terms, are increasingly the object of dissatisfaction. There is an apparent double standard, with the majority of academics receiving their reward in the form of a salary, while a minority receive both salaries and promotions simply because of the focus of their work – research. It is particularly galling for those who are asked to 'go the extra yard/metre' in order to create the resources and practices demanded by the university managers (as is the case for academics involved on the Logan Campus). To make this commitment to institutional goals means that they sacrifice possibilities of promotion, or, in some cases, even continuing employment. As noted by the Dearing Committee, academics do want criteria for promotion which reflect the wider range of relevant skills that they can and do offer. One of the realities is that while, in Australia at least, staff can be promoted on a range of criteria, the perception held by academics is that this possibility is seldom realized.

A number of factors are contributing to this perception. One is that the majority of staff achieve promotion because of their research achievements. That is, there is an empirical basis to the perception. Another factor involves a tendency for promotion to be based on ever more demanding standards of performance. The criteria might be fixed, but standards attached to them are becoming tougher – an 'inflationary' effect. An important additional factor is that achievement in research is seen to be based on peer review in ways that achievements in other areas are not. That is, research achievements have a credibility which is based on the traditional claims of academic identity. Student ratings of teaching, by comparison, have no such authority, and very few academics have access to any form of peer evaluation of teaching that readily equates to the anonymous, external peer review system for publications.

But there are additional issues being played out in the context of change. One is the increasing instrumentalization of work, and therefore recognition and reward. This results from the formalization of work practices in the context of the need to generate additional revenues and increasing accountability for how academics actually spend their time. It is increasingly evident that the activities and achievements that will be recognized and rewarded are those that most closely align with the needs of a university, rather than those achievements that might be lauded by peers. In addition, there is a process of ever-increasing specification of the outcomes that will be recognized. For example, in Australia, the activity of research has been progressively narrowed in terms of recognition to include only specific types of publication, and sources of research funding – in both cases recognition is closely aligned with processes of peer review. Publications or funded research that lie outside those parameters are largely ignored. Thus, while the institutional and role boundaries blur and disappear, the boundaries around 'recognition and reward' are drawn with more clarity, and more tightly.

A second issue involves the actual outcomes of these processes of recognition and reward. There is increasing evidence that the benefits flowing to the organization as a result of successful innovation are disproportionally distributed to the organization and its managers, compared with 'the workers'. The extensive research of Drago *et al.* (1992) shows this in industries other than higher education, while the research of Aronowitz (1997) and Randle and Brady (1997) suggests this is also the case in higher education. To date the literature on higher education conveys a sense of institutional crisis, with an implied intention to have academics work differently in order to ensure the survival of their university. What is less clear is how, or if, the rewards of survival will be distributed. Institutional survival may involve more 'targeted sacrificing' than 'recognition and reward' at the level of those who will contribute most labour to that achievement, i.e., those who do the teaching. This possibility is clearly evidenced in the view of future careers offered by the Dearing Committee – fewer core employees and the erosion of pay structures.

Non-core work

Academics are also spending a greater proportion of their time doing work which most do not enjoy – non-core work as McInnis (1996) describes it. Surveillance and accountability measures are proliferating, penetrating and punctuating academic work. This is evidenced in the commitment by management to the use of performance indicators (McDaniel 1996) and the process of performance appraisal (Imrie 1996). This means that academics are spending more and more time responding to:

> the demands of institutional competition and accountability. Work related to quality assurance includes processes associated with induction and mentoring, appraisal, student evaluation of teaching, and providing data for institutional profiles and submissions.
>
> (McInnis 1996: 111)

Like the teachers in Sharon Gerwitz's (1997) study, academics are meeting more often, and for longer periods of time, and the agendas they are addressing are often set by those above them. There are decreasing opportunities for collaboration around issues of their own determination, while opportunities for collaboration in projects nominated by the institution proliferate. It seems that collegiality is being reinterpreted to mean 'entrepreneurial teamwork'. Other, more reflective or social forms of collegiality that are a proven source of satisfaction for academics are increasingly seen as indulgent and unnecessary.

This non-core work clearly has the potential for undermining the exceptionally high level of satisfaction academics get from their work and the control they are used to exercising over both the processes and the outcomes (McInnis 1996). In particular, the non-core work intrudes into the time that would otherwise be used for research purposes. This time is not protected from intrusions by the requirements of teaching, although the move to more 'flexible' forms of teaching can give the impression that even the time it requires can be treated as discretionary. My point is that effective research requires high-quality time – uninterrupted time – and the increase in non-core work is severely compromising that possibility.

Careers and emergent work conditions

There is a range of additional issues that impact on academics' identities, cultures and commitments – issues that are rarely if ever discussed in the literature on change in higher education. I explore three such issues that are potential sources of dissatisfaction with emergent work conditions: the built environment; conditions of employment; and the emergent academic underclass of non-tenured academics.

The built environment

The use of space impacts on the conditions of employment in very important ways, providing another symbol of management priorities in economically stressed times. Earlier this year I visited an Australian campus that has been built in the last five years, and was struck by the limited possibility of student discussions outside formal teaching spaces. This is a campus in a sub-tropical region, but it had no outdoor seating, no roofed areas in which students might meet informally for conversation or debate. But it did have impressive car parks and public transport facilities. Student movement to and from the campus seems to have been a priority in the design of the campus, while informal conversation was not.

Closer to my work, academics at the Logan Campus will have less office space than is provided for their colleagues on other campuses of the university. But they have been assured by facilities managers that the amount of floor space they are allocated is 'in excess of current benchmark levels for professional staff in industry'. This management-speak implies that all office work is the same – an office is an office, end of story. Importantly, these facilities managers are also trialling the concept of 'hot desks' for staff whose 'home office' is not on the Logan Campus. These desks are located in open spaces, and are to be used on a 'first-come-first-occupied' basis for only the time that the staff member is on the campus – a form of desk hotelling. Academics are expected to carry any resources they might need with them – an office-in-a-briefcase.

It is also interesting to observe that economic stringencies are tending to limit the hours and extent of operation of many food and beverage outlets on campuses. In some instances this includes the conversion of 'coffee lounges' into self-service facilities which allow coffee making, but rule out 'lounging'. These conversions have particular meaning for me, given my first taste of European universities earlier this decade. There I found that the ritual of morning coffee was sacred, and provided a welcome and well-used opportunity for rich scholarly conversation. When I returned to the Australian university at which I was working at the time, I found that no one wanted to acknowledge the contribution of the built work environment to the achievement of a culture of research, an outcome which that university was anxious to achieve.

I am suggesting that the nature of the physical work environment is an outcome of management decisions, and should be given very careful consideration in terms of what it symbolizes and offers by way of amenity for both student and staff morale, and for academic work.

Conditions of employment

This section draws on a postgraduate research project into the industrial regulation of work in higher education. The work was undertaken by a colleague, Dr Linda Hort, and was written up as a dissertation which I supervised. Her study, 'The tiger hunt: collegiality, managerialism and shaping academic work' (1997), examines the development of a performance review scheme for academic staff in one Australian university, a scheme arising from conditions established under requirements of the Australian industrial arbitration system. Hort's analysis is that current working conditions for academics are the outcome of processes that have been, to a significant degree, externally imposed, with the fine details being negotiated at the institutional level.

She uses the expression 'culture shock' to represent the current experience of academics as a former culture, characterized in terms of collegiality, confronts a new culture, characterized in terms of managerialism. The collegial culture is characterized in terms of values including: intellectualism; the centrality of learning; criticism of ideas and of society; academic freedom; autonomy; and collegial decision making. Managerialism, on the other hand, is characterized by perspectives and values including: economic rationalism; corporatization of the public sector; 'state' intervention in university management; a 'productivity' view of work; and a 'market' orientation. Hort is interested in how this confrontation came to be – the conditions that gave rise to it. Her explanation focuses on changes in the industrial awards governing academic work in Australia.

The historical evolution of the process of 'enterprise bargaining' is important to her discussion. The first move to establish a national industrial body for academics occurred in 1952, with the establishment of the Federal Council of University Staff Associations of Australia, which acted more as a professional than an industrial association. However, it was not until 1983 that higher education came to be recognized as an industry in terms of the operation of the mechanisms of industrial regulation. And it was not until 1987 that any registered agreement recognized academics as 'employees'. This recognition involves a very significant revision of the status of academics, reclassifying them as employees, rather than members, of their university. Any claim to 'corporate collegiality' was undone by this agreement.

A 1988 industrial agreement required the formation of 'Joint Union Management Consultative Committees' to negotiate the specifics of staffing policies arising from the awards – a form of worker participation which other industries may have seen as a major advance for the employees. However, in the context of higher education, the employees were regaining a very different version of what they had lost in 1987. The 1988 outcome involved levels of formalization of role description and processes for career advancement which were unheard of less than twenty years before, and these formalizations have generally been welcomed. Hort notes that:

> Prior to the 1970s, the professors had held almost autocratic power in relation to Departmental matters and staffing. The 'god professors' had, in practice, operated as the sole authority as 'supervisors' of staff, and had perpetrated injustices on academic staff . . . Such actions were based in scholarship (and elitism and sexism) not in relation to an 'employment contract'.
>
> (Hort 1997: 65)

Hort's case study traces the process of 'worker–manager' negotiation at the level of a performance management agreement for academic staff. The process of negotiation was controlled by an agenda and timeframe set by the terms and conditions of the award which were common to all Australian industries which sought registration under it. That is, the process of enterprise bargaining was generic to all industries, and required the use of a set of generic principles and practices, irrespective of their appropriateness to a specific industry. The negotiation process was adversarial in nature, and involved tight timelines and pressures to compromise.

The implication here is that the general language and specific practices of managerialism were as much imposed on university management as on the employees. Her evaluation of the scheme and its implementation is that it failed on every criterion she nominated. However, Hort argues that:

> It was the intention of neither the union nor the management side to create a poor and unworkable performance management scheme in

the University, nor to have the training underfunded and unsupported at senior levels. In fact it would be reasonable to assert that both sides were committed . . . to create a positive process that would benefit the staff and the University.

(Hort 1997: 185)

The explanation for this negative outcome relies on the fact that, in universities, the cultural clash does not involve conflict between workers and management. Rather than seeing academics as victimized by managers, 'it is the academics (at a certain level, and for certain, usually brief periods) who are the managers' (p. 195). This reminder sits in stark contrast to some views, including that of Tony Becher (1989), who called for a greater sense of mutualism between academics in different fields:

as a better defence against intrusive managerialism which seeks to impose a crude form of accountability, based on false assumptions about the nature of intellectual endeavour, and bolstered by insensitive and often spurious 'indicators of performance'.

(Becher 1989: 171)

Importantly, Hort's work acknowledges that academic careers (in Australia at least) are increasingly governed by formal agreements which set minimum industrial conditions and requirements. The recency of some of these changes means that colleagues and folklore may be quite misleading.

An academic underclass

It is clear that an academic career is not the same thing for those who are not on the tenure track as for those who are tracking to tenure, or have achieved it. The largest employer in the USA is now a temporary agency, Manpower, Inc. According to Cary Nelson:

Over the last two decades the percentage of college and university teaching done [in the US] by underpaid part-time faculty across the country has risen to about 45 percent. Very few schools hire their own part-time faculty for permanent positions when they open up, so these part-timers instead become a permanent underclass.

(Nelson 1997: 4)

The Dearing Report's reference to the trend to a smaller proportion of an institution's staff remaining as core employees implies, and endorses, a growth in Nelson's 'permanent underclass'. Margaret Brown's (1998) work suggests that many researchers are also part of this underclass, particularly those who are attempting to start an academic career.

This is an extension of a global trend that began several decades ago. According to Castillo (1997) it had been noted as early as the 1970s when it was discussed as 'the dual crisis of work':

On the one hand, this was a *crisis of quantity*, that is, job losses; on the other hand, and what was then considered more important, it was a *crisis of the quality work* and, with this, of its social significance and meaning for individuals.

(Castillo 1997: 416 – original emphasis)

Castillo discusses two approaches to this crisis. One focuses on the crisis of quantity and issues of technological determinism – the 'havoc of progress' (p. 417), while the second attends to the crisis of quality – the meanings of work. The former agenda dominated during the 1970s and 1980s, and continues to typify many of the critical responses to the current situation of the underclass of academic workers. The second agenda engages with issues such as:

complex systems of production demand[ing] a more involved workforce, one with broader and more holistic skills . . . [and] the need for workers who, paradoxically, would be involved in their work but to whom the company [or university] no longer would be tied in any way.

(Castillo 1997: 417)

In this scenario, work of a high quality is expected, but the 'psychological contract' between worker and employer is being radically altered, as I discuss more fully in Chapter 6. Thus, the disappearance and precariousness of employment is one of the postmodern conditions – this is 'the era of a disposable, rootless worker' (p. 418).

In his discussion of the decline of the professoriate in the United States, Philip Altbach (1997) notes that the proportion of the professoriate in tenured and tenure-track positions is steadily declining and is now around 44 per cent of all faculty. However, the goal of tenure is likely to remain 'the "gold standard" to which all aspire' (p. 321). That is, while there are multiple employment tracks, only one is esteemed. Universities will increase their use of non-tenured staff primarily because this strategy involves reduced costs, and increases the flexibility of their academic workforce primarily through decreasing the cost of discontinuing employment. On the other hand, Altbach suggests that the tenured professoriate have greater loyalty to both the institution and the profession – they constitute 'the traditional core of the university' (p. 322). This suggestion contains yet another ahistoric myth – Stanley Aronowitz (1997: 202) points out that tenure as a formal condition of employment 'is barely a half-century old', having begun only after World War II in American universities.

Nevertheless Altbach is correct to point out that the underclass – or as he calls them, the 'untouchables' – are primarily employed to teach. That is, rather than occupy the traditional academic role, they are employed to undertake a quite specific and limited form of academic work. Trowler (1998) reports research which demonstrates that this underclass is gendered – disproportionately the 'untouchables' are women. Margaret Brown's (1998) work suggests that this tendency to short-term employment encompasses a single-role focus for researchers as well as teachers. She speaks of these researchers spending considerable time applying for research grants that might enable their work *and* employment to continue. That is, the employment opportunities of the underclass are restricted in the amount and nature of the paid work available to them.

Altbach suggests that this underclass will form a rapidly expanding pool of workers, especially in the less prestigious institutions – the community colleges and the non-elite research universities – where student demand can both fall and be fickle. While many 'untouchables' have very similar levels of research qualifications to 'the tenured Brahmins', they are 'hired to teach a course or two, provided no benefits, often given no office space, and expected simply to show up to teach a class' (1997: 322). His reference to a type of caste system is deliberate, highlighting the difference in prestige, and drawing attention to this system as a hierarchy within the academy, a hierarchy which challenges the more egalitarian assumptions of collegiality. Those challenges extend to opportunities for involvement in institutional governance, and to support for research and publication.

While Altbach appears to lament this trend, Cary Nelson condemns it outright. His story elaborates the experiences of 'the underclass' at Yale University during the period 1994–6, including an extended period of strike activity in 1995–6. Nelson's perspective suggests a less benign state of affairs, one that challenges some of the implicit comfort of those who, because they are on the 'right track', are not particularly concerned with the interests of the underclass. He suggests that 'higher education as a whole has become structurally dependent on a pool of cheap labor to teach its lower-level courses' (1997: 5). He points to this as part of a larger trend in campus employment patterns involving downsizing, subcontracting, outsourcing and the like. Those trends have tended to impact mostly on the general staff, another group for whom the Brahmins tend not to show great concern.

But that is not the case in all instances, as Nelson's work demonstrates. In fact, the actions of the Yale University led to the formation of very untraditional 'coalitions of resistance', as 'permanent faculty, adjunct faculty, graduate students, secretaries and maintenance workers suddenly acquired common interests and reasons to build working alliances' (p. 6). Those 'reasons' are important. In a community in which the university is a major employer, as is the case with Yale, a shift to decrease the employment conditions of one group rapidly 'bleeds' into the agendas of both the larger community and other occupational groups on the site. Thus, the growth of an underclass can tend to make universities 'insecure, oppressive, and embittered places to work' (p. 5), even for 'the tenured Brahmins'. The phenomenon of 'coalitions' also challenges notions of academic autonomy and freedom – tensions between 'individual and collective notions of identity' (p. 6). Thus, while unionism may be seen as an undesirable intrusion on individual freedom and autonomy, when employment conditions are the focus of change, 'the general inability of faculty to act collectively now threatens the existence of the university as we know it' (p. 7).

The existence of an underclass calls into question many of the assumptions that underlie the ethics of higher education, especially commitments to serving their local communities, and to equity and justice. Nelson concludes that 'most faculties have maintained no ongoing conversation about the nature and social function of higher education' (p. 24). This is consistent with the characterization, in Chapter 1, of universities as non-literate cultures. It is also reminiscent of Joni Mitchell's assertion that 'you don't know what you've got 'til it's gone'. The possible importance of 'communities of practice' as a pedagogical concept would be compromised in an employment context in which 'community' was based on academics' shared experience of resistance, fear and frustration.

But what is a career?

The concept of a career is modernist. It draws on employment-related expectations such as predictability, security, loyalty, a 'ladder' of progress, and assumptions like:

- a long-term, even permanent, mutually rewarding association between individuals and their employers;
- a progression within that association that is predictable, and which involves a series of relatively discrete increases in both responsibilities and remuneration;
- a parallel change in the nature of the work, from an initial involvement in doing 'productive work' to later engagement in the supervision of 'productive workers'.

Careers have a decidedly gendered history – they were for men, but that has changed markedly in the last decade or so. Individuals, rather than organizations or groups, have careers. Professionals and white-collar workers have careers, while unskilled and blue-collar workers have jobs. Issues of status are strongly related to an individual's sense of career, and individuals can gauge their success in life, in part, on the development of a career path, i.e., achieving employment that includes a career ladder, and achieving progression up that ladder.

Academics have careers that are referenced both to employment-related advancement and to research-related recognition. Thus one can progress up a sequence of levels of appointment with corresponding salary increments. And one can advance a career through achievement of particular discipline-related research goals, for example the achievement of principal researcher in a particular type of research project, principal author of an internationally refereed journal article, or membership of certain councils of scholars or professional bodies.

Career decisions are important. They signal intentions and expectations. But those decisions have to make contact with the wider set of life experiences, and with the very different conditions of employment that exist, and are emerging, within universities and in the wider community. Many of the more traditional expectations and assumptions attached to the term career act to constrain thinking in quite unhelpful ways. I want to examine this idea by reflecting on the career decisions of a colleague.

The colleague came to work with me less than six months ago. She had been working in another local university, on a series of short-term non-academic staff contracts over a period of three years. I had worked with her in the conduct of a four-day regional seminar two years ago. When she applied for the academic position we had advertised as a one-year contract, she indicated the importance she attached to the opportunity to move to undertake an academic role. She has achieved exceptional outcomes in the brief time she has been employed by my university.

Five months after starting in this position she told me of her decision to resign. Her partner had been unable to find suitable work locally. She had been offered a position similar to the one she is currently undertaking in another city, where her partner stood a better chance of gaining the employment opportunities they were seeking. The contract there was for three years, at the same level of appointment as her existing position.

Three weeks after that conversation she told me that another section of my university had offered her a position that involved a significant increase in her salary, a three-year contract, but employment as a member of the non-academic staff. She accepted the offer. The increase in salary allows her partner to consider full-time study.

How helpful is the concept of a career to the young woman in this story? She changed jobs twice in the period of six months. In each case she has relied on particular opportunities offered by a position to justify her decisions. This story resonates with that told in Paula Caproni's paper, 'Work/life balance: you can' get there from here' (1997). In that paper she argues that the very notion of 'Work/life balance' reflects 'the individualism, achievement orientation, and instrumental rationality that is fundamental to modern bureaucratic thought and action' (p. 46). Her advice is 'not [to] settle for balancing or juggling' (p. 54). In many ways her paper is an argument against the technological rationality that Heidegger identifies – flexibility and efficiency for their own sake. Her response is to look to purposes other than these, purposes that 'privileged tranquillity over achievement, contribution over success, and choice over status' (p. 54). This response is very similar to those I have found in conversations with colleagues of either gender.

The term career brings with it implications of pre-existing 'structures' which become both the path and the means of advancement. That is, these structures map a pathway, providing guidance on what is valued, and what is more optional. Tierney (1997), in a report on socialization into academic careers, notes that his respondents found this pathway very poorly lit in universities – 'the goals for tenure were unclear' (p. 12), and 'grand markers that conveyed institutional meaning were absent' (p. 13). These structures – tenure and schemes for internal promotion, and the existence of journals to publish in, or funding bodies – provide a quite specific and limited set of options by which advancement might be achieved. While they offer limited options, they really do not guarantee advancement. Some achieve promotion very quickly, while others toil for little obvious reward. However, these structures did offer security.

Career conditions

One way of thinking about a career involves the metaphor of a 'treadmill'. This metaphor acknowledges the structure that surrounds a career, a structure which is not changed by an individual's career advancement. It also acknowledges the amount of work that must go into achieving that advancement. It seems that career treadmills have gone out of fashion in many, if not most, industries (Rousseau 1997). Because their 'treadmills' are not broken, many academics are having their sense of security taken away unexpectedly, and without good reason. A new set of career conditions seems to be emerging. The following statements capture some of these new conditions.

It is now the norm for organizations to have no fixed career paths, and for individuals in them to see no further than one or two years ahead, if that, in their own careers.

(Peiperl and Baruch 1997: 7)

With fewer external guides for work, greater value is placed on improvisation and learning.

(Rousseau 1997: 518)

Competence and hard work no longer guarantee continued employment.

(Peiperl and Baruch: 7)

Promotions and formal status gains are being reduced and replaced by lateral moves presented as 'career-building' assignments.

(Rousseau 1997: 520)

Impression management – particularly with superiors – [is a way of managing performance appraisal and of accessing] rewards beyond an individual's actual level of performance.

(Rousseau 1997: 519)

The changes in the ways our *work* is organized will make the biggest differences to the way we all will *live*.

(Handy 1989: 5)

Collectively these requirements suggest two major challenges to the assumptions underlying the concept of a career. First, the old psychological contract between employer and employee, represented in the concepts of loyalty and career, has been broken. The future will involve a psychological contract with the self and one's work rather than with an organization (Hall and Moss 1998: 25). Indeed, 'the underlying message is less to serve the present employer, than to protect against dependency upon it' (Defillippi and Arthur 1994: 310).

This change does not, in one sense, represent a significant challenge for many academics, given their loyalties to their disciplines and valuing of autonomy. The large and growing number of part-time and casualized academic teachers – the academic underclass – have already experienced the failure of this contract. Nelson's (1997) comments on the experience of Yale University staff highlight the trauma that this failure can cause, emphasizing the significance of grief associated with loss of expectations. For this group, occupational-focused (i.e., teaching-focused) professional associations could offer significant forms of support.

The second challenge is that the concept of career advancement will be increasingly unstructured. It will lack an obvious and pre-formed path, and the means to move up that path. That path was once mapped out by the organization, and movement along it was largely taken care of by the organization. The new situation will include neither path nor means, as they are currently understood. The path may have been poorly lit, but its removal is causing very significant levels of anxiety among academics in many institutions. Here the sense of grief reflects a loss of direction as well as of expectation.

Organizations are also being restructured. One model of the future structure – the 'shamrock structure' – is described by Charles Handy (1989). The reference to the 'shamrock' alludes to the 'three-leaved' structure he describes. The first leaf is the core of the business – the organization. It includes the 'permanent' employees, including the directors, managers and other well-qualified people who are needed to direct the organization and conduct its core business. These people will be committed to the organization and dependent on its success: a significant proportion of their income will be performance based. Handy speaks of these people working very long hours in an organizational context that is like a professional partnership.

The second leaf is 'the contractual fringe'. These are individuals and firms to which the organization outsources specific aspects of its work – subcontractors. Outsourced work will either demand skills that core staff do not have, or be too tedious for or of no interest to those people. These subcontractors will have a relatively permanent form of employment, but they will only be paid for results.

The third leaf is 'the flexible labor force' – the part-time and casual staff who are employed to work on a needs basis. Handy's discussion recognizes this form of employment, and the workers it involves, as essential to the capacity of the organization to change the size of its workforce quickly in response to changes in demand for its products. These are the 'just in time' workers.

This model of the organization is consistent with trends in many existing universities to outsource specific work, and to increase the use of part-time academic teachers. In a more extreme form it is very similar to the structure of universities in the digital age proposed by Brown and Duguid (1996). It is also consistent with the future career patterns suggested by the Dearing Committee, as discussed earlier in this chapter. For this reason it may be time to recognize and take stock of the direction of organizational evolution being experienced by universities. Indeed, it may be helpful for those who have tenured positions to think carefully about their location in the organizational core. Some academics might want to question whether the term 'shamrock', which Handy links to the three-leafed Irish plant, might better be understood in terms of 'sham-rock', implying deceit rather than naturalness and certainty.

Handy's description of the career of core workers is very organization-focused in ways that academics are not. However it is understood, it seems that the new breed of academic managers is adopting positions that are consistent with the concept of core worker. They are working long hours themselves. That is they are attempting to realign academics' loyalties with the institution rather than their discipline. Individually, academics need to think carefully about the relationship they want with their university, and how that relationship might be achieved in the future.

These challenges have been recognized for some time, with some organizations and their employees having negotiated new relationships. In their review of such experiences, Douglas Hall and Jonathen Moss (1998) offer three scenarios: 'lost in the trees'; 'sees the forest'; and 'comfortable in the woods'. In the first situation, employees are lost and grieving the loss of the old contract (p. 27). The second scenario reflects settings where the drastic changes occurred 'a long time ago'. As a result, the grieving is over, and a new sense of 'acceptance' has developed, with 'many employees now embracing the new arrangement, with its greater freedom, [and] responsibility' (p. 27). The success stories involved firms which showed 'exceptional leadership and high employee involvement' (p. 28), which allowed the relationship to change gradually. This meant there was no sense of unexpected loss, more a process of continuous (and continuing) learning and adjustment. One of the features of these firms is their commitment to staff. However, the new psychological contract is focused on the achievement of the firm's goals – it is a performance-driven contract, which rewards loyalty through achievement. That is, a form of mutually beneficial loyalty, a loyalty which extends to customers as well as staff.

This loyalty is referred to by Hall and Moss (1998) as 'the new protean career contract'. Their work, like most of the other work I am referring to here, is written for managers, rather than employees (although Handy is writing for both). The view adopted by those authors tends to privilege the organization over the employee, and to promote thinking that is consistent with the technological, flexibility and efficiency imperatives. I am uncomfortable with this view. While it engages with issues related to possible future conditions of professional work, it tends to be directed towards ends that are decidedly narrow. Perhaps my reaction is telling me that my preferred relationship lies outside Handy's organizational core. If the future involves a 'structureless career' what strategies might be helpful to provide a sense of personal direction and advancement during a work-life?

Work-life self-management

Once the challenge was to get on the advancement treadmill. Now it seems that it might be helpful to get off the treadmill, even to ignore it. Universities are finding it difficult to fulfil the increasing range of expectations which employees and clients are voicing. Investing in a psychological contract that is fixed, immutable, based on 'modernist' assumptions, and focused on institutions as providers of a career path seems pointless. Rather than careers, some commentators refer to a 'portfolio of projects' – some paid, some unpaid, while others might be underpaid in the interests of expanding one's attractiveness to potential employers. The message of the authors who write of 'boundary-less' and 'protean' careers is that it may be better to think in terms of a professional career *and* of relationships with employers. Denise Rousseau (1997) suggests that attachment to their employers places employees at greater risk if their employment contracts are violated. The advice is to separate the self from the employment as part of a reshaping of the self as an individual who can be productive in an uncertain world.

Employment relationships and professional careers can be managed so as to optimize the possibility of financial security and personal satisfaction. That task is increasingly shared between individual academics and their supervisors. Universities are developing organizational policies and procedures that govern this process in their interests – seen largely in terms of needs for increased flexibility and efficiency. That is, university management has recognized emerging opportunities and challenges, and is tending to invest attention and resources in the development of self-interested responses. But there is little evidence that academics have begun to recognize their own emerging opportunities and challenges. They tend to be focused on their disciplines – the self-help book industry has not been boosted by sales to academics. Management issues are the concern of managers, and most academics want as little to do with them as possible.

However, academics need to recognize what is happening to their career opportunities, and to invest in the development of responses. The literature on 'borderless' and 'protean' careers offers some very useful suggestions. Robert Defillippi and Michael Arthur (1994) suggest a need to develop three types of competencies – *know-why, know-how*, and *know-who* competencies. Their meanings, adapted to fit my intentions, are as follows.

- *Know-why* competencies are related to motivation, personal meaning and identity. They require a competence in self-awareness in terms of beliefs and values as they inform decisions about work-life. Without any 'treadmill' or 'pathway' academics will have little choice but to look to their own beliefs and values as the basis for setting directions and managing their employment opportunities and professional identity. This awareness needs to extend to the multicultural identities, particularly disciplinary and employee allegiances. It also extends to an awareness of the values and beliefs inherent in specific opportunities for employment. The point of this competence for self-management is the possibility of pursuing goals that are financially rewarding and personally meaningful. Because beliefs and values change in both nature and significance over time and circumstances, competence in this area will be amenable to completion but not ever finished.

- *Know-how* competencies underpin work-life expertise. They are the professional competencies – the skills and understandings related to disciplinary scholarship, including teaching, research and service, and to work-life, accumulated throughout an individual's life. Most academics are used to representing their achievements in a *curriculum vitae*, but *know-how* competence refers to capacities rather than achievements. That is, self-management in this area requires individuals to identify the nature of the professional and work-life skills and expertise which they have, and to be able to provide evidence of the extent to which they possess them.

  The SEDA accreditation procedures are an emergent example of what this might mean. Those procedures are based on recognition of eight key tasks (objectives) of university teaching and six principles and values that should underpin their work and the attainment of those objectives. Those principles and values are:
  - an understanding of how students learn;
  - a concern for students' development;
  - a commitment to scholarship;
  - a commitment to work with and learn from colleagues;
  - the practising of equal opportunities;
  - continuing reflection on professional practice.

  The procedures allow for any course or programme of training for teachers in higher education to be accredited through demonstrating achievement. The identified objectives are assessed to ensure their demonstration in ways consistent with the principles and values. The scheme is outlined in some detail at the SEDA web site address: http://www.seda.demon.co.uk/acrdmenu.html.

- *Know-who* competencies are based on work-life relevant networks. Academics know of the importance of networks to their research, and to reputations. One of the explanations for the capacity of some individuals to increase the speed of the old treadmill lies with their capacity to network, and to find mentors. Use of email has made networking easier, and has emphasized its value to learning. The email networks of which I am a member allow access to extensive discussions on the changing roles of academics. In particular, I find the 'aahesgit' network run by Steve Gilbert for the American Association for Higher Education extremely informative and active. The url for their Web site is <http://www.aahe.org>, and registration for this network is available there. The trend in employment is that more opportunities are created through personal recommendation than through relatively anonymous applications. So networking and mentoring will be of increasing importance for managing both a professional career, and employment.

Academics need to manage the development and the value of their skills, expertise and relationship networks. This requires a high level of personal awareness and responsibility, and an awareness of trends in the professional environment in which they are working or seek to work. One of the questions academics constantly need to research is 'what areas of work, projects, responsibilities, learning would I like to engage in over the next two to three years, and how am I going to achieve this?' Definite answers to questions like this will help to ensure that performance evaluation and activity planning discussions with supervisors serve the processes of self-creation for 'advancing' academics.

Looking over the horizon

The existence of a group of academic workers characterized as an 'underclass' can be seen as a portent of the future roles of the majority of academics in the next ten to twenty years. For that reason I want to conclude this chapter by discussing briefly some of the implications that stem from the current fragmentation of the concept of academic, returning to earlier questions and themes.

I asked whether 'the cumulative experience of change was causing shock to academic identities'. In light of the preceding discussion, some responses to this question can now be offered. Rather than shock caused by surprise and horror, it seems that the effect is better characterized as fragmentation, associated with an increase in the scope and range of roles that academics are expected to occupy, and new employment conditions and practices. Rather than a cumulative experience of change, there seems to be an accumulation of particular changes around particular roles, especially (but not limited to) the role of teaching. In terms of that role, what is becoming less clear in some institutions is whether the current privileging of research over teaching will give way to a complete separation of the operation of teaching from research functions in those universities.

In these circumstances, an identity – referring to a sense of belonging, a feeling of persistent significance, a sense of continuity and coherence – becomes an increasing improbability. Organizational continuity and coherence give way to fragmentation and opportunistic interinstitutional and intertribal alignments. It is clear that academics' identities will need to be increasingly distanced from their institutional commitments in the era of the disposable, rootless worker. Because a greater proportion of academic work will involve the role of teaching, it will become more useful to develop a sense of identity which is anchored in more cosmopolitan values related to teaching (rather than researching) a discipline.

During the time that this reidentification takes place, it seems likely that academics' experiences of shock will have more to do with a sense of loss of opportunity and of trust in their institutions and the managers of those institutions, than of actual change in their roles within those institutions. That is, morale will suffer more because of symbolic than substantive losses. In these circumstances, it is likely that academics will engage in strategic compliance with their managers' priorities – accepting their 'definition of constraining circumstances whilst retaining reservations' (Bloor and Dawson 1994: 290). Thus, work may tend to be engaged with in terms of instrumental, even technical, rather than professional values. Academics may also come to see themselves more as knowledge workers than as knowledge makers, in keeping with a former change when academics became knowledge makers after having primarily been custodians of knowledge.

The most credible long-standing tradition of universities to which we can point is the tradition of change – of adapting to external constraints and opportunities. My contribution here has been to engage with a range of constraints and opportunities resulting from a change in the environment in which academics work, and to offer ways of thinking about those changes, and the opportunities, at the level of academic work. The next chapter explores changes at the level of academic managers.

6

How May We Be?

The shift we are trying to define is away from 'professionalism' as the ideology of service and specialist expertise; away from 'professionalism' where the status of the occupation is at stake; and towards a 'professionalism' which focuses on the quality of practice in contexts that require radically altered relations of power and control.

(Nixon *et al.* 1997: 12)

Whatever future there will be for academics, as active, committed, valuing individuals, they will have to talk and write and advocate it into being. This is a constant, ongoing task – forever incomplete. Change requires new words, new ideas, new questions – new thinking. The issues of possibilities and becoming are central to the web of rules that govern academics' work. The position adopted here is that these rules are the *achievements* of academics rather than an imposition on them. Academics have an opportunity to become more literate about their practices. They can develop a greater awareness of the historical nature of those rules, and a language with which to discuss and to help imagine changes in that web. They have more opportunities than they recognize to resist the intolerable. They are freer than they feel to explore new possibilities.

In this chapter I discuss those opportunities and possibilities, including issues related to the concept of an academic 'profession' in the broadest sense and also at the level of the individual academic.

The academic 'profession'

The term 'profession' has been much devalued. Now everyone – from shop assistants to shoe shiners – can claim that they are professional. Indeed, they ought to do so. More thorough discussions of the concept refer to work which is of a principled and ethically reflective more than technically efficient character, and characterize professionalism in terms of virtues rather than skills (Carr 1994: 47). In spite of this devaluation, its use continues to offer opportunities and possibilities in terms of the redevelopment of academics' identities, and to mobilize efforts towards such achievements. There are those who argue that the new management of education requires a new sense of professionalism, one more in keeping with the postmodern condition (Nixon *et al.* 1997). But it is clear that 'professionalism' is a contested concept, as evidenced by Cary Nelson's (1997) discussion of the industrial disputes at Yale. This contestation is productive given that it forms the basis of its continued achievement and development.

In her discussion of the triumph of 'the Oxbridge ideal' over civic universities, Sarah Barnes (1996) notes that the development of the civic universities represented a revival of university education as a preparation for the professions in the mid-nineteenth century. Unlike the medieval universities, the purpose involved explicit training in the fields of science and particularly in forms of thinking associated with science and rationalism more generally: 'in a society increasingly dominated by professional experts, higher education emerged as a gatekeeper for entrance into an educated elite' (p. 288). Here 'professionalism' was associated with the possession of highly valued technical capacities, capacities acknowledged through the achievement of particular qualifications, often awarded by universities. The Oxbridge universities, on the other hand, tended not to award such qualifications, except in the case of the elite professions of theology, law and medicine.

But they could not remain aloof from changing community expectations, so the meanings of the term professional were adapted to the core values of these institutions. Barnes describes this process as involving two steps. First, the concept of 'professional' was redefined:

> to include qualities normally associated with the nineteenth-century English ideal of the gentleman – honesty, responsibility, self-discipline, and devotion to duty . . . [T]he gentleman-professional was seen as one who relied on expert knowledge, selection by merit, and the judgement of peers to rise by merit. Placing service to his fellowman above profit, the gentleman-professional earned his reward by proving his indispensability to society.
>
> (Barnes 1996: 288)

The second step involved abandonment of the last sentiment expressed in the above quotation – disdain for the profit motive. Accordingly, just as earlier the term 'professional' had been redefined to encompass the qualities of the gentleman, the conduct of business itself was now elevated to the status of a profession. It is clear that both changes were made as an accommodation with external pressures. Thus the Oxbridge universities came to provide a form of training for the elite of the worldly professions, 'one that was connected with the national elites of politics, administration, business, and the liberal professions and designed to mould character' (p. 289). This is the notion of autonomous professionalism that is currently associated with higher education.

This brief review shows how 'traditional' understandings of academics' sense of professionalism are neither fixed, nor closed. It shows them to be social constructions – partial, patchy and incomplete – as also argued by Nixon *et al.* (1997). Thus, the project of exploring new opportunities and possibilities has greater 'traditional' validity than do the accusations that such an exploration might put the so-called 'traditions' of academic autonomy and freedom at risk.

The development of the concept of academic professionalism

In his review, Göran Blomqvist (1997) provides a historical view of the development of the concept of academic professionalism. He observes that, in Europe, there has been a general trend towards greater respect for the occupation – or profession – of university teacher, and the self-awareness of university staff has grown accordingly. Blomqvist distinguishes two concepts to represent opposing foci for professionalism: autonomy and heteronomy. Autonomy is equated with 'academic freedom', involving scholarship 'pursued for its own sake, with its own organization and a system of thought and rules that only academics can judge' (p. 172). It includes a commitment to research and teaching that are pursued independently of short-term external expectations and demands. It is a view of professionalism which 'is more self-conscious and oriented towards the professional interest and status of academics as a body' (p. 194).

Heteronomy, on the other hand, involves a sense of professionalism in which the interests of society are sovereign – teaching and research are pursued in ways which both respond to social needs and are valued in terms of their contributions to the 'social good' as defined by others. Here the emphasis is on social responsibility 'and the role of the scholar as bearer of culture' (p. 194). It is interesting to note that Blomqvist, in the closing paragraph of his review, chooses to use the term 'professional' only in relation to 'autonomy' while his earlier discussion shows how the concept of professionalism was contested throughout the period of his review, i.e., 1820 to 1920. This symbolizes the 'naturalness' of this version in the current historical moment.

The concept of 'autonomy' has also evolved. Blomqvist's account of the ongoing tension between these two versions of professionalism points to autonomy as being preferred, in the main, by the academic community, while the state and wider social interests tended to prefer heteronomy. Neither preference is surprising. What *is* surprising is that the academic community has at times been divided in terms of its interpretation. Before 1852, autonomy was considered only in terms of obligations to the corporate community of the university, and to the role of this community as a bearer of culture. However, the relative priority of these two obligations was disputed. Scholarship in the form of publication only became part of the 'job description' of Swedish academics after 1852. Since then, autonomous professionalism has tended to be defined in ways which privilege the individual over the corporate, and research over 'the bearing of culture', paralleled by the rising allegiance of scholars to their disciplines (and Departments) rather than to their institutions.

Related ideas have also changed. The notion of 'corporate community' is now understood in terms of organizational departments, i.e., the communities of disciplinary scholars discussed by Becher (1989). The term 'bearer of culture' was contested by those who sought to have the national culture championed in some way, and by those who saw 'culture' as referring, in a generic way, to Western culture – initially to Hellenic culture, and later to the Enlightenment culture with its focus on science and rationality. Indeed, when discussed 'within the fold', the professionalism evidenced by academics seems to have far more in common with Blomqvist's notion of heteronomy than with the implied unity of 'autonomy'. Thus the terms autonomy and academic freedom have been associated with broad sets of evolving meanings. These meanings become visible and articulated (in both senses) only when the academic profession is under serious external threat. Mind you, I am talking about a profession that seems to have seen itself as enduring a constant state of threat.

Developing role-based identities

This discussion can be related to other discussions on the extension of expertise. Borrowing ideas from Bloor and Dawson (1994), I want to make some of these continuities explicit. They refer to 'dominant subcultures' within organizations with multiple groups of professionals, and issues of hierarchical dominance. Rather than dominance, I want to focus on the possible value of extending the three levels of academic identity discussed in Chapter 2 to include a role-focus. The majority of academics already identify their preferred role as 'teacher', as noted by Sheehan and Welch (1996), and this could provide a strong basis for a professional identity, as argued by Jon Nixon (1996). What they lack is a well-developed conceptual understanding to underpin that identity – they are 'closet teachers'.

Learning to be an academic is largely informal – on-the-job – as implied by the Dearing Committee:

> The skills associated with academic work: teaching, scholarship, research, and administration, have traditionally been acquired within higher education itself. Possession of a good degree and postgraduate research qualification have been the traditional entry qualification for academic staff.
>
> (NCIHE 1997: para. 14.5)

Academics are trained as researchers, yet their roles involve more than this. In particular, the work of most academics is focused on teaching. The educational knowledge underpinning their teaching is largely accumulated through experience and transmitted orally, rather than through texts or formal educational activities.

Achievement of the role changes discussed in Chapter 5 will rely on relatively sophisticated educational understandings consistent with the student-centred, learning-oriented approach to teaching discussed by David Kember (1997). The crucial matter is that, whatever form the academic teaching roles take, they will increasingly focus on helping students to make use of information, rather than being their primary source of information.

The changes will also require that academics develop their existing under-standings of how students learn in the context of their disciplines, and the particular learning environments in which learning occurs, and how they can intervene to increase the effectiveness of that learning.

One of the immediate challenges for a teaching-based identity would involve the broad distinction between the disciplines. Bender (1997) distinguishes the humanities from the social [and natural] sciences. Becher (1989: 153) makes a very similar distinction, separating disciplines with restricted knowledge which have clearly defined boundaries (i.e., the sciences), from those which deal with unrestricted knowledge characterized by 'unclear boundaries, problems which are broad in scope and loose in definition, a relatively unspecific theoretical structure, a concern with the qualitative and particular, and a reiterative pattern of inquiry' (i.e., the humanities, including education).

These distinctions seem to parallel rather neatly the view of academics' conceptions of teaching provided by Kember. He identifies two opposing orientations to teaching: one teacher-centred and content-oriented; the other, student-centred and learning-oriented. It is rather easy to suggest that academics involved in teaching 'the sciences' would tend to the former orientation, while those in the humanities would hold the second. In fact, that correlation tends to hold only when the academics have little concep-tual understanding of their teaching. Once academics from either disciplin-ary group engage with the research literature on education, and use it to inform their thinking about teaching, there is a stronger likelihood that they will identify with the latter orientation, irrespective of the discipline that they teach. This outcome is exemplified in the comments of two aca-demic scientists, John Dearn (1998) and Darryl Jones (1998), who describe their disciplined engagement with the educational literature. I explore those comments in more detail later in this chapter. My point is that identifica-tion with student-centred, learning-oriented approaches could form the basis for a more cosmopolitan sense of academic teacher.

The existing sense of 'professionalism' and its implications

I have explored issues related to the broad issue of academic professional-ism in earlier chapters, as well as in the preceding section. Collectively, that exploration highlights the importance of two 'indexes' for academics' sense of professional identity:

- the cosmopolitan values of academic freedom and autonomy, including relational values of collegiality, peer-based review and recognition; and
- more local, discipline-focused values related to knowledge and research expertise.

The local values reflect the process of socialization that both Tony Becher (1989) and David Damrosch (1995) discuss. That process involves an extended period of discipline-focused training, including both undergraduate and postgraduate studies. Thus the path to an academic identity is based on many years of intensive training. The intensity of the doctoral programme, and its formative influence on personalities of academics, is well argued by Damrosch, who views its achievement with considerable ambivalence. Given the length, intensity and selectivity of such apprenticeship programmes, it should come as no surprise that the sense of professional identity is so closely aligned with disciplinary world-views, including research methodologies.

This sense of professionalism accommodates disciplinary diversity but works against other forms of difference. In particular it privileges the function of research over those associated with either teaching or service, as noted by many commentators, including the Dearing and West Committees. The reports of both Committees, while acknowledging the importance of research, call for a more balanced focus on all aspects of academic work. In a sense they call for an elaboration of the *indexes of self* to include both service and teaching, but their calls are directed more to the assumptions underlying system- and institution-level practices. While the academic identity is based in the notion of academic researcher, for universities, the equivalent pinnacle is the research university: the triumph of the elite and research-focused 'Oxbridge' style universities over the majority of current universities whose origins are consistent with 'civic' purposes – teaching for the professions and applied research.

The need for such an elaboration springs from a number of imperatives. First, while research is an essential feature of the charter of universities, that charter places an emphasis on teaching. Service remains a core role of universities, particularly those with strong links to their local communities. Second, teaching is the most important role of the majority of academics. Those academics, and their commitment to teaching, are marginalized by the privileged status of research. This marginalization is exacerbated in very profound ways for the growing group of part-time and casualized academic teachers. Third, it would represent a powerful symbolic response to the chorus of complaints that universities are failing to provide teaching of the quality and type required. In this sense, it is a form of 'decoupling' (as explained in Chapter 4), which can provide a symbolic defence against pressures to instrumentalize the curriculum.

This call has been argued at length by other commentators, most notably by Ernst Boyer, in the influential book *Scholarship Reconsidered: Priorities of the Professoriate* (1990). He proposed four interdependent components of scholarship: the scholarship of discovery; the scholarship of synthesis; the scholarship of application; and the scholarship of teaching. These four components clearly extend beyond 'knowledge and research expertise'. Notions of 'service' are related to the scholarship of application, while 'teaching' is clearly equated with the 'scholarship of teaching'. What Boyer provides is a strategy for articulating teaching with scholarship and, via the interconnections with the other forms of scholarship, with research. Teaching is given status as a form of applied research, a particular form through which the scholarship of discovery is re-presented to those who wish to become more knowledgeable of the discipline. And its status as a distinct form of scholarship is accentuated. In turn, Boyer's work has spawned attempts to define and exemplify scholarly teaching. Here the link with the relational values of collegiality, peer-based review and recognition becomes central.

Is it possible to anchor the academic identity to both research and teaching? At the moment, the answer is 'yes', but only one anchor has any weight – research. Most academics see themselves as both teachers and researchers, as evidenced by the international studies reported by Sheehan and Welch (1996), and the Dearing Committee. Future employment opportunities seem likely to disrupt this, offering employment to some full-time academics on a teaching-only basis. The current deployment of the term professional would mark these individuals as second-class members of the academic profession. So why does only research count?

Academic researchers and academic teachers

Teaching in universities is seen to be unprofessional. Thomas Angelo, a visiting American academic to Australia, is reported to have suggested that university teaching as a profession is, in 1998, where the medical profession was in 1858 (*The Australian* 27 May, 1998: 36). By implication, university teachers are craft-workers, learning to teach largely through a process of imitation during an observation-only apprenticeship as a student. This tends to be the case for all aspects of their work–teaching, scholarship, research and administration – as noted earlier.

Andy Hargreaves (1997) provides an overview of four historical phases in the changing nature of school teachers' sense of professionalism and their professional learning. His four ages/phases are:

- the pre-professional age – pre-1960s;
- the age of the autonomous professional – from 1960s;
- the age of the collegial professional – from mid- to late 1980s;
- the post-professional age – the future.

(I have indicated the period that Hargreaves suggests each phase began, but I think it is possible to see ongoing traces of all previous 'phases'. That is, each phase is 'sedimented' onto, rather than a replacement of, previous thinking.)

It is difficult to argue that academics have moved beyond the first of Hargreave's phases. During it 'teaching was seen as managerially demanding but technically simple, its principles and parameters were treated as unquestioned commonsense, one learned to be a teacher through practical apprenticeship, and one improved as a teacher by individual trial-and-error' (pp. 90–1). This view of teaching calls for enthusiastic teachers who know their stuff, know how to get it across, and some tricks of the trade. So there is little need for anything more than brief pre-service training, and certainly no need to support ongoing professional development beyond irregular and infrequent workshop sessions connected to latest policies. In fact, such sessions are more likely to be seen as an interruption of work than as a way to develop the quality of that work. This is/was an age where teachers had little professional status, and teaching was too often seen as 'women's work', i.e., 'real men' were off doing other types of work (in universities they are busy researching).

The age of 'autonomous professional' is linked with moves to 'empower' teachers as curriculum developers and decision makers. In its fullest expression, responsibility for curriculum development was delegated to schools, where detailed curricula had previously been developed by central authorities. It was a time of great innovation, but those innovations were only known to those most directly involved with them. In this sense autonomy inhibited the wider adoption of those innovations, so many classroom practices remained rather traditional. More importantly, 'the age of professional autonomy provided teachers with poor preparation for coping with the dramatic changes that were headed their way and against which their classroom doors would offer little protection' (p. 95). This seems to have a familiar ring to it as academics face the new millennium.

The current 'collegial' age involves a move beyond individualism to collaborative, networked professionalism. One of the major reasons involves the requirement for teachers 'to teach in ways they had not been taught' (p. 95). The collegial focus includes:

> efforts to build strong professional cultures of collaboration to develop common purpose; cope with uncertainty and complexity; respond effectively to rapid change; create a climate which values risk taking and continuous improvement . . . [which are linked more closely] to the priorities of the school.
>
> (Hargreaves 1997: 98)

In many senses these are the issues now facing academics, and academic management is pursuing these agendas. But academic culture remains wedded to notions of individual autonomy in ways that school cultures do not. In this sense, the professional culture in both settings is expanding, but the values underlying that expansion are different, contested and emergent.

The final age is 'the future'. Here Hargreaves is speculating rather than documenting. Using ideas consistent with 'end of enclosure', he suggests that 'teachers and principals are having to turn outwards toward wider publics as they plan, prepare and defend what they teach' (p. 101). Interestingly, he notes that while the boundaries between schools and their surrounding communities are 'dissolving', 'schools are increasingly seen as providing a possible focal point for retaining and regenerating community' (p. 102). Here the parallel with universities is significant, but while some academic leaders in both the UK and America are calling for greater attention to the local communities, this sense of becoming a focal point for retaining and regenerating community is less evident. In its place is a narrower concern with local business – the commercial community. The opportunity to focus on a wider sense of community seems just as important, if not more so, for higher education.

This discussion suggests that academics are facing very similar demands to teaching professionals in school settings. What is missing is the strong sense of professional identity that was developed during the period from the early 1960s, as school teachers came to recognize the value of claims to professionalism, and the implications of those claims for their own education and work. Of course, that recognition involved their employing authorities and the educational bureaucracies. This was a period of mutual adjustment, adjustments that are ongoing. My point is that school teachers are better placed than academics to be players rather than pawns in this process.

Professionalism, like identity, is an achievement – always in the making, and based on emergent expertise. Discontinuous change and the end of enclosure speak to a form of professionalism that moves beyond the paternalism of 'public service' and occupational monopolies. Nixon *et al.* (1997) explore this emergent teaching professionalism. They suggest that it will focus on an ongoing need for learning, and its actions will be guided by principles and values. It will be based on a recognition of plurality and multiculturalism. Thus, deliberation about possible actions will be inclusive, in the sense that actions will be an outcome of explicit agreements between the professional and her/his clients. I return to these issues later in this chapter when I explore issues related to both conversation and multiculturalism.

Making teaching count

Research has a long-standing tradition of 'collaborative, networked professionalism'. It left the pre-professional age with the rise of scientific research towards the end of the nineteenth century, and adopted the collaborative approach early in this century. The Manhattan Project represents one of the best-known examples of orchestrated collaborative, networked professionalism in research. Research also counts because its outcomes are relatively concrete. Papers can be read, patents are filed. While students do graduate, it is much more difficult to attribute that outcome to teaching, and even more difficult to identify the contributions of any specific teacher. So how might the specific contributions to student learning of academic teachers be recognized?

Recognizing 'scholarly teaching'

While there is a strong sense of community surrounding the concept of scholarly teaching, the question of how it might be subject to peer review and recognition has to be answered. To date, attempts to achieve this have involved two strategies: credentialling and accreditation, and teaching portfolios.

The development of formal programmes to 'accredit' the educational value of academics' teaching practices is a relatively recent phenomenon. Confidence in the value of these programmes has spread quickly and widely. As a result many credential-awarding programmes have been developed, with a wide array of practical and philosophical underpinnings. The diversity of pathways by which these credentials might be achieved has raised the question of their comparability, and their 'professional status'. Entry level requirements for other professions are set by the members of that profession. This implies that academics must set standards for teaching in order to have their credentials 'recognized'. Such a requirement is difficult for academic teaching credentials, as there is no 'professional body' of academic teachers. In this sense, the claim to professional status requires the establishment of a 'professional body'.

The most systematic high-level focus on accreditation of academics as 'professional' teachers is provided in the report of the Dearing Committee (NCIHE 1997: Chapter 14). They note widespread support for a system of accreditation and argue that:

> higher education teaching needs to have higher status and be regarded as a profession of teaching. To support this we have proposed the establishment of a professional Institute for Learning and Teaching in Higher Education, one of whose roles would be to accredit programmes of higher education teaching training.
>
> (NCIHE 1997: para. 14.28)

This Institute will provide national (UK) recognition for programmes of teaching training provided for academics during the probationary period of their career, i.e., before they are awarded tenure. In this sense, it will act as a surrogate professional body for academic teachers.

The Dearing Committee's suggestion follows the existing programme run by the UK Staff and Educational Development Association (SEDA), which was established in 1993. The SEDA programme allows universities to have their formal programmes of staff development 'recognized', and then awards certificates of accreditation to graduates of those programmes. It is not limited to UK universities – the Graduate Certificate in Higher Education which my university offers has been recognized by SEDA, although it is one of a very few non-UK courses to seek and achieve this. The SEDA programme specifies a set of professional commitments and areas (of academic teaching) in which those commitments have to be evidenced. The process of recognition requires the staff who offer the 'programme of teaching training' to show how that programme achieves and evidences these commitments. Evaluation of the adequacy of graduates' work requires extensive use of peer review and feedback.

While I support the accreditation of programmes of teacher training, the very words 'teacher training', and the proposed location of involvement within the 'probationary period' imply limitations in this approach. It is focused on 'beginning academics', while the current availability of 'probationary positions' suggests that graduates of such training will be a very small minority within any Department. As a minority, and as novices, their presence is unlikely to have other than a very marginal impact on the academic culture, or the status of teaching within it. The word 'training' implies a focus on the development of basic skills and attitudes. The SEDA requirements are consistent with this, and require engagement with a rather traditional teaching role. Thus, rather than promote doubt or change, the requirements for accreditation are likely to reinforce rather traditional and superficial attitudes to teaching. Finally, the approach offers little to those who are already working as academic teachers – those whose scholarship of teaching is likely to be the most sophisticated. For example, all of the lone rangers located through our EIP investigation had many years of teaching experience. Indeed, their sense of doubt about the status quo, and their commitment to experiment with alternatives, arose in and through those experiences.

The concept and practice of using 'portfolios' to evidence the scholarliness and value of teaching practices is also rather recent. The earliest reference I have found in the education literature to the use of teaching-focused portfolios is a 1989 article, followed soon after by the very influential book by Edgerton *et al.*, *The Teaching Portfolio: Capturing the Scholarship in Teaching* (1991). The concept has been borrowed from other areas of work, especially from the creative arts, where portfolios of completed work have long been used to represent an individual's existing capacities. Donald Schön's book, *The Reflective Practitioner* (1983), provided significant intellectual momentum for the concepts underlying the use of professional portfolios, and for learning from other professions. Portfolios are proposed as a mechanism to make aspects of teaching available for peer review and, therefore, peer recognition. The portability of the portfolio lends itself to such a possibility, while the opportunity for individual academic teachers to select what they include in their portfolio allows considerable scope for diversity. Many universities, particularly in America, now require academics to provide 'teaching portfolios' as part of the documentation required for processes of tenure review and confirmation, and for internal promotion.

Their increasing use, however, appears to have done little to enhance the status of teaching, or to validate the claims of scholarly teaching. That possibility requires answers to a number of questions. The concept and related practices have been in use for a relatively short period of time. How can the 'social inertia' associated with the use of these practices be increased, so that they are seen to have greater value? How might the 'rules' for making a claim of scholarly teaching be established? Neither the authors nor the reviewers have the confidence or competence to identify or authorize those rules in most cases. Indeed, rules usually follow practice, so it is likely that those rules will only emerge once sufficient experience has accumulated, and then only in fragmented, partial and incomplete ways. How can the development of these practices be distanced from other bureaucratic impositions? That is, how can these practices, including the responses academics produce, be recognized as professional rather than instrumental? Finally, the actual knowledge base for their creation and review tends not to have been add-ressed. The instructions are instrumental. They reflect the fact that just as there is no 'professional body' of academic teachers, there is also a lack of 'collective conviction' concerning the values and knowledge which should underpin academic teaching expertise, either generally or in relation to specific disciplines. How can the knowledge base which might underpin the professionalism of academic teaching be developed in those who wish to claim this as part of their academic identity?

Looking to the possibility of an academic teacher identity

The previous section illustrates two mechanisms to give greater recognition to the profession of university teaching. However, both arose in a context of increased accountability – institutional accountability and system account-ability. Earlier it was noted that the concept of autonomy has evolved primarily as a form of defence against external threats. These responses are also defensive – of institutions and the wider system of higher education.

But they are not being driven by academics – they are not identity work. Identity work is self-work. Reasons why academics might be slow to develop a response which unites them in a collective defence of their teaching role are not difficult to imagine. Some may well see schemes such as these as intrusions, motivated by managerial necessities and values other than those associated with teaching. That perception could be supported by the fuller description of the role of the Institute for Learning and Teaching offered by the Committee:

> The Institute . . . would be concerned with all aspects of teaching and its pedagogy, and . . . would give priority to developing assessment practices and strategies, which would become a key part of the initial training and continuing professional development of teaching staff. It was also suggested to us that accreditation arrangements should encompass all aspects of 'academic practice', for example, management/administration, use of Communications and Information Technology . . . and research.
>
> (NCIHE 1997: para. 14.31)

This is an instrumental, not a professional, agenda.

Others suggest that research is being swamped by teaching and other duties. Academics in the pre-1992 (research) universities in the UK are expressing the greatest sense of stress (NCIHE: para. 14.17). Sheehan and Welch (1996) suggest that academics whose primary role used to be teaching are now enjoying the possibility of research. This implies that academics, irrespective of their institution, see research as 'the way to go', and regard intrusions on research time negatively. There is very little recognition or reward for involvement in teaching.

This seems like a Catch-22 situation. Academics are unlikely to unite in defence of teaching because it represents a barrier to their career prospects. Yet the only way to make teaching a valued career path, rather than a barrier to career development, is to achieve a collective commitment to valuing it. Un-catching this situation will not be easy, and certainly will take time to achieve. What are some possibilities?

Issues of values and valuing

While academics individually value their work in teaching and service, this valuing is not being translated into professional recognition. That is, while academics value their own contributions in these areas, they tend not to value the contributions of others. For example, the service role of 'public intellectual' is a very important one. But those who take it on are more likely to be seen by some peers as 'media performers', with a focus on the performance aspect of this role, than as scholars or intellectuals engaging with the public via the media. Similarly, academics who are much admired by their students are unlikely to have that expertise seen as scholarly. It seems that the only appropriate audience for scholarship is other scholars, hence the significance of peer review for recognition.

One possible reason for this involves the difference in the understandings underlying research by comparison with teaching and service. The research apprenticeship is extensive, intensive and, most of all, selective. While the number of doctoral graduates is increasing rapidly, the award of a doctorate continues to represent a very significant achievement. It is character forming in its requirements for perseverance and diligence. It is personality selecting in that those who have a strong capacity for individual and isolated engagement with intellectual issues are more likely to succeed. It is attitude forming, through its requirements for the methodical pursuit of understanding. Perhaps more than anything else, those who succeed may well come to realize the limits of their knowledge – to recognize their profound ignorance. This is the basis for their capacities for doubt, and for scepticism. The awarding of the doctorate is immensely symbolic. It recognizes the achievement of these attributes – of the capacity for research. It continues to represent entry to a very select club.

There is no such sense of exclusivity attached to teaching or service. Of course teachers have to know something about the subject matter, but so many academics have to teach outside the area of their specific expertise that their expertise as knowers is seldom exercised. Some simply stay 'one step ahead' of the students, as they work through the curriculum. Service is seen as optional in many situations. So the need for specific expertise is much less than for research. That is, teaching and service are seen as less valuable because 'anyone could do it'. On the other hand, there is a view that only a very select few can do research, and each has their own specific specialization. A specialization and the publications that evidence it, i.e., the *curriculum vitae*, forms the basis of an individual research career, which, in turn, forms the basis of an academic career.

The attribution of research expertise relies on processes of peer review. The examination of the doctoral thesis involves a range of practices, and includes expertise external to the university in which the candidate is studying. The actual nature of that research expertise is itself taken for granted by peers from other disciplines. Similarly, the status of the doctorate, or the research profile, is not related to the 'subject' of the research. The symbolic value of the title 'Dr' crosses disciplinary boundaries in ways that teaching achievements do not. Why is this?

The issues that characterize the holders of the title, and those who engage in research without the title, tend to be the attitudes and values that underlie research. That is, the capacity for perseverance and diligence, for individual and isolated engagement with intellectual issues, for the methodical pursuit of understanding, and for doubt and scepticism, and so on. These bring a particular commitment to the cosmopolitan values of academic freedom and autonomy, including relational values of collegiality, peer-based review and recognition. They express the taken-as-uniform core of the academic identity.

There is no equivalent 'taken-as-uniform' set of attitudes and values underlying teaching or service. Indeed, my experience suggests that many academics have great difficulty expressing the commitments that underlie their teaching practices in anything other than a rather superficial or half-hearted way. It is very difficult for academics to value teaching without a formal process that engages in the task, i.e., identity work, of coming to identify, understand and recognize the values that might underpin it. The capacity to teach is seen as a relatively 'pre-professional' low-level competence which can, and should, be acquired largely 'on-the-job' – through experience. There is no requirement that comes anywhere near the demands of the research thesis to formalize and defend a position on teaching. These more cosmopolitan teaching values might address issues such as:

- diversity – equity, access, non-discrimination;
- the negotiation of intentions;
- supporting student learning – advocacy for students, the quality learning environments, assessment and feedback, the cost to students of participation;
- the nature of learning outcomes – social responsibility, lifelong learning; and
- the pursuit and defence of excellence.

Issues of a knowledge base for teaching

Research expertise is constructed on a knowledge base. The attitudes and values are inculcated in the context of a specific and extensive research exercise, but they are related to an existing and detailed formal knowledge base of the subject matter. The undergraduate degree assures certain intellectual skills, and a broad understanding of related subject matter, but that knowledge base is transformed – sharpened and deepened – during the doctoral programme. This transformation extends to the candidate, as she or he is formed into an expert in those aspects of the discipline/s relevant to the research method/s and topic.

Teaching expertise, by comparison, is based on the application of discipline-related understandings. The pedagogical knowledge base remains for most academics that of experience – tacit and informal. While all academics reflect on that experience, the basis of reflection is itself likely to be other everyday experiences – a comparative exercise. This is the knowledge base of pre-professionals. But what would any 'educational training' contribute to this knowledge base, given that academic teaching is always discipline-specific, or at least disciplined (in the sense that it is methodical – based on a system of rules or underlying principles and/or values which are made explicit)?

'Training' is unlikely to contribute anything beyond an improved set of teaching skills. That is not to deny the importance of skills, or to suggest that academics will learn them through their everyday experience. Practice-focused change tends to be 'technical' rather than professional, and thus unlikely to change beliefs, or to develop new attitudes, let alone value positions. Those who receive the training may have very little opportunity to step back from practice, to question the value of existing and proposed practices. In this sense, academic teachers are very poorly prepared to cope with the dramatic changes which they are experiencing and against which claims to academic autonomy offer little protection. The capacity to question educational practices (and through questioning and disciplined experimentation develop new practices) requires a knowledge base. The discipline we call *education* has developed in response to that need. All disciplines have developed for similar reasons.

The discipline of education has developed largely because of the need for new practices in the compulsory education sectors. The move to mass higher education means that academic teachers now need to develop a disciplined approach to their teaching. While the educational knowledge base has been developed for primary and secondary education, it provides a rich resource for the development of a knowledge base focused on the needs of academic teachers. Just as the 'taken-as-uniform' research values were developed in relation to a deepening understanding of a discipline-focused knowledge base, an understanding of a set of values for academic teaching is most likely to be achieved in the context of education-specific knowledge. Unfortunately, education is a low-status discipline within universities, and this does little to increase its attractiveness to academics, particularly those whose home discipline is aligned with the tight subfields and objectivist methods of the sciences (Bender 1997: 30).

My experience in teaching an education-specific course for academics leads to optimism in terms of these possibilities. That is, I regard the development of a shared value-related educational knowledge base for academics as very achievable, irrespective of the discipline focus of their teaching. Once they have developed familiarity with aspects of the educational literature, they bring the skills and capacities of their research training to the application of these ideas to educational practices. That is, they use their capacity for perseverance and diligence, for individual and isolated engagement with intellectual issues, for the methodical pursuit of understanding, and for doubt and scepticism, to the improvement of their teaching. But those skills and capacities are now informed by educational values, rather than the attitude that teaching is a low-level competence. These academic teachers now value their own teaching, and the teaching of colleagues, with a 'collective commitment' and an informed passion.

A recent newsletter of the Higher Education Research and Development Society of Australasia – *HERDSA News* – includes two brief statements from academics who have engaged with aspects of this knowledge base. One, Darryl Jones (1998), undertook the Graduate Certificate in Higher Education at my university. His comments exemplify the arguments I have offered. He reports being confronted by a student who said 'Let me get this straight: you got your job here because you study sex in birds? So, you have never actually been taught how to teach!' He comments on learning through experience: 'Any "learning" was rather unconsciously incorporated into my skills.' Then of beginning to doubt, and his refusal of 'traditional' explanations:

> Sharing these puzzlements and concerns with others was not particularly easy either. It soon became apparent that the most common approach to these ubiquitous problems was to blame the students . . . I still wondered about what was really going on behind those expressions of my seemingly attentive, busy congregation.
>
> (Jones 1998: 8)

He writes of his early attempt to distinguish between 'teaching' and 'learning', and of reading Paul Ramsden's book, *Learning to Teach in Higher Education* (1992), as his first sustained encounter with educational literature.

> This may be either pathetically obvious or hopelessly obtuse to many readers but these were and are revolutionary concepts, which greatly enhanced my interest in the connections between teaching and learning. But such an interest does not necessarily translate into improved practice. What was needed was an immersion into the field [of education] itself, to have an opportunity to explore these often complex issues with colleagues suffering similar levels of frustration and fascination.
>
> (Jones 1998: 8)

John Dearn, from the University of Canberra, pursued a more independent path which resulted in his receiving the inaugural Australian Award for University Teaching in the category 'Science'. But his journey has many similarities to that of Jones, as these extracts suggest:

Having come from a very rigorous background of research and teaching in the biological sciences, mastery of the knowledge domain became less and less of a problem for me while gradually another set of equally fascinating issues emerged in the area of teaching and learning. In this sense the focus of my scholarship gradually shifted [expanded?] from issues related to evolutionary biology to those related to how people come to know about and interpret their world . . . Since then I have been on a path of discovery, delving into the labyrinths of constructivist epistemology, intellectual development and education as a cultural phenomenon . . . During that period I 'discovered' many ideas for the first time, perhaps the most important being the evidence that exists on the failure of traditional didactic teaching for most students, at least in the sciences. In terms of my classroom practice, this has resulted in me gradually exploring ways of creating a learning environment that better reflect students' ways of knowing.

(Dearn 1998: 10)

These two stories tell of the implicitness of experiential learning, and of the deliberate application of doubt and curiosity to motivate their explicit educational explorations and experimentations. They exemplify development of scholarly teaching.

Collectively, educational values and knowledge base provide an intellectual basis for a cosmopolitan academic teacher identity. This is a very different base to that provided by the traditional craft-based apprenticeship of observation and experience, in that it requires engagement with the discipline of education. It is also different from the 'teacher training' approach suggested by the Dearing Committee, given its focus on values and broader understandings in addition to skills. Most importantly, those who achieve it are able to use it to continue learning about, and extending their approach to, teaching of their particular discipline through the use of their research capacities. Research and evaluation expand our imagination about what to try, why, and what errors to watch out for – they increase our sensitivity to the boundaries of possible performance (Steve Ehrmann: 24 June 1997 AAHESGIT email list, post 152).

Cosmopolitan academic teachers would be well placed to resist and reform the wave of instrumentalization and commodification of education that is currently sweeping through higher education. Indeed, it is probably essential to possess these values and understandings in order to respond to the opportunities for involvement in, and forming, the CIT agenda for higher education. In the specific instance of academics negotiating their involvement in the Logan Campus initiative, the opportunity to draw on a credible academic teaching identity would have been extremely helpful.

For teaching to be recognized and valued, what is needed is for academics to develop an educational knowledge base for their teaching, and for that knowledge base to be underpinned by a set of educational values. Those values must reflect the ethical commitments of academic teachers.

That is, they must be owned and respected by academics. These achievements are most easily achieved in the context of courses of formal education, although other more flexible possibilities are also available. Some academics read in the area of education because that is where their curiosity has led them. Others work in situations where discussion of teaching and educational issues becomes part of the everyday experience, as does their documentation. For example, this can happen in the context of the development of open learning or similar teaching resources, and is happening for some of the academics involved in the Logan Campus work. But it is extremely difficult to achieve this without support, and the motivation to represent these understandings in scholarly ways.

Spreading the word

Rewards for academics are located in cultural systems. But teaching-focused activities, on their own, tend to create enclaves of academic teachers. They do little to advance the awareness or recognition of those values in the wider community – to include them in the cultural systems in which their work is located. Those values need to achieve a cosmopolitan status as a response to the perennial cry for teaching to be recognized and celebrated more universally. This work could be done through professional bodies established and controlled by academics. The agenda of a body like the Institute for Learning and Teaching in Higher Education proposed by the Dearing Committee could be refocused on these issues. However, it is unlikely that any government would initiate or invest in a body whose function is to mobilize academics to help defend their professional interests.

There are other possibilities. This sort of work might also be done by extending the agenda of existing academic organizations. In the UK there is the Society for Research into Higher Education (SRHE), in Canada the Society for Teaching and Learning in Higher Education (STLHE) and in America the American Association for Higher Education (AAHE). The Australasian equivalent is the Higher Education Research and Development Association (HERDSA). My experience of HERDSA suggests that, while these bodies do invaluable work in providing a focus for the scholarship of teaching, the value of an educational knowledge base or of educational values is not necessarily evident in their publications or their conferences. The various academic staff associations and unions could extend their work in this direction, as could the various professional associations of academic managers and administrators. Their strong support for this type of work, as distinct from fiscal and staff management issues, could also be of great assistance, especially its potential use as a 'decoupling' strategy, and as a way to increase the possibility of recognizing 'civic' ideals for universities.

And then there is a myriad of less formal professional networks. It seems to me that these offer excellent possibilities for capturing a burst of enthusiasm for a project based around the issues that I am advocating.

Email has made these networks extremely flexible in terms of geographically dispersed participation, and in terms of the speed with which ideas can be formalized and offered for comment – peer-review. These changes would have impacts beyond their obvious targets.

Anticipating some new opportunities and challenges

I have argued that universities are already multicultural contexts, and that academics are also multicultural in terms of their identities and their role-focused practices. The discussion suggests a future in which the range of role-focused practices is going to increase, and that those practices will rely on access to multiple forms of expertise. One way of accessing that expertise is through teamwork – multiple contributors. A second approach involves the development by individuals of multiple forms of expertise. In a sense, the stories of Darryl Jones and John Dearn referred to earlier illustrate this second approach, as they developed teaching expertise to complement their expertise in the subject matter they teach, and in the research practices that give rise to those disciplinary understandings.

Opportunities for conversation

One of the major benefits of a team approach involves the opportunity for conversation across tribal/cultural boundaries. But 'conversation' is an open concept – its meaning is not fixed. Patrick Jenlink and Alison Carr (1996) distinguish four types of conversation, three of which are relevant here: dialectic, discussion and dialogic. Dialectic conversation is seen as disciplined inquiry in whatever is being examined, where disciplines are the sources of the arguments, and the holders of the 'truths'. It involves bringing alternative truth claims to bear, in a debating-style conversation. Discussion conversation involves negotiation, and tends to draw on opinion and supposition. Negotiation proceeds from an advocacy of beliefs, and seeks to protect personal assumptions. It can draw like-minded people together, but fragmentation along lines of preferred opinions is an equally likely outcome. Dialogic conversation involves collective formation of meaning. Thus, it is a community-building form of conversation, creating a conscious collective mindfulness – a collective commitment. It recognizes the importance of multiple perspectives and opinions in ways that require the suspension of personal preferences and avoidance of judgements. This version of dialogic conversation is consistent with Stephen Brookfield's (1996) description of 'critical conversation'. It is also consistent with Jon Nixon's (1996) call for a 'learning profession', and the elaboration of that call in his later work (Nixon *et al.* 1997).

Dialogic conversation implies acknowledgement of dimensions other than 'task work' in team-based activities, dimensions which are seldom acknowledged, resulting in many team-based conversations being restricted to the level of discussion. In particular, it recognizes that time spent clarifying and agreeing values and intentions before starting work is usually time well spent. William Isaacs (1996) explores the conditions under which dialogue is likely to be achieved. He suggests that the initial stages of a conversation must resolve issues related to safety and trust. The next stage is likely to involve a struggle with issues of belief and assumptions. Its resolution requires their suspension, while failure leads to fragmentation, and a 'discussion conversation'. Discussion in turn is likely to lead to a dialectic debate, and rhetorical engagement. On the other hand, if beliefs and preferences are suspended, participants can then explore issues without needing to defend or deny preferences. As collective understandings are built, consensus on the need to seek new ways of thinking or acting can arise, leading to a final stage of generative thinking. This involves creatively moving beyond the set of ideas brought to the discussion.

This form of conversation is a process of collective sensemaking around 'arguable objects', with all the implications that holds for collective action. It has both political and ethical ramifications (Brookfield 1996; Nixon *et al.* 1997). The politics involve a commitment to share all one knows, to uncover assumptions, and to enact collective decisions. The ethics involve issues like valuing diversity, being respectful of others and the process, being open to outcomes, and being reflective. These requirements are very ambitious, and, unfortunately, are seldom achieved. However, the explication does provide a basis for monitoring the development of conversations. Elaine Martin (1999) provides a very useful discussion of collaboration in Chapter 7 of her book. In it she provides extensive advice on how to make collaborations work. The framework for that discussion is the tension between collaboration and independence, a tension well known to the academic community.

Protecting and enhancing the 'cultural capital' of academic work settings

While most organizations value their human resources, often those resources are seen primarily in terms of material resources, i.e., the individual workers. James Coleman (1990) distinguishes between human capital, the work-related competencies of the workers, and social capital, which refers to the social relations among individuals and those aspects of the social and organizational structures which facilitate productive action. The concept of social capital overlaps with Gamst's (1995) discussion of the web of rules. Gamst suggests that these 'structures' are likely to include both implicit and explicit rules, and emphasizes the value of social relations and rules to productive action. My point is that there is a need to recognize the 'social capital', and to value it in the current context where resources which do not have a 'market value' can be overlooked, and undervalued.

There are valuable actions for building 'social capital'. They are very similar to those recommended to generate dialogic conversations. The building of social capital begins at the social level – the 'getting to know you' conversation that involves awareness and trust building without task-focused pressures. Social activities that explicitly seek to build links with other groups in the institution, or outside it, provide more structured opportunities for this possibility. Access to common social facilities like coffee lounges also assists. Dialogic conversation contributes to community building – to the building of common purpose, mutual obligations and trust. Recognition of individual and collaborative contributions and achievements builds social capital. Activities of these types can enrich the working conditions of all.

But social capital can also be reduced as well as augmented. Some employment trends are likely to put at risk the social capital of universities. The increasing employment of academics on a part-time and casual basis can decrease the sense of mutual obligation and shared ownership of activities. On the other hand, it can enhance these by providing an opportunity to make the taken-for-granted social capital more explicit. For example, the full-time coordinator of a course might establish regular meetings with the part-timers who assist in teaching it, including activities that have a social purpose, such as sharing of backgrounds and interests. In fact staff who are not full-time can add a sense of freshness and life that may have been gradually eroded within the full-time staff. This freshness is easily squashed when the jaded only pay lip-service to welcoming the fresh ideas, or where they simply exploit the energy of the part-timers.

The practice of outsourcing tends to deny 'insiders' the opportunity to build social capital around those activities. I have found the non-academic staff who undertake the maintenance, security and cleaning functions among the most long-term employees of the institutions in which I have worked. They tend to be extremely knowledgeable about the local community, and the institution. I suspect the social capital associated with the general staff is a most neglected resource in terms of institutional 'boundary maintenance' functions. General staff control access to many of its more important resources (anyone who thinks that the Principal is in charge of a school obviously has not met the janitor or ground keeper). I have found such individuals very open to conversation, and that social and professional relationships with them always pay off. But now I see moves to outsource their work and to make them less visible in the daily life of universities. Thus, cleaning is increasingly carried out during the night, and the cleaners have left the premises before we academics arrive. Where once I could quickly and personally ask for a favour I now have to make an impersonal and official request. The community fragments and social capital decreases as organizational arrangements and structures militate against, rather than facilitate, informal, inclusive and social interactions.

As practices become more focused on tasks, and budget officers look to issues of cost minimization in financial terms only, institutions are becoming more ordered and clinical, less human and user friendly. The irony is that, as universities become more 'peopled', they seem to be becoming less 'social'. As the pace of work-life increases, and the numbers of students increase, universities come to take on some of the characteristics of shopping malls. Perhaps this is consistent with moves to make the curriculum more like a smorgasbord, and to make accessing it more like a supermarket experience. Trading off gains in productivity against losses in social capital is obvious, and part of the larger 'technologising project' that Heidegger discusses in his later work (see Dreyfus 1996: 8). The goal of that project is increasing flexibility and efficiency *for their own sake.* Should universities engage with purposes other than these?

Living multiculturally

I am arguing for universities to support a multiplicity of cultures, rather than to engage in processes of assimilation or homogenization, and for academics to become more aware of, and to extend, their own multicultural identities. Pluralism has added value in a situation of change – it enhances adaptability (Berry 1997).

Cross-cultural studies of migration tell us about the outcomes of contact between culturally distinct groups of people – the process of acculturation. John Berry (1997) notes that the individual experience of acculturation is influenced by both cultural and individual factors. He suggests that bicultural acculturation – a mutual accommodation (sedimentation) strategy – leads to better outcomes for individuals than the domination of one culture by another. But 'accommodation' is not homogenization. Berry argues for 'policies that neither force cultural shedding, nor ghettoisation', and for strategies which 'promote an appreciation of the benefits of pluralism' (p. 28). He points to evidence of the protective benefits provided by a strong cultural identity in situations of cultural conflict. Those benefits are enhanced if individuals also attempt to understand and accept the core values and basic norms of the cultures around them. The implication is that institutions should adopt policies and practices that promote pluralism and culturally sensitive thinking. Individuals cope with cultural contestation better if they are more knowledgeable about those cultures – including the historical basis of those values and traditions.

While institution-based and occupation-based cultures are ongoing, individuals have to be socialized into them. William Tierney (1997) uses the distinction between modernist and post modernist perspectives to 'take issue with many of the common assumptions we share about organizational socialization' (p. 1). The modernist perspective involves a view of culture as the sum of activities – symbolic and instrumental – that exist in the organization and create shared meaning, while socialization is a process through which new members come to understand and incorporate those activities. Thus, culture is seen as relatively constant, and it 'teaches people how to behave, what to hope for, and what it means to succeed or fail' – it is 'coherent and understandable' (p. 4).

Tierney's postmodern account recognizes multiple possibilities, incoherence, inconsistency and contestation. From this perspective, culture 'is not so much a definition of the world as it is, but rather a conglomeration of the hopes and dreams of what the organizational world might be' (p. 6). Socialization is seen as 'an interpretive process involved in the creation, rather than the transmittal, of meaning'. It is a sensemaking process, which draws on the understandings and experiences that all individuals bring with them, and allows for the development of new cultural identities in ways consistent with the strategy of 'sedimentation'. That is, old identities are not 'lost', but are supplemented by new context-specific assemblages that include both former and new aspects. Socialization is a creative process, and leads to the possibility of a new identity for the individual, and for the individual to create a new identity within the organization.

Perspectives such as Tierney's allow for thinking about socialization in ways very similar to Berry's suggestions on acculturation. The challenge of socialization becomes less a matter of the adjustment of the individual to the organization, and more a matter of taking advantage of the experiences/identities that new members bring with them. It means an organization should use 'the ideas of excellence and difference, rather than similarity, as its overriding ethos' (Tierney 1997: 14). Tierney invites a shift in the discussion of socialization from the new recruits to '*us* – those who establish organizational norms' (p. 15). The implication is that valuing of pluralism requires a shift from modernist to certain postmodernist 'hopes and dreams'. He calls for strategies which 'orchestrate action', and for multiple approaches to promotion and tenure – a shift in managerial strategies from controlling to conducting.

Looking back, looking forward

In looking to the future of academic work I have attempted to draw on some of the threads of thinking signalled earlier in the book. One thread involves the recognition that the language through which academics think is evolving. The meanings of terms like 'autonomy' and 'professional' have changed, and will continue to change. The related implication is that academics should be careful to distinguish between beliefs that are based in experience, beliefs that are based in disciplined awareness, and beliefs that are based in myths. Academic training should privilege disciplined awareness, and it does. But many aspects the work-life of an academic lie outside the boundaries of her/his discipline. Thus, many beliefs that are advocated or defended with great passion have not been subjected to rigorous consideration.

I am not arguing that one type of belief is better than any other. Pre-literate and pre-professional beliefs continue to inform 'indexes of the academic self' in valuable ways. But I am arguing that beliefs that are unknowingly held anchor their holders in unconsidered experience and myth. Those anchors are problematic in an age of relentless change. They impose a rigidity that militates against elegant, engaging and timely responses. Their nature limits academics' capacities to engage in conversation about circumstances, and to generate considered and collegial responses. They imply an obstinacy that is quite antithetical to the capacities for doubt and creativity that mark academic scholarship.

A second thread involves the postmodern condition – that is, the recognition of the limitations of assumptions of rationality, predictability, uniformity and progress associated with the Enlightenment Project, and the resulting sense of existential anxiety and fragmentation. I have given considerable attention to the discussion of the increasing diversity of organizational cultures, and to the sense that this diversity represents a resource rather than a threat. Further, I have argued that academics need to attend to the indexes of the self which contribute to their sense of professional identity. In particular, strengthening the index of academic teacher has potential in terms of both opportunities for employment and resisting and redirecting some of the challenges that threaten the very concept of 'academic'.

The third thread recognizes both the constructedness of the academic identity and its multicultural dimensions. Thus, rather than a unified construct, this story reveals a multitude of possibilities beyond the media image of this label. While this comes as little surprise to those within 'the academy', those who seek its reform hold a more essentialist interpretation. That is, the 'label' sticks to all, and serves to unify in ways that serve their purposes. Academics, and universities, need to resist these unifying discourses, to emphasize their differences as well as their similarities. While there might be strength in unity, evolutionary survival depends on diversity.

This shift from a modern to a postmodern perspective has implications that spill over into self-management. We need to recognize and value that we *are* multiple selves, and that we are always in a process of becoming. These multiple selves have increasing value in a time when self-work requires us to think less in terms of a continuous career, and more in terms of complexity, choice, self-awareness, learning, and short-term 'relationships' with projects, and those who employ us. My sense is that academics are extremely well placed to engage with these possibilities, but successful engagement will require particular attention to the *know-why* and *know-who* competencies discussed in Chapter 5.

These threads are mutually informing rather than 'coming together'. I am not attempting to knit them together to reveal some coherent and comforting garment for academics to 'slip into'. There are no solutions. But there are opportunities, better ways of thinking, and more useful questions to think about.

7

Moving On

People cannot reconcile themselves to the loss of the familiar attachments in
terms of some impersonal utilitarian calculation of the common good. They
have to find their own meaning in these changes before they can live with them.
Hence the reformers must listen as well as explain, continually accommodating
their design to other purposes, other kinds of experience, modifying and
renegotiating, long after they would like to believe that their conception
was finished.

(Marris 1974: 156)

In this final chapter I want to revisit and elaborate earlier themes. In particular I want to focus on academics' self-management, and on strategies that
might assist them to continue to co-adapt with universities in their changing
environments. To do both is to revisit the theme of sensemaking, and the
conservative cognitive functioning of autopiloting, extending these to include
issues of identity. In particular, I want to discuss how change necessarily
involves ambivalence and loss. It is through grieving this loss that 'moving
on', in a sustainable way, becomes possible.

Sensemaking in changing contexts

The earlier discussion highlights the absence of any systematic attempts to
help academics recognize that their roles will change during their careers.
Instead of systematic attempts to create an expectation of change, socialization into an academic career seems to be treated primarily as a function of
a non-literate academic culture – e.g., the words of wisdom from a respected
elder over coffee in the staffroom. This wisdom, necessarily, tends to be
steeped in academic traditions. Thus, rather than looking to change –
to discontinuities – it speaks from and to continuity. Such a pattern of
socialization sets academics up to be disrupted by change – to be *shocked*.

How are we to understand academics' current experiences of change?
Both the Dearing and West Committees report that the pace of change has
increased, and that it is likely to accelerate. The report of the Dearing
Committee also indicates the morale of university staff in the UK is suffer-
ing. To return to Alvin Toffler's terminology of over two decades ago,
academics are experiencing a form of future shock, which is linked to the
institutional crises discussed in the earlier chapters. But their shock is

always experienced in relation to specific locations and identities – their own and those of others. As a consequence, their shock is always associated with, and linked to, specific local conditions.

Sensemaking, cognitive functioning and autopilots

It is clear that human cognitive capacities are most effective in situations of relative stability. We sensemake by looking to our prior experiences, understandings and values, drawing on the frames of reference that our biography has led us to construct. In everyday life the majority of actions are planned without conscious attention, using a cognitive 'autopilot' which is 'programmed' by previous experiences, particularly by beliefs and attitudes. Individuals 'go into the future' paying little conscious attention to new experiences, relying on existing frames of reference to help make sense of the expected as well as the unexpected in those experiences. This form of cognitive functioning, is effortless – it just happens. Thus, cognitive functioning 'programmes' individuals to expect the future to be maximally continuous with the past.

There are other features of cognitive functioning that become important in changing contexts. First, the 'frames of reference' are highly interlinked. Meanings are abstractions based on networks of relational understandings. While it is relatively easy to strengthen those networks, or to add additional 'ideas' to them, changing the frames themselves is quite difficult. It requires restructuring of the networks – establishing new links between existing ideas *and* weakening existing links. The more elaborate our 'frames', the more difficult and disruptive it is to restructure them. Not only is experience a good teacher, but the success of what is learned through it makes its revision extremely difficult. In fact, individuals tend to overlook or ignore events that might require a restructuring of existing beliefs or frames.

Second, cognitive functioning is not 'cold'. Those 'frames' are associated with affect and purpose, not just ideas. Beliefs and understandings are inseparable from purposes, which are less open to change than are ideas. Thus, new factual information can be learned, yet behaviour can continue in ways that is quite indifferent to that information. Indeed, the formal knowledge learned through instruction tends to be easier to revise *because* it is relatively 'cold' information. Autopilots tend to be governed by purposeful beliefs, rather than the totality of our knowledge. The meaning of events includes their perceived emotional consequences – good, bad, or indifferent. Thus, restructuring involves more than rational processes.

Third, autopilots function in context-specific ways. That is, memory functions to make available to an autopilot the 'programmes' for behaviour that are expected to be relevant to the situation into which the individual is moving. This is done through remembering 'what worked' in similar contexts in the past. When I reach to put the key in the ignition of my car, I do not have to think about the location of the ignition switch. We subconsciously monitor the contexts for which planning is required, and quickly select plans so as to allow competent behaviour. My 'programme' fails when I get into a car with which I am not familiar. Then I have to search for the ignition switch, and the switch to activate the windscreen wiper, and so on. Thus, there is a powerful contextual priming of cognitive functioning that is reflected both in what is learned and then in what is planned. That is, individuals learn in context, and find it very difficult to transfer that learning to new situations. Transfer requires an interruption of autopiloting.

On the other hand, this capacity for cognitive context-specificity allows access to relatively distinct sets of context-specific beliefs and purposes. It is what I rely on to drive home in the evenings without conscious attention at times. It allows individuals to step out of their academic roles when they leave the office to go home, or to become daughters/sons or sisters/brothers or aunts/uncles when they are with their extended families. It allows an individual to lecture to a large group of first-year undergraduate students, then join a staffing committee discussion, without having to think about how to enact herself/himself, that is, how to behave appropriately. It allows sensemaking in context-specific ways, and the enactment of relatively context-specific identities.

This capacity for cognitive context-specificity allows individuals considerable flexibility. It is the basis for every individual's multicultural capacity, and for multiple indexes of the self. Context-specific frames of reference include expectations of the interpersonal relationships. Thus, a sense of efficacy and emotional well-being reflect expectations of how others will react to an individual in a given context, that is, the quality of the relationships they have with the people they regularly encounter in those situations. Those relationships form a very significant component of the indexes of self that are activated in those contexts. Thus, the sense of cohesion and continuity, of self and of the environment are relatively context-specific.

But those senses also depend on continuity within that context. Once that continuity is disrupted, autopilots produce less competent behaviour. Sensemaking becomes a quite demanding process, as individuals try to interpret novel information, and unexpected consequences of their behaviour. As the degree of novelty increases, individuals have to pay increasing amounts of attention to that environment, and plan to act in quite deliberate ways. Cognitive functioning becomes increasingly effortful, requiring mental concentration to cope with uncertainty. But sensemaking and uncertainty reduction can only be accomplished on the basis of prior experiences. Cognitive functioning provides a limited capacity for coping with change or uncertainty.

Strategies for coping with uncertainty

A capacity to cope with uncertainty is a requirement of many forms of employment. Indeed, people are employed because of their capacity to deal with novel situations. However, their problem-solving strategies do not violate the three features of cognitive functioning discussed above. These problem-solving capacities rely on the use of strategies which have been learned, and which rely on familiarity with the context of the problem. Rannan Lipshitz and Orna Strauss (1997) have investigated how decision makers conceptualize and cope with uncertainty. Consistent with the discussion here, they suggest that 'uncertainty in the context of action is a sense of doubt that blocks or delays action' (p. 150). Thus, uncertainty is essentially a subjective experience triggered by a sense of doubt that interrupts routine action, i.e., doubt that interrupts the autopilot.

Lipshitz and Strauss point to the importance of context-specific values and personal identity in responding to uncertainty. Their subjects (members of the Israel Defence Forces) had individual styles of decision making in these situations, but adjusted those styles according to the issue generating the uncertainty, and the source of the uncertainty. Their subjects tended to attribute uncertainty to subjective sources (i.e., doubt due to inadequate understanding and ambivalence) rather than to a lack of information. In all cases, the coping strategies relied on the decision maker's initial attempts to make sense of the situation, and then generate acceptable actions, or forestall decision making. Actions ultimately depend on the imposition of some form of sense on the situation, through strategies including assumption-based reasoning, weighing pros and cons of alternative course of action, or simply suppressing uncertainty (through tactics like denial or rationalization). Decision making in these contexts becomes a reasoned but non-rational process.

The context-specific nature of these coping strategies suggests that their use is learned in context. Professional expertise involves the capacity for problem solving under conditions of uncertainty, but only in the general domain of that expertise. It is simply not possible to impose a 'sense' on situations with which an expert has no familiarity. Thus, the problem-solving strategies identified by Lipshitz and Strauss are consistent with the three features of cognitive functioning mentioned earlier. In addition, their work emphasizes the subjective and non-rational basis of decision makers' responses to uncertainty.

Change, uncertainty and ambivalence

'Problem solving' is focused on sources of uncertainty which are everyday yet unpredictable, even random. Uncertainty generated by organizational change is different from more 'natural' causes in at least two senses: it implies an intention; and it involves a disruption of familiar contexts. When universities change their practices, most academics tend to assume that there are 'good' reasons underlying the decisions – that the need for the change and the processes by which it will be achieved have been considered carefully. Thus, there is a sense that change is imposed in an intentional and reasoned way. But change-focused decision making is made necessarily under conditions of uncertainty. For this reason, it is an outcome of the sort of decision-making process described by Lipshitz and Strauss. As the external conditions require academic managers to deal with uncertainty, their decisions necessarily involve elements of ambiguity, and the outcomes cannot be predetermined.

There are three problems here. One involves the expectation, on the part of academics, that university management knows what it is doing. This is an attribution of certainty, where uncertainty is the case. The second involves a compounding of this expectation when academic managers represent their decisions as 'solutions', rather than as 'best guesses'. This is an emulation of certainty, when much more tentativeness is called for. The third problem is that the first two problems mutually reinforce each other. The expectation of leadership generates both leaders and followers.

There is another important problem. Managerial functions include scanning of the environment and maintenance tasks, as noted in Chapter 4. They are engaged with the external environment in ways which academics tend not to be. As a consequence, when managers come to make change-focused decisions they do so after lengthy engagement with issues related to that decision. Academics, on the other hand, tend to focus on issues related to their discipline, relying on administrators to look after their interests and those of the institution. As a consequence, academics tend not to have engaged with the issues that may have been the focus of managerial thinking for some time. Managerial decisions can, therefore, appear to come out of the blue – to surprise, even shock some academics.

Intentional change involves a disruption of familiar contexts. That disruption necessarily involves the loss of aspects of the familiar, and related loss of meaning and relationships. This is quite different from problem solving involving novelty, where the problem and the novelty co-occur and the intention of problem solving is to restore the status quo. With intentional change, the purpose is to develop responses that are different from the status quo. In this sense, intentional change involves a form of decision making where the preferred outcomes, as well as the processes by which they might be achieved, are uncertain. Thus, the process can be experienced more as a severance from the familiar, than its disruption. Severance from the familiar can lead to anxiety, as individuals struggle to defend or recover a pre-existing pattern of relationships. Peter Marris (1974: 1) notes a characteristic ambivalence which marked these reactions, an ambivalence which 'seemed always to inhibit any straightforward adjustment' to the new situation. He uses the concept of grieving to describe the less straightforward process of adjustment.

While uncertainty is associated with external factors, ambivalence is a concept that refers to internal ambiguity. That is, ambivalence refers to 'the simultaneous existence of attraction and repulsion, of love and hate', that is '*opposing affective orientations* toward the same person, object or symbol' (Smelser 1998: 5 – his italics). Smelser suggests that ambivalence provides an essential addition to thinking about individual behaviour and social institutions to that provided by explanations that focus on the rational. His argument is that in any situations of emotional attachment, ambivalence invariably arises, and 'moving on' from them necessitates dealing with that ambivalence. Situations that provoke emotional commitment are also likely to provoke ambivalence and the emotional response, particularly anxiety. Separation from those situations evokes strongly ambivalent reactions – anxiety. These reactions bear the same features as those associated with death and separation – shock, anger, grief and recovery.

The sense of loss that accompanies the process of change involves more than a loss of meaning. It also involves a loss of expectation:

> [I]t is obvious that we do have unspoken and even unacknowledged expectations for the future, and the loss of these expectations demands from us minor or major adjustments. Adaptation is perhaps the crucial skill for mankind's survival, but because of circumstances, upbringing, inherited characteristics and other factors, there are many who are ill-equipped to cope with the 'changes and chances of this mortal life,' and who are greatly in need of assistance in achieving the adjustment and acceptance, to enable them to compromise between the expectations and the reality.
>
> (Bright 1986: 9)

Thus, disruption of the familiar also generates a sense of anxiety, which reflects ambivalence about the choices involved in 'adjustment and acceptance'. While death has to be accepted, deliberate change – deliberate disruption of the status quo and the expectations attached to it – is not accompanied by the same sense of absoluteness. It can be resisted, and the status quo can be defended.

Conservatism and grieving

Cognitive functioning and sensemaking are inherently conservative. They rely on prior learning as the basis for interpreting current experiences. The impetus to defend the 'thread of continuity' of life, its predictability and promises, is bound to the need to make life sensible – to maintain the value of investments in relationships, in understandings, in expectations, and in a sense of self. Change severs that thread; deliberate change does so knowingly. But resistance can be seen as irrational:

> When we argue about the need for social change, we tend to explain conservatism away as ignorance, a failure of nerve, the obstinate protection of untenable privileges – as if the resistance could be broken by exposing its irrationality.
>
> (Marris 1974: 5)

Ruth Bright expresses this view somewhat differently, suggesting that conservatism can be seen as a moral, rather than an intellectual, failure. This is because:

we are expected by society to adapt to change, to carry on as usual despite loss and disaster, to put a premium on stoicism not only in physical disease but in the dis-ease of the spirit, we feel bound to hide our feelings for fear of not living up to people's expectations, and – perhaps a still stronger influence – for fear of seeing ourselves as weaklings who are unable to cope. Capacity to cope seems to have become a measure of moral fibre in Western society.

(Bright 1986: 83)

In contexts of change, former strengths may come to look like inflexibility. Thus, the consistency of purpose that enables individuals to impose sense can be interpreted as obstinacy. The very conservatism that is the basis of a rationality for behaviour, and a rationality for sensemaking, can be seen as irrational, even an indicator of moral weakness, in the context of change. Reformers and managers who have invested considerable time and intellectual energy in a change-focused sensemaking process can equate 'conservatism' with obstinacy and weakness. In so doing they are caught by what I referred to in Chapter 5 as the 'transformer trap' – the problematic assumption that change in an identity is easily achieved, requiring only a rational acknowledgement of what is obvious, and what is reasonable.

The ability to handle change relies upon the conservation of the frames of reference developed during a lifetime. The challenge is to adopt strategies that make those frames useful for sensemaking, yet sufficiently flexible to be adaptive. Marris (1974) suggests that one way to achieve this is to 'formulate principles in terms abstract enough to apply to any event we encounter' (p. 17). These principles become very powerful sensemaking tools, allowing the imposition of sense. They also assist individuals to cope with the unexpected by allowing distance from the immediacy of events. This capacity, and the principled frames of reference that underlie it, form the intellectual basis of expertise.

All of the academic disciplines reflect this intellectual capacity. The development of an educational knowledge base for academic teachers would offer this capacity to them. This potential is illustrated in the findings of the EIP investigation (Taylor *et al.* 1996), in which it was concluded that those academics who possessed an educational understanding of their teaching practices were best placed to interrogate their existing practices, to evaluate new practices, and to imagine alternative practices. They demonstrated an optimism about the future uses of communication and information technologies which was notably lacking in those who were unable to 'step back' from their anxieties. That is, the development of a principled knowledge base allowed a less emotive attachment to former commitments and encouraged proactive engagement with change.

Irrespective of the ultimate reactions, change tends to be experienced ambivalently as a mix of continuity and discontinuity, growth and loss. Cognitive functioning ensures that the discontinuity and the loss are noticed first. The immediate consequence of noticing is likely to include a sense of distress, and a tendency to become inert and to retreat within oneself. The experience of ambivalence, like the experience of uncertainty, interrupts a sense of security and routine action. The experience involves 'oppositional' alternatives – continuity and discontinuity, loss and growth – and the interruption results from the perceived necessity to choose between what appear to be equally valid, yet opposing, interpretations, i.e., ambivalence. It is associated with a sense of grieving over what is irretrievably lost. Successful grieving allows an individual to acknowledge ambivalence, loss and disruption, and to use the remaining elements of continuity as the basis for growth. That is, on the recovery of a sense that what was lost can still give meaning to the present.

Grief arises from the need to acknowledge and resolve issues of ambivalence and loss, including loss of trust, as they impact on the self. The achievement of change ultimately depends on continuity of purpose and continuity of meaningful circumstances, as they relate to the individual. However, Marris (1974) implies that the achievement of 'continuity' involves more than a simple extension of the past into the present and future. He suggests that grief is mastered, not by ceasing to care for what has been lost, but by 'abstracting what was fundamentally important in the relationship and rehabilitating it' (p. 34). This process of abstraction increases the range of circumstances with which existing purposes might be associated. Thus, existing purposes can be associated with new circumstances, and through that association, add meaning to those circumstances. This applies equally to continuing circumstances, i.e., these too may take on new meanings. By implication, while individuals are focused on their sense of loss, their ability to engage in sensemaking, and therefore their capacity to learn, will be impaired.

Some implications for managing change

The process of grieving cannot be treated as a simple rational process. Injunctions to 'get on with it' (i.e., to endure), or to 'have faith' in the change process (i.e., suspend doubt), are unhelpful. They ignore, and may interfere with, the need to acknowledge ambivalence and to reconnect with what has been lost. They also ignore one of the characteristics of grief, namely the loss of faith in any possible reward. So activity can become increasingly meaningless, as individuals simply 'go through the motions' with little purpose and even less sense of accomplishment. Rather than 'activity', grief and mourning call for 'time out' for introspection and reflection because they:

> involve taking something inside, but not in order to be 'full up', to achieve emotional satisfaction. Rather they involve loss in the outside world and for a while at least they emphasise internal loss, internal inadequacy: our confusions and conflicts are emphasised.
>
> (Craib 1994: 158)

Thus there is real value in 'time out' during change processes so that individuals can give necessary attention to 'going inside' to allow them to reconnect old purposes with new activities or circumstances.

Traditional mourning rituals provide a form of 'time out'. They tend to be used to 'mark out' the beginning and end of a period during which grieving is both sanctioned and expected. In the context of change (rather than death) the period of mourning might be marked by things as simple as timelines for the introduction of new practices. The symbolic value of mourning as a containment of grieving has great potential to assist the process of change. Rituals towards the beginning of the period could be used to help individuals focus on what has been lost, and what 'continues', and to articulate their sense of grief. Rituals towards the end could focus more on re-establishing a sense of community, inviting individuals to come together to share their new practices, to renew a sense of shared purpose, and to celebrate progress toward the achievement of the intended change. That is, to transform what Weick (1995) refers to as individual intersubjective meanings into a shared social reality, or intersubject meanings.

But change in an organization has elements that distinguish the more localized sense of loss associated with mourning, and the collective loss associated with organizational change. In particular, collective grief can give rise to conflict in situations of intentional change. In these circumstances, it is relatively easy to identify 'winners' as well as 'losers'. Conflict may express a search for identity in ambiguous circumstances. This search is most likely to focus on 'former' identities.

That focus can be interpreted in at least two ways. On the one hand it can be seen as evidence of obstinacy, of melancholy, of resistance. This view is most likely to be adopted by those who are advocates of change. On the other hand, it can be interpreted as a necessary stage in the process of change, a stage that requires acknowledgement rather than condemnation. Marris (1974) argues that:

> Every attempt to pre-empt conflict, argument, protest by rational planning can only be abortive: however reasonable the proposed changes, the process of implementation must still allow the impulse of rejection to play itself out. When those who have the power to manipulate changes act as if they have only to explain, and, when their explanations are not at once accepted, shrug off opposition as ignorance or prejudice, they express a profound contempt for the meaning of lives other than their own.
>
> (Marris 1974: 155)

This positive view is consistent with the notion of 'voice' discussed by Smelser (1998) in relation to the acknowledgement of ambivalence. Encouraging 'voice', as distinct from exit or loyalty, involves attempts to change, rather than to escape from, an objectionable situation. Clearly 'voice' can be an individual as well as a group issue, but Smelser discusses it as a productive and political aspect of organizational life.

There are two issues to elaborate in terms of Marris' comments. Earlier I suggested that academic managers are more likely than academics to have been thinking about issues related to any planned change for a relatively long period of time. They therefore have had an extended period in which to 'come to grips with' the need for change. On the other hand, the changes that they implement are likely to impact more on other members of staff than on themselves. In a profound sense, loss is shared unequally because the change directors force change on others rather than on themselves. The irony is that those who have the least time to consider change have the greatest need for a period of time in which to adjust to it. While those at the coalface are looking for support in dealing with their sense of loss, the managers have long moved on.

This difference in starting positions is true of staff as well. Individually they confront any proposal for change with varying degrees of awareness, and differing levels of preparedness to accept the need for change, and to develop new practices. The lone rangers may well encourage academic managers to fall into the 'transformer trap', seeing their anticipation of change as evidence that if some can do it, all can do it. In addition most advocates for change, and most change processes, focus most attention on the easily converted. One result of this is that those who need most support are least likely to be given that support in ways that respond to and engage with their starting position. After several experiences of being left out of the process, individuals can become disenchanted with the prospect of being asked to change again next week, next month, next year. These individuals become the casualties of change.

Second, by forcing the speed of change, managers can 'refreeze' change processes long before they have achieved their potential. Holding an organization in a state of conflict may be difficult, and threatening, but premature resolutions are unlikely to achieve the desired outcomes. Some conflict can be productive for a number of reasons. Anger seems to be a necessary stage in any successful process of grieving. Anger and hostility are signs of engagement with change, rather than signs of denial. Anger with others precedes reformulations of the self. Conflict allows for issues of disappointment to be raised, and shared, thus affirming individuals' sense of loss and allowing for a new sense of group identity to emerge. Conflict can dramatize a transition, helping to make that transition both visible and meaningful. I have found that the most useful initial response to those on whom change is being imposed is to acknowledge frustration or anger rather than to reply by reinforcing the need for change, or by debating their response. I have seen academics change their position with respect to a proposal for change in a relatively brief period of time (less than an hour) once their sense of loss had been acknowledged.

There is an additional bonus for those who knowingly achieve deliberate change – change itself can come to be understood. In an environment that is characterized in terms of the permanence of change, the need to develop change-focused competence is urgent. Successful grieving becomes a learning experience through which such competencies can be developed. Indeed, it is the *only* context within which they can be developed. This suggests that those who manage change should pay considerable attention to the value of making the process of change *visible* to those who are experiencing it, and particularly to the discussion of the experience after it has been completed. Again, this calls for time out, but at a different time, and for a different purpose. This is particularly important for those whose change-competence is least well developed.

Most change processes in universities appear to focus on the easily converted, and tend to leave 'the others' behind, expecting that the weight of time will wear them down. What these approaches ignore is that confidence is also worn down – by the loss of rewards, by the stigma of 'othering'. As the scope and speed of change increases, universities will not be able to afford the luxury of leaving these damaged individuals to languish. What begins as a few is likely to multiply. Therefore efforts need to be made to develop change-competence in all, rather than continuing to rely on the change-ready.

Action for change

Change is achieved through action. I have suggested that change involves a constant interaction between rational and non-rational processes. Generating action is likely to involve both intuition and plans. But change, and ownership, is achieved though action, rather than either intuition or plans. While Weick (1995: 57) points out the value of plans to action in bringing order to the world, and in prompting action, the preceding discussion suggests that the generation of plans needs to be preceded by actions which prepare people for change, and during which plans are negotiated. However, Weick points out (p. 55) that it is action rather than planning that leads to change, implying that the process of negotiation should focus more on sensemaking than on the generation of plans. Similarly, Trowler (1998: 154) argues that both ownership and change are 'developed and sustained by hands-on experience and by giving room for experimentation and adaptation', issues which I have explored elsewhere (Taylor 1998). Of course it is possible to plan for experimentation and adaptation.

Change of the type that I am discussing always involves uncertainties about the nature, scope and consequences of outcomes. In this sense, change requires a suspension of doubt, and a boldness to create. All knowing is partial, as Weick implies:

> Biased noticing may be bad for deliberation, but it is good for action. In a world that is changing and malleable, confident, bold, enthusiastic action, even if it is based on positive illusions, can be adaptive. Bold action is adaptive because its opposite, deliberation, is futile in changing a world where perception, by definition, can never be accurate.
>
> (Weick 1995: 60)

In this sense, there can never be certainty, given the incompleteness of our capacity to know. The implicit condition of ambiguity is extended by action. Intentions evolve and change during action, which means that the perceptions of the value of the existing circumstances, and the desired outcomes, are also evolving. However, while action creates change, the outcomes of that change are understood in terms of frames of reference that are brought to them. Sensemaking creates those outcomes. In conditions of uncertainty, abstract principles and purposes provide the most appropriate basis for sensemaking. Those abstractions allow a progressive clarification of meaning, and the concurrent imposition of a reality on experience by naming it.

My experience suggests that most academics are willing to go with the flow of action-driven change. But that willingness follows acknowledgement of their need to grieve the loss implied by that flow. This implies a process of individualized change, very similar to that achieved through lone ranging. What tends to be missing are sustained attempts to convert their personal learning into a shared outcome, that is, to convert intersubjective sensemaking into an intersubject 'social reality'.

On the other hand, change is often plan-driven. The rise of managerialism within universities has accentuated the reliance on plan-driven change. It has also led to attempts to guide both change and sensemaking through the use of benchmarking, performance indicators and similar concrete measures of outcomes rather than abstract principles and purposes, or even assumptions. This has the effect of emphasizing a form of rationality that sees grieving as self-indulgent, and privileges action over purpose, and information over negotiation and dialogic conversation. It also locates the decision-making processes and actions as separate, unconnected or poorly connected activities. The irony here is that the subjective and non-rational are being banished at the same time as the flexible and open are sought.

An alternative approach to change

While the preceding discussion has acknowledged the non-rational aspects of change, the sense of self that the change process draws on tends to be context-bound. I have referred to the context-specific nature of identity that allows for multiple versions of self. But this suggests that each 'identity' is produced and activated quite automatically. Similarly, grieving the loss of identity tends to have a context-specific dimension to it. However, this is less context-bound than is the automatic activation of identity. That is, loss 'bleeds' across boundaries in ways that routinized behaviour does not.

The question I want to pose here is based on the discussion of grieving. The literature on it suggests that 'moving on' from grief is achieved through an abstraction of purpose, even of personal significance, from the object of loss. Through abstraction, individuals are able to step back from the experience of ambivalence and loss. This allows them to restructure their sensemaking so as both to recognize and value what was lost, and to imagine future relationships and circumstances that are meaningful and rewarding.

But is it possible to abstract the indexes of the self, so that individuals are better able to deliberate on the relationship between their context-specific identities and their experiences of those specific contexts?

The answer is that this may be possible. There is common-sense evidence that those who are most able to influence others have a capacity to project a 'self' which conforms to the expectations or needs of their audience. These are the capacities that are most readily associated with salespeople, public relations officers and politicians.

However, I am suggesting a considered rather than a 'common-sense' approach to change. Unlike institutionally driven change, this approach to change is directed to the level of the individual. It involves deliberate self-management. Unlike lone ranging, which seeks to develop new capacities that may or may not be valuable in changing contexts, this approach speculates on the management of one's identity so that the sense of loss associated with change can be resolved more quickly. It does not deny ambivalence or loss, but anticipates strategies by which individuals might develop capacities to recognize the relationship between their sense of loss and their sense of self. This recognition offers the possibility of limiting the sense of loss, and identifying the aspects of identity that will continue to offer meaning and reward in the emergent circumstances.

This approach draws on the work of Alan Schrift (1995) and Hubert Dreyfus (1996) who make applications of the work of Foucault, Heidegger and Neitzsche. Schrift's discussion focuses on the issues of the self, drawing on the work of Neitzsche and Foucault, while Dreyfus focuses on issues of being, self and power, drawing on the work of Heidegger and Foucault. Their work can be seen as projects that apply the idea that an individual's sense of self, or 'indexes of self', are produced rather than given. Thus, the sense of self that emerges from consideration of their work recognizes 'a subject that is both autonomous and disciplined, both actively self-forming and passively self-constructed' (Schrift 1995: 34). The self is social – created out of the cultural resources at hand. Those resources – the experiences, languages, histories, myths – constrain self-forming while, at the same time, they provide possibilities which can be used for deliberate self-formation.

This calls for recognition of the conditions that inform the *indexes of self*, and how those conditions are enacted and experienced in specific contexts. Here 'conditions' refer to both material resources and discourses – the systems of language use – which constitute the 'context'. While those 'conditions' constrain the possibilities for self-formation, that constraint is relative rather than absolute. The conditions work as texts that make self-formation possible through structuring 'the possible field of action' (Foucault, cited in Dreyfus 1996: 3). Similar possibilities are argued by Trowler (1998) who draws on the concept of 'agency' and 'actor' in suggesting that academics have considerable opportunity and intellectual resources at their disposal to engage in what I am referring to here as self-formation.

Dreyfus comments on how this governance is enacted in the 'everyday practices of individuals and groups . . . so as to produce, perpetuate, and delimit what people can think, do and be' (1996: 3). This is also how modern power – 'bottom-up, diffuse, continuous, invisible, discretely in the micropolitics, and constantly on the move' (p. 9) – is exercised. In this sense, power controls actions while none the less leaving them free. For example, Schrift argues that while 'relations of power are inevitable, . . . we need not accept as inevitable the particular forms in which those relations have emerged' (1995: 34). The imperative here is not that 'we can do as we like' but that it is possible for individuals to be active within certain prescriptions for action. This view allows the possibility of, and value of, a self-knowing form of self-interested activism. I want to address 'self-knowing' and 'activism' in terms of what they offer a discussion of grieving and change.

Self-knowing

Self-formation always involves working out of language systems and everyday practices. Autopilot functioning allows automatic planning of everyday practices, while language systems also provide well-rehearsed vocabularies with their related frames of reference for the process of sensemaking. Through the context-specific functioning of these systems – one based on personal experience, the other on the linguistic practices in that context – everyday practices come to appear both 'natural' and effortless.

Reflexive or self-conscious 'self-knowing' requires an effortful interruption of this 'naturalness'. That is, it requires thinking that is focused on increasing one's awareness of the index of self that underlies context-specific behaviour and sensemaking, and of the conditions and assumptions which govern its construction. It is through such 'double' self-forming techniques that those conditions can be made visible, and options that are available within them opened for deliberate exploration. Thus, rather than automatic activation of context-specific identity, reflexive self-formation makes possible an engagement with a deliberate process of identity examination. This 'denaturalising' of the self allows the possibility of the revision, even expansion, of the *indexes of the self.*

Self-interested activism for academics

Self-interested 'activism' involves issues of purpose. Heidegger saw the process of governance as representing a technological world-view, focused on the goals of flexibility and efficiency for their own sake. But academics are committed to other purposes. I hear academics speak with enormous enthusiasm about their desire to increase the accessibility and quality (for students) of their teaching practices, and their personal versions of the scholarship of discovery, synthesis, application and teaching. These are the purposes in which academics' identities are anchored.

Self-interested activism calls for strategies that go beyond reflexive self-knowing. In particular it invites academics to consider the ways in which power works, and options to locate their work nearer to the margins of the core imperatives for efficiency and flexibility, particularly through reference to notions of educational effectiveness. The current 'core' technologies extend to all aspects of academic work. While funding for research, and specification/quantification of research outcomes, have been aligned with the goals of efficiency and flexibility, there is relatively little evidence of attempts to align the actual practice of research with these goals. One explanation lies in the very creativity of the process of research – it is a 'practice of creativity'. Research is located towards the margins rather than with the core imperatives. Indeed, it is seen as a means by which those margins might be extended. Thus, while it is engaged with the core imperatives, it prioritizes goals like creativity, discovery, invention and rethinking.

At the other extreme lie the work of institutional organization and administration. In these aspects of academic life, efficiency and flexibility are used to justify a raft of practices focused on re-engineering, restructuring, and resizing universities. The 'challenges' facing higher education, discussed in Chapter 1, evidence the significance of these two goals. Internally, universities are restructuring to increase efficiency largely through centralizing administrative functions, especially those functions related to quality assurance and accountability, while decentralizing budget responsibilities. The increasing use of CITs is exacerbating these trends. The irony is that universities are tending to adopt many of the organizational practices which the commercial sector is abandoning. The discussions of Perry *et al.* (1995), and Drago *et al.* (1992) provide an empirical basis for this claim, while Charles Handy's (1989) work provides a more rhetorical and conceptual basis for it.

University teaching is increasingly influenced by these goals. The recent publication by the Carnegie Endowment for the Advancement of Teaching, *Reinventing Undergraduate Education: A blueprint for America's Research Universities* (Kenny 1998), examines undergraduate teaching, and, like studies in other countries, finds that students are treated as second-class citizens as universities focus on issues other than teaching. The introduction of CITs is almost unanimously seen by those who are most aligned with the core purposes as the 'best bet' to increase both efficiency and flexibility, as exemplified in the reports of both the Dearing and the West Committees. The expectation is that on-line and/or multimedia-based courses will allow access anywhere, any time, by anybody to higher education. Once the necessary instructional resources have been developed, the costs of delivery will be reduced because campus facilities will no longer need to be provided, and the cost of teaching support will be reduced through the use of part-time and casualized academic teachers. I have offered a critique of this thinking elsewhere in this book, particularly in Chapter 4.

One of the problems for academic teachers is the fragility of their grasp of the educational values underlying their teaching, as discussed at some length in Chapter 5. Academics who do have access to a more extended knowledge and value-base for their educational work are better placed to argue that it is also a 'practice of creativity'. Unfortunately too much university teaching undermines that claim. The fact is that there is little reason to oppose efficiency-motivated change in those instances. However, there is little evidence that the use of CITs, or any other efficiency practice, contributes to the achievement of the goal of cost-efficiency. Instead, through routinizing teaching and focusing on the 'delivery' of information, the more immediate outcomes of CIT-based teaching tend to include a decrease in the status of teaching, and a separation of decision making from the actual context of teaching. Quite different outcomes from their use might be achieved through prioritizing educational and creative purposes over issues of efficiency and flexibility.

Self-interested activism works through strategies that give 'voice' to purposes in addition to efficiency and effectiveness. Those alternative values are likely to be more easily advocated if the practices to which they attach are seen as serving multiple purposes. Academics have a very significant responsibility to focus discussions of teaching in particular on issues of access and educational effectiveness – that is, to engage in dialogic conversation around specific issues related to their teaching. Again, this calls for a greater capacity to argue the importance of these additional purposes, and to achieve them. However, individual academics can focus their own teaching on these purposes, particularly with their own students. Even then, there is good reason to engage in dialogic conversation with these students around the same issues. This is because there is a need to align expectations within a community of course participants.

Self-interested activism and individual power

Before leaving this issue I want to comment on self-interested activism in terms of the issue of power. Core management practices tend to emphasize a concern with leadership for change. In Chapter 4 I noted that a focus on leadership implies an expectation of followership – the two are mutually constructing. I see evidence of increasing timidity on the part of academics, reflected in the rising sense that 'the cause' of many current problems lies with management. If the cause lies there, then, by implication, so does 'the solution'. This is timid behaviour, attributing power to those who occupy managerial positions.

Foucauldian scholars offer a very different analysis of power, focusing on its relationship to everyday practices (Dreyfus 1996). Power is not centralized, but is capillary, working in and through everyday practices. Academic managers interviewed as part of the EIP project (Taylor *et al.* 1996) commented on their own sense of powerlessness, but the everyday attitudes of academics as 'governed selves' contributes to their sense of powerlessness. Once individuals expect others to make decisions for them, they give away their own power. This is not to suggest that an academic has as much power as a Vice-Chancellor, Rector or President. It is to suggest that academics have more freedom to influence – more autonomy to choose – than they realize, and that it is in their interests to exercise that freedom and autonomy.

Similarly there is too much followership and too little self-management. The claim that everyone is a leader can be taken seriously, and used to pursue purposes beyond efficiency and flexibility. But by 'self-interest' I do not mean either 'selfish' or 'individualist' interest. I have in mind a form of 'self' which is relational rather than isolated. It recognizes the tensions between self and community interests, while emphasizing that only individuals can act to form, re-form and advocate those interests. Where once collegiality was enacted to provide a sense of collective power, it is now often limited to representative committee work. Similarly, autonomy was once community-focused, now it is individualized. Revitalization of collective academics seems imperative if effective responses to the incursions into their tribal territory by both academic managers and general staff are to be mounted. Long-term collective engagements might best be pursued through discipline-focused associations – a form of professional-identity politics. On the other hand, within institutions it might be useful to think in terms of short-term alliances around specific issues – a form of issue or 'complaint' politics (Hughes 1994). These alliances might include more than just academics, as exemplified by the Yale University actions (Aronowitz 1997 and Nelson 1997, discussed in Chapter 5).

Just as universities are no longer the beneficiaries of state patronage, academics cannot rely on unrelenting patronage from their managers. The emergent conditions of academic work call for greater self-knowledge. This knowledge ranges from understanding focused on the immediate conduct of work (what difference my work makes, and how I know this), to understanding the purposes of that work (what I am attempting to achieve, and whose interests these achievements might serve), and to knowledge of self (what beliefs inform my sensemaking, what values motivate my work, how I enact myself in context-specific ways, how I enact my autonomy). These forms of self-knowledge are necessary for self-interested activism through which academics might be players rather than pawns in the ongoing processes of change in universities.

In conclusion

Academics need to exercise and extend their capacity for thinking. This capacity represents an ideal of academic work. It has, in most instances, been developed largely in the context of discipline-focused scholarship. Thinking is effortful, requiring a commitment to interrogate the taken for granted, and a capacity for scepticism and doubt. As more of the taken-for-granted academic world comes under pressure to be changed, the need to think about what has been taken as given becomes more urgent. I suggest that effortful thinking offers at least two benefits over automatic rejection or acceptance of change. It builds a capacity to engage with ongoing change, to respond critically and insightfully to proposals for change, even to initiate change. More importantly, it builds a capacity to grieve what is lost, and to 'move on' through stepping back from the immediate context and linking *what was* to *what might be.*

Academics are under increasing pressure to align their thinking with purposes that reflect universities' commercial interests and the imperative to increase efficiency and flexibility. This book acknowledges that those purposes have long been associated with higher education – they are not a new phenomenon. Academics need to engage with them, but in ways which address additional values and purposes. This is why academics should extend their capacity for thinking to include all aspects of their work, especially their teaching. The capacities for thinking, for scepticism and doubt, need to be applied equally to traditional practices as to those that are emergent. Those capacities offer the potential to interrogate both sets of practices and to extend and refine their understanding of and engagement with the values and purposes that underlie each.

The capacity for thinking helps avoid the misrecognition of the conditions of one's life-work as 'problems'. 'Problems' invite 'solutions' which may invite the creation of more or less radical alternatives to the status quo. 'Conditions' are seen as setting limits on self-formation – limits on what is possible. They offer only incremental change because they are expressed through language systems. As language changes, so do the conditions, but there is little scope for any radical reformation. However, there is always wriggle room – constrained opportunities for self-formation and autonomy.

Out of this discussion arise principles for the management of change (extending the suggestions of Marris 1974: 156).

- The process of change should engage with both the rational and the non-rational aspects of identity and experience, and of change itself. Ambiguity and uncertainty are inherent in any change process, and are experienced by both leaders and followers. The rational and non-rational aspects of change will constantly interact.
- The sponsors of change should warn those who are to enact change that they are likely to experience both grief and decreasing competence during the initial stages of the change process. The scope of change should be acknowledged, particularly if it is going to involve changes to identity.
- The process of change should anticipate and even encourage conflict. Followers should be encouraged to recognize what can no longer be, and to express their disappointment, in order that they can move on.
- The process must respect both the individuality of experiences and reactions, and the sense of collective loss.
- Grieving must be allowed to run its course. This requires time and patience, so that conflicts can be worked through, and the rehabilitation of beliefs and purposes achieved.
- The process of change should itself be made visible and understandable to those who achieve it. This can only occur after success, but builds an ongoing capacity for change.

In turn, the discussion suggests a further six principles for academics' self-management of change. Adoption of those principles needs to be linked to the adoption of the first set. That is, academics should find these useful irrespective of the principles underlying the management of change in their institution. The principles are:

- to develop a disciplined knowledge base for the roles in which they are primarily engaged, including an awareness of the beliefs and attitudes underlying their everyday practices, and the values and purposes that those practices serve. These values and purposes should provide a sense of direction for their work;
- to expect their roles to change. They should be prepared to engage with opportunities for change primarily in terms of consideration of values and purposes, in addition to issues of practice;
- to expect to experience grief during any change in role. Further, they should learn to distinguish between doubt and grief. Doubt grows out of a questioning of practice, and is a productive basis for the improvement of practice. Grief grows out of emotional attachment to 'things' which are threatened by change, or to which they have ambivalent attachment. Grieving provides a basis for 'moving on';
- to develop their awareness of the basis of their academic identities in terms of both their context-specificity and their underlying values and purposes. That awareness allows a distancing from experience which might otherwise be personally destabilizing;
- to extend their capacity for self-interested activism, including their collective engagement with colleagues in support of shared values and purposes. Their voice has to advocate for values beyond efficiency and flexibility;
- to develop strategies that allow continuing professional support and growth outside their immediate place of employment. Academic careers will increasingly be built through these extra-institutional networks.

These principles reflect the themes that I nominated in the first chapter of this work.

- Engagement with change at the level of *individual academics* and their sense of *academic identity*.
- A *respect for ambivalence* and a *valuing of scepticism* – those who resist and/or express uncertainty, and those who question visions of certainty, should be listened to with care and interest.
- The characterization of my approach to the challenge of discussing academics' changing roles as *sensemaking* – developing a set of ideas with explanatory possibilities rather than as a body of knowledge.
- The need to acknowledge and deal with issues of *loss associated with change* together with the importance of the *non-rational* in the sense-making process, and in any other engagement with change.

I have developed these themes within discussions of the historical, the current, and the emergent conditions of academic work. They have provided a basis for recognizing and imposing continuity across these conditions.

This work offers ways of thinking about these conditions which allow for forms of engagement which refuse a direct alignment of the interests of the individual academic with the interests of universities. The value of that differentiation is suggested by the following statement: 'I want to be involved, but not necessarily committed. It's like a breakfast of bacon and eggs. The hen is involved; the pig is committed.' Universities invite commitment, and seek loyalty. Academics' interests might be better served by strategies and alliances that focus on involvement – scepticism and qualified optimism. That is, there are good reasons for academics to disentangle their professional career paths from those of the institutions known as universities, especially when both are under pressure to change.

Academics are well placed to refocus and extend their expertise in ways that will serve their interests, and the interests of those contributions they wish to make to their communities. But this refocusing is no simple matter. It will require the development of new expertise, new capacities – new learning. While learning is a risky business, it remains the best bet for ensuring personal satisfaction and a continuing role for academics into the future.

References

Altbach, P.G. (1997) An international crisis? The American professoriate in comparative perspective, *DÆDALUS*, 126 (4): 315–38.

Aronowitz, S. (1997) Academic unionism and the future of higher education. In C. Nelson (ed.) *Will Teach for Food: Academic Labor in Crisis*. Minneapolis, MN: University of Minnesota Press.

Baba, M.L. (1995) Work and technology in modern industry: the creative frontier. In F.C. Gamst (ed.) *Meanings of Work: Considerations for the Twenty-First Century*. Albany, NY: State University of New York Press.

Barnes, S.V. (1996) England's civic universities and the triumph of the Oxbridge ideal, *History of Education Quarterly*, 36: 271–305.

Barnett, R. (1996) Situating the learning university, *International Journal of University Adult Education*, 35 (1): 13–27.

Bauman, Z. (1998) What prospects of morality in times of uncertainty?, *Theory, Culture and Society*, 15: 11–22.

Becher, T. (1989) *Academic Tribes and Territories*. Milton Keynes: Open University Press.

Bender, T. (1997) Politics, intellect, and the American university, 1945–1995, *DÆDALUS*, 126: 1–37.

Bergquist, W.H. (1992) *The Four Cultures of the Academy: Insights and Strategies for Improving Leadership in Collegiate Organizations*. San Francisco, CA: Jossey-Bass.

Bergquist, W.H. (1995) *Quality through Access, Access with Quality: The New Imperative for Higher Education*. San Francisco, CA: Jossey-Bass.

Berry, J.W. (1997) Immigration, acculturation, and adaptation, *Applied Psychology: An International Review*, 46 (1): 5–34.

Bloland, H.G. (1995) Postmodernism in higher education, *Journal of Higher Education*, 66: 521–59.

Blomqvist, G. (1997) State, university and academic freedom in Sweden: the Universities of Uppsala and Lund between 1820 and 1920, *Minerva*, 35: 171–94.

Bloor, B. and Dawson, P. (1994) Understanding professional culture in organizational context, *Organization Studies*, 15: 275–95.

Boyatzis, R.E. (1982) *The Competent Manager: A Model for Effective Performance*. New York: John Wiley and Sons.

Boyer, E.L. (1990) *Scholarship Reconsidered: Priorities of the Professoriate*. Princeton, NJ: Carnegie Endowment for the Advancement of Teaching.

Bright, R. (1986) *Grieving*. St Louis, MO: MMB Music.

Brookfield, S. (1996) Fostering critical conversation in the learning university, *International Journal of University Adult Education*, 25 (1): 48–60.

Brown, J.S. and Duguid, P. (1994) Borderline issues: social and material aspects of design, *Human–Computer Interaction*, 9: 3–36.

Brown, J.S. and Duguid, P. (1996) Universities in the digital age, *Change*, 28 (4): 11–19.

Brown, M. (1998) Educational researchers in universities: the condition of the workforce, *British Educational Research Journal*, 24: 125–39.

Caproni, P.J. (1997) Work/life balance: you can't get there from here, *Journal of Applied Behavioral Science*, 33: 46–56.

Carr, D. (1994) Educational enquiry and professional knowledge: towards a Copernican revolution, *Educational Studies*, 20: 33–52.

Castillo, J.J. (1997) Looking for the meaning of work, *Work and Occupations*, 24: 413–25.

Coleman, J.S. (1990) *Foundations of Social Theory*. Cambridge, MA: Belknap Press.

Cooper, D.J., Hinings, B., Greenwood, R. and Brown, J.L. (1996) Sedimentation and transformation in organizational change: the case of Canadian law firms, *Organization Studies*, 17: 623–47.

Craib, I. (1994) *The Importance of Disappointment*. London: Routledge.

CRHEFP (Committee of Review of Higher Education Financing and Policy) (1998) *Learning for Life: Final Report. Review of Higher Education Financing and Policy*. Committee chaired by Roderick West. Canberra: Australian Government Printing Service. Available at *http://www.deetya.gov.au/divisions/hed/hereview*

Damrosch, D. (1995) *We Scholars: Changing the Culture of the University*. Cambridge, MA: Harvard University Press.

Davies, J.L. (1997) The evolution of university responses to financial reduction, *Higher Education Management*, 9 (1): 127–40.

Dearn, J. (1998) Reflections on the Australian awards for university teaching, *HERDSA News*, 20 (1): 10–11.

Defillippi, R.J. and Arthur, M.B. (1994) The boundaryless career: a competency based perspective, *Journal of Organizational Behavior*, 15: 307–24.

Deleuze, G. (1992) Postscript on the societies of control, *October*, 59: 3–7.

Drago, R., Wooden, M. and Sloan, J. (1992) *Productive Relations? Australian Industrial Relations and Workplace Performance*. North Sydney: Allen and Unwin.

Dreyfus, H.L. (1996) Being and power: Heidegger and Foucault, *International Journal of Philosophical Studies*, 4: 1–16.

Edgerton, R., Hutchings, B. and Quinlan, K. (1991) *The Teaching Portfolio: Capturing the Scholarship in Teaching*. Washington, DC: American Association for Higher Education.

Ehrmann, S.C. (1996) Responding to the triple challenge facing post-compulsory education: accessibility, quality, costs. In OECD Documents – *Information Technology and the Future of Post-Secondary Education*. Paris: Organisation for Economic Co-operation and Development.

Elliott, G. and Crossley, M. (1997) Contested values in further education, *Educational Management and Administration*, 25: 79–92.

Elmore, R.F. (1996) Getting to scale with good educational practice, *Harvard Educational Review*, 66: 1–26.

Everett, J.E. and Entrekin, L.V. (1994) Changing attitudes of Australian academics, *Higher Education*, 27: 203–27.

Firestone, W.A. (1996) Images of teaching and proposals for reform: a comparison of ideas from cognitive and organizational research, *Educational Administration Quarterly*, 32: 209–35.

Ford, P., Goodyear, P., Heseltine, R. *et al.* (1996) *Managing Change in Higher Education: A Learning Environment Architecture*. Buckingham: The Society for Research into Higher Education and Open University Press.

Foucault, M. (1985) *The Use of Pleasure: The History of Sexuality Volume 2*. Harmondsworth: Penguin Books.

Gamst, F.C. (1995) The web of rules in comparative work relations systems. In F.C. Gamst (ed.) *Meanings of Work: Considerations for the Twenty-First Century*. Albany, NY: State University of New York Press.

Gerwitz, S. (1997) Post-welfarism and the reconstruction of teachers' work in the UK, *Journal of Educational Policy*, 12: 217–31.

Goodman, J. (1995) Change without difference: school restructuring in historical perspective, *Harvard Educational Review*, 65: 1–29.

Hall, D.T. and Moss, J.E. (1998) The new protean contract: helping organizations and employees adapt, *Organizational Dynamics*, Winter: 22–37.

Handy, C. (1989) *The Age of Unreason*. Boston, MA: Harvard Business School Press.

Hargreaves, A. (1997) The four ages of professionalism and professional learning, *Unicorn*, 23 (2): 86–114.

Heidegger, M. (1977) The end of philosophy and the task of thinking. In D.F. Knell (ed.) *Basic Writings*. New York: Harper and Row.

Herron, J. (1988) *Universities and the Myth of Cultural Decline*. Detroit, MI: Wayne State University Press.

Hort, L. (1997) The tiger hunt: collegiality, managerialism and shaping academic work. Unpublished Master of Higher Education thesis, Griffith University.

Hudson, R., Maslin-Prothero, S. and Oates, L. (1997) *Flexible Learning in Action: Case Studies in Higher Education*. London: Kogan Page.

Hughes, R. (1994) *Culture of Complaint: The Freying of America*. London: Harvill.

Imrie, B.W. (1996) Performance planning, appraisal and development, *Higher Education Management*, 8: 87–104.

Isaacs, W.N. (1996) The process and potential of dialogue in social change, *Educational Technology*, 36 (1): 20–30.

Jenlink, P. and Carr, A.A. (1996) Conversation as a medium for change in education, *Educational Technology*, 36 (1): 31–8.

Johnston, R. (1997) Distance learning: medium or message, *Journal of Further and Higher Education*, 21 (1): 107–22.

Jones, D. (1998) Confessions of a slow learner, *HERDSA News*, 20 (1): 8–9.

Kellner, D. (1998) Zygmunt Bauman's postmodern turn, *Theory, Culture and Society*, 15: 73–86.

Kember, D. (1997) A reconceptualisation of the research into university academics' conceptions of teaching, *Learning and Instruction*, 7: 255–75.

Kenny, R.W. (1998) *Reinventing Undergraduate Education: A Blueprint for America's Research Universities*. Available at *http://notes.cc.sunysb.edu/pres/boyer.nsf*

Kerr, C. (1994) *Higher Education Cannot Escape History: Issues for the Twenty-first Century*. Albany, NY: State University of New York Press.

Kotter, J.P. (1990) *A Force for Change: How Leadership Differs from Management*. New York: Free Press.

Laurillard, D. (1993) *Rethinking University Teaching: A Framework for the Effective Use of Educational Technology*. London: Routledge.

Lipshitz, R. and Strauss, O. (1997) Coping with uncertainty: a naturalistic decision-making analysis. *Organizational Behavior and Human Decision Processes*, 69: 149–63.

McDaniel, O.C. (1996) The theoretical and practical use of performance indicators. *Higher Education Management*, 8: 125–39.

MacFarlane, A.G.F. (1995) Future patterns of teaching and learning. In T. Schuller (ed.) *The Changing University?* Buckingham: The Society for Research into Higher Education and Open University Press.

McInnis, C. (1996) Change and diversity in the work patterns of Australian academics, *Higher Education Management*, 8 (2): 105–17.

McNay, I. (1995) From collegial academy to corporate enterprise: the changing cultures in universities. In T. Schuller (ed.) *The Changing University?* Buckingham: The Society for Research into Higher Education and Open University Press.

Marris, P. (1974) *Loss and Change*. London: Routledge and Kegan Paul.

Martin, E. (1999) *Changing Academic Work*. Buckingham: The Society for Research into Higher Education and Open University Press.

Miller, H.D.R. (1995) *The Management of Change in Universities: Universities, State and Economy in Australia, Canada and the United Kingdom*. Buckingham: The Society for Research into Higher Education and Open University Press.

Mitchell, T.R. (1997) Border crossings: organizational boundaries and challenges to the American professoriate, *DÆDALUS*, 126 (4): 265–92.

Montgomery, K. and Oliver, A.L. (1996) Response by professional organizations to multiple and ambiguous institutional environments: the case of AIDS, *Organization Studies*, 17: 649–71.

Morrison, T.R. (1995) Global transformation and the search for a new educational design, *International Journal of Lifelong Education*, 14: 188–213.

Nadler, D.A. and Tushman, M.L. (1995) Types of organizational change: from incremental improvement to discontinuous transformation. In D. Nadler, R. Shaw, and E. Walton (eds) *Discontinuous Change: Leading Organizational Transformation*. San Francisco, CA: Jossey-Bass.

NCIHE (National Committee of Inquiry into Higher Education) (1997) *Higher Education in the Learning Society*. Committee chaired by Ronald Dearing.
Available at *http://wwwd2.leeds.ac.uk/niche*

Neave, G. (1996) Higher education in transition: twenty-five years on, *Higher Education Management*, 8 (3): 15–24.

Nelson, C. (1997) Between crisis and opportunity: the future of the academic workplace. In C. Nelson (ed.) *Will Teach for Food: Academic Labor in Crisis*. Minneapolis, MN: University of Minnesota Press.

Neuhauser, P. (1988) *Tribal Warfare in Organizations*. Cambridge, MA: Ballinger Publishing Company.

Nixon, J. (1996) Professional identity and the restructuring of higher education, *Studies in Higher Education*, 21: 5–16.

Nixon, J., Martin, J., McKeown, P. and Ranson, S. (1997) Towards a learning profession: changing codes of occupational practice within the new management of education, *British Journal of Sociology of Education*, 18: 5–28.

Oakley, F. (1997) The elusive academic profession: complexity and change, *DÆDALUS*, 126 (4): 43–66.

Peiperl, M. and Baruch, Y. (1997) Back to square zero: the post-corporate career, *Organizational Dynamics*, Spring: 7–21.

Perry, M., Davidson, C. and Hill, R. (1995) *Reform at Work: Workplace Change and the New Industrial Order.* Auckland: Longman Paul.

Posnock, R. (1997) How it feels to be a problem: Du Bois, Fanon, and the 'impossible life' of the black intellectual, *Critical Inquiry*, 23: 323–49.

Prichard, C. and Willmott, H. (1997) Just how managed is the McUniversity?, *Organization Studies*, 18: 287–316.

Ramsden, P. (1992) *Learning to Teach in Higher Education.* London: Routledge.

Ramsden, P. (1998) *Learning to Lead in Higher Education.* London: Routledge.

Randle, K. and Brady, N. (1997) Managerialism and professionalism in the 'Cinderella Service', *Journal of Vocational Education and Training*, 49 (1): 121–39.

Riffel, J.A. and Levin, B. (1997) Schools coping with the impact of information technology, *Educational Management and Administration*, 25 (1): 51–64.

Robbins Committee (1963) *Report of the Committee on Higher Education*, cmnd 2154. London: HMSO.

Rousseau, D.M. (1997) Organizational behavior in the new organizational era, *Annual Review of Psychology*, 48: 515–46.

Sarros, J.C., Gmelch, W.H. and Tanewski, G.A. (1997) The role of Department Head in Australian universities: changes and challenges, *Higher Education Research and Development*, 16: 9–23.

Sarros, J.C., Gmelch, W.H. and Tanewski, G.A. (1998) The academic dean: a position in need of a compass and clock, *Higher Education Research and Development*, 17: 65–99.

Schon, D.A. (1983) *The Reflective Practitioner: How Professionals Think in Action.* New York: Basic Books.

Schrift, A.D. (1995) Reconfiguring the subject as a process of self: following Foucault's Nietzschean trajectory to Butler, Laclau/Mouffe, and beyond, *New Formations*, 25: 28–39.

Schwalbe, M.L. and Mason-Schrock, D. (1996) Identity work as group process, *Advances in Group Processes*, 13: 113–47.

Shapiro, S. (1994) Re-membering the body in critical pedagogy, *Education and Society*, 12: 61–79.

Shattock, M.L. (1995) The university of the future, *Higher Education Management*, 7: 157–64.

Sheehan, B.A. and Welch, A.R. (1996) *The Academic Profession in Australia.* Report 96/1 of the Evaluations and Investigation Program. Canberra: Australian Government Printing Service.
Available at *http://www.deetya.gov.au/divisions/hed/operations/eippubs.htm*

Smelser, N.J. (1998) The rational and the ambivalent in the social sciences, *American Sociological Review*, 63: 1–16.

Spender, J.-C. and Kessler, E.H. (1995) Managing the uncertainties of innovation: extending Thompson (1967), *Human Relations*, 48 (1): 35–56.

Srikantia, P. and Pasmore, W. (1996) Conviction and doubt in organizational learning, *Journal of Orgnaizational Change*, 9 (2): 42–53.

Taylor, P.G. (1991) Developing and promoting a constructivist view of learning. Unpublished Doctor of Philosophy thesis, University of Queensland.

Taylor, P.G. (1997a) Preparing for internationalisation: messages from an EIP project. In R. Murray-Harvey and H.C. Salins (eds) *Learning and Teaching in Higher Education: Advancing International Perspectives.* Proceedings of the Higher Education Research and Development Australasia Conference held in Adelaide, South Australia, 8–11 July.

Taylor, P.G. (1997b) Creating environments which nurture development: messages from research into academics' experiences, *International Journal for Academic Development*, 2 (2): 42–9.

Taylor, P.G. (1998) Institutional change in uncertain times: *lone ranging* is not enough, *Studies in Higher Education*, 23: 269–79.

Taylor, P.G., Lopez, L. and Quadrelli, C. (1996) *Flexibility, Technology and Academics' Practices: Tantalising Tales and Muddy Maps*. Report 96/16 of the Evaluations and Investigation Program. Canberra: Australian Government Printing Service. Available at *http://www.deetya.gov.au/divisions/hed/operations/eippubs.htm*

Teichler, U. and Kehm, B.M. (1995) Towards a new understanding of the relationships between higher education and employment, *European Journal of Education*, 30: 115–31.

Tierney, W.G. (1997) Organisational socialization in higher education, *Journal of Higher Education*, 68: 1–16.

Toffler, A. (1970) *Future Shock*. London: Pan Books.

Trow, M. (1997) The development of information technology in American higher education, *DÆDALUS*, 126 (4): 293–314.

Trowler, P. (1997) Beyond the Robbins Trap: reconceptualising academic responses to change in higher education (or . . . Quiet Flows the Don), *Studies in Higher Education*, 22: 301–18.

Trowler, P.R. (1998) *Academics Responding to Change: New Higher Education Frameworks and Academic Cultures*. Buckingham: The Society for Research into Higher Education and Open University Press.

Weick, K. (1995) *Sensemaking in Organizations*. Thousand Oaks, CA: Sage Publications.

Weick, K.E. (1976) Educational organizations as loosely coupled systems, *Administrative Science Quarterly*, 21: 1–19.

Index

The Society for Research into Higher Education

The Society for Research into Higher Education exists to stimulate and coordinate research into all aspects of higher education. It aims to improve the quality of higher education through the encouragement of debate and publication on issues of policy, on the organization and management of higher education institutions, and on the curriculum and teaching methods.

The Society's income is derived from subscriptions, sales of its books and journals, conference fees and grants. It receives no subsidies, and is wholly independent. Its individual members include teachers, researchers, managers and students. Its corporate members are institutions of higher education, research institutes, professional, industrial and governmental bodies. Members are not only from the UK, but from elsewhere in Europe, from America, Canada and Australasia, and it regards its international work as among its most important activities.

Under the imprint *SRHE & Open University Press*, the Society is a specialist publisher of research, having over 70 titles in print. The Editorial Board of the Society's imprint seeks authoritative research or study in the above fields. It offers competitive royalties, a highly recognizable format in both hardback and paperback and the worldwide reputation of the Open University Press.

The Society also publishes *Studies in Higher Education* (three times a year), which is mainly concerned with academic issues, *Higher Education Quarterly* (formerly *Universities Quarterly*), mainly concerned with policy issues, *Research into Higher Education Abstracts* (three times a year), and *SRHE News* (four times a year).

The Society holds a major annual conference in December, jointly with an institution of higher education. In 1996 the topic was 'Working in Higher Education' at University of Wales, Cardiff. In 1997, it was 'Beyond the First Degree' at the University of Warwick and in 1998 it was 'The Globalization of Higher Education' at the University of Lancaster. The 1999 conference will be on the topic of higher education and its communities at UMIST.

The Society's committees, study groups and networks are run by the members. The networks at present include:

Access	Mentoring
Curriculum Development	Postgraduate Issues
Disability	Quality
Eastern European	Quantitative Studies
Funding	Student Development
Legal Education	Vocational Qualifications

Benefits to Members

Individual

Individual members receive:

- *SRHE News*, the Society's publications list, conference details and other material included in mailings.
- Greatly reduced rates for *Studies in Higher Education* and *Higher Education Quarterly*.
- A 35 per cent discount on all SRHE & Open University Press publications.
- Free copies of the Proceedings – commissioned papers on the theme of the Annual Conference.
- Free copies of *Research into Higher Education Abstracts*.
- Reduced rates for the annual conference.
- Extensive contacts and scope for facilitating initiatives.
- Free copies of the *Register of Members' Research Interests*.
- Membership of the Society's networks.

Corporate

Corporate members receive:

- Benefits of individual members, plus:
- Free copies of *Studies in Higher Education*.
- Unlimited copies of the Society's publications at reduced rates.
- Reduced rates for the annual conference.
- The right to submit applications for the Society's research grants.
- The right to use the Society's facility for supplying statistical HESA data for purposes of research.

 Membership details: SRHE, 3 Devonshire Street, London W1N 2BA, UK. Tel: 0171 637 2766. Fax: 0171 637 2781. email: srhe@mailbox.ulcc.ac.uk
World Wide Web: http://www.srhe.ac.uk./srhe/
Catalogue: SRHE & Open University Press, Celtic Court, 22 Ballmoor, Buckingham MK18 1XW. Tel: 01280 823388. Fax: 01280 823233. email: enquiries@openup.co.uk

CHANGING ACADEMIC WORK
DEVELOPING THE LEARNING UNIVERSITY

Elaine Martin

Higher education has changed enormously in recent years. For instance, it now serves a more diverse range of students and is under closer government scrutiny and control. There is consequently a significant number of academics who are uneasy with current values and practices and who work with them reluctantly. Universities may speak publicly of efficiency and effectiveness but they cannot function successfully if their academic staff are disillusioned.

Changing Academic Work explores the competing tensions in contemporary work: the need to balance individualism with collaboration; accountability with reward; a valuing of the past with preparation for the future. The aim is to help staff build a contemporary university which is as much a learning organizaiton as an organization about learning. Elaine Martin develops a set of simple but sound principles to guide academic work and, through case study material, she provides engaging and convincing illustrations of these principles in action. She offers insight and guidance for academic staff at all levels who wish to make their working environment more satisfying and productive.

Contents
Preface – Changes in academic work – Experiences of change in academic work – Learning and teaching in higher education – Organizational change and learning organizations – Finding a way forward – Visions and missions and reality – Collaboration and independence – Accountability and reward – Encouraging change: valuing the past, preparing for the future – A final word: a better working life – Bibliography – Index.

c.192pp   0 335 19883 X (Paperback)   0 335 19884 8 (Hardback)

THE ADULT UNIVERSITY

Etienne Bourgeois, Chris Duke, Jean-Luc Guyot and Barbara Merrill

In most universities there are now more adults as students than young people straight from school. Yet many universities continue to act as if no such change had taken place. *The Adult University* examines theoretically and practically key issues of broader participation in higher education. It asks:

- What are university access policies and how do they connect with practice; do universities behave in ways which encourage or thwart wider access?
- How do adults experience universities; and how far do universities adapt to assist adults?
- What can universities realistically do to improve both the access to and experience of university for adults.

This is a genuinely international study by a transnational team which is grounded in research into two institutions in two major European university traditions. Its focus is both on national systems and local interactions, on macro level policy and students' own voices.

The Adult Univesity is essential reading for all those interested in the development of our mass higher education system. It points to ways in which individual universities and the system of higher education could and should evolve in advanced industrial societies.

Contents
Introduction – Changing to survive: the modern university in its environment – Are universities organized to facilitate access and participation? – Adult students: getting in and keeping out – Staying in and coming to terms – Innovation and the university: the struggle for adultification – The adult university: from adult education to lifelong learning? – References – Index.

c.192pp   0 335 19907 0 (Paperback)   0 335 19908 9 (Hardback)

HIGHER EDUCATION: A CRITICAL BUSINESS

Ronald Barnett

Barnett reviews what the academy customarily means when it talks about critical thought, explains why that talk is so often shallow and pessimistic, and holds up for contemplation a positive conception of a 'very wide self' formed through education . . . He breathes completely new life into the dead notion of academic as intellectual.

> Professor Sheldon Rothblatt, University of California,
> Berkley and Royal Institute of Technology, Sweden

Higher Education: A Critical Business is a bold statement about higher education in the modern age. It continues Ronald Barnett's thinking of his earlier books but offers a completely new set of ideas in a challenging but engaging argument.

A defining concept of the Western university is that of critical thinking, but that idea is completely inadequate for the changing and unknowable world facing graduates. Instead, we have to displace the idea of critical thinking with the much broader idea of critical being. In this idea, students reflect critically on knowledge but they also develop their powers of critical self-reflection and critical action. This critique is transformatory. An education for critical being calls for a new approach to the process of higher education. It also has implications for the organization and management of universities, and for the relationship of universities to the wider worlds of work, professionalism and intellectual life.

Anyone interested in understanding how we might develop universities and higher education for the modern world should read this important book.

Contents

208pp   0 335 19703 5 (Paperback)   0 335 19704 3 (Hardback)